You Say You Want A Revolution

Reed E. Hundt

Yale University Press   New Haven and London

You Say You Want A Revolution

A Story of Information Age Politics

Designed by Sonia Scanlon
Set in Adobe Garamond type by The Composing Room of Michigan, Inc., Grand Rapids, Michigan.
Printed in the United States of America.

Library of Congress Cataloging-in-Publication Data

Hundt, Reed E., 1948–
You say you want a revolution : a story of
    information age politics /
    Reed E. Hundt
        p.   cm.
Includes index.
ISBN 0-300-08364-5 (cloth : alk. paper)
1. United States. Telecommunications Act
    of 1996.   2. Telecommunication pol-
    icy—United States.   3. Information
    superhighway—Government policy—
    United States.   4. Internet (Computer
    network)—Government policy—
    United States.
HE7781.H88   2000
384.3'3'0973—dc21   99-059629

A catalog record for this book is available from the British Library.

The paper in this book meets the guidelines for permanence and durability of the Committee on Production Guidelines for Book Longevity of the Council on Library Resources.

10   9   8   7   6   5   4   3   2   1

To Betsy, Adam, Nathaniel, and Sara

CONTENTS

Preface   ix

Cast of Characters   xiii

PART 1. EXPERIENCE KEEPS A DEAR SCHOOL

1. Coincidence
   JULY 1992 – NOVEMBER 1993   3

2. Cockiness Goeth Before
   NOVEMBER 1993 – JANUARY 1994   18

3. On the Chin
   FEBRUARY 1994 – APRIL 1994   33

4. Learning the Ropes
   APRIL 1994 – JULY 1994   49

5. On a Roll
   JULY 1994 – OCTOBER 1994   63

PART 2. CHANGES AND CHOICES

6. On the Floor
   NOVEMBER 1994 – FEBRUARY 1995   81

7. Finding a Way
   MARCH 1995 – SEPTEMBER 1995   102

8. Politics Matters
   OCTOBER 1995 – JANUARY 1996   130

PART 3. REMEMBER WHO YOU ARE

9. Chance of a Lifetime
   FEBRUARY 1996 – MAY 1996   151

10. Help!
JUNE 1996 – OCTOBER 1996   176

11. Elections Matter
NOVEMBER 1996 – APRIL 1997   201

12. Exit and Outcomes
MAY 1997 – NOVEMBER 1997   213

    Index   227

In 1992, the United States economy was moribund. Most felt the country was headed in the wrong direction. Voting for Bill Clinton and Ross Perot, and against George Bush, two-thirds of American voters called for change. In the following years, American self-confidence surged and the American economy boomed. A major cause and the most salient manifestation of these changes was the communications revolution.

I had been Al Gore's friend since high school and an adviser to him in his 1984 Senate campaign, 1988 presidential campaign, 1990 Senate campaign, and 1992 run with Bill Clinton for the White House. I had known Bill Clinton since we were in law school together. These coincidences and the essential bit of political luck that consists of being on the scene made me the chairman of the Federal Communications Commission—as described in the headline of *USA Today,* the "Top Cop of the Information Superhighway." In that job, I followed the leadership of Al Gore and an eclectic set of other political allies to help shape what is now called the New Economy of high growth, low inflation, productivity gains, and explosive entrepreneurial enterprise.

The communications revolution has had technological, economic, and political dimensions that are each and all beyond precedent or expectation. This multifaceted revolution would not have had such grand scale and scope but for the new laws that, in an era of extreme political disharmony, were enacted in the first term of the Clinton-Gore Administration. These laws—the 1993 Omnibus Budget Reconciliation Act and the 1996 Telecommunications Act—reversed one hundred years of pro-monopoly policy in the telephone and cable industries.

These legal reforms delegated to the Federal Communications Commission the responsibility for writing and enforcing the rules that introduced competition, and vast technological change, to communications markets. By passing such power to my much-maligned administrative agency, the Congress gave me a stunning opportunity to succeed or fail on the biggest stage on earth: the real-world theater that is important public office in Washington, D.C., the capital of America and the world. Now, several years after the events of my story, it appears that by a combination of design and luck, the Commission's economic and social decisions, embodied in hundreds of rulemakings and adjudications, have helped foster the rise of not only the New Economy but the Internet Society as well. These twin phenomena have created more wealth and more opportunity to enhance the quality of life for all citizens than any nation has ever enjoyed.

The coincidence of new technologies, a pro-competitive legal framework, and a balanced budget caused the information sector to double its share of the total American economy from 1992 to 1998. It has been the domain of two-thirds of all new jobs and one-third of all new investment. It is now one-sixth of the United States economy—twice the size of its share of most other countries' economies. Global desire to imitate this growth was a principal reason why the United States government was able in 1997 to convince most of the world to adopt our pro-competition communications reforms in a World Trade Organization treaty. More than a trillion dollars in additional global economic growth over the next decade will come from this negotiating success.

In our time at the FCC, my marvelous team also believed that all Americans had an inalienable right to share equally in the opportunities that technology creates. Our central effort, based on a vision articulated by Al Gore, was to have the federal government guarantee that new communications technology would be at the fingertips of every child in every classroom. Against vigorous political opposition, we fought from 1994 to 1997 to create the largest national program to benefit elementary and high school education in our country's history.

If the purpose of public office in America is to do the right thing for the people, the way to perform this duty is not self-evident. The meanings of "right" and "people" elude firm grasp. "Acting"—that is, using the power of government to enact rules, issue judgments with legal force, or effect results by setting an agenda—is also shrouded in uncertainty: what steps lead to what results? Even when the path is clear, political journeys are torturous. In our current era of politics, many factors militate against changes in policies. The self-styled Republican Revolution of November 1994 intensified the degree of difficulty for my group's ambitions, as the new leaders of Congress insisted vehemently on a narrow vision of the uses of government. My experience in public service was a battle, but exhilarating and rewarding.

Tom Wolfe, in *The Electric Kool-Aid Acid Test*, wrote: "I have tried not only to tell what the Pranksters did but to re-create the mental atmosphere or subjective reality of it. I don't think their adventure can be understood without that." I tried to put Wolfe's method (if not his inimitable style) into effect here so that the reader can form a judgment about public service in our time.

I did not take verbatim notes during my four years in government, but to the best of my ability I have accurately depicted the events described. For the detail-minded, my reference material includes records of meetings, speeches (on the World Wide Web at www.fcc.gov), and trade and general publication accounts of our doings at the FCC. The ultimate arbiter of facts has been memory. In aid thereof, however, I obtained comments on the manuscript from my friends and colleagues Nick Allard, Karen Brinkmann, Michael Buas, Jackie Chorney, Tom Craft, Gary Epstein, Ira Fishman, Jon Garcia, Julius Genachowski, Don Gips, Judy Harris, Peter Knight, Karen Kornbluh, Greg Lawler, Blair Levin, Richard Metzger, Ruth Milkman, Bob Pepper, Greg Rosston, Gretchen Rubin, Bob Sussman, Paul Taylor, Richard Tedlow, and Bill Young, all of whom were witnesses, participants, and soul mates in these events. They, and many others on our side, also were always "on the bus," as Ken Kesey put it. I also wish to acknowledge the friendship of Charles Firestone and the generosity of the Aspen Institute, whose assistance made this book possible; the great care, high skill, and fine loyalty of my assistant, Michael Gollust; the boundless support and vast wisdom of the best of agents and advocates, Andrew Wylie; the grace and insight of my editor, Jonathan Brent; and the infinite tolerance, support, and love of my family.

CAST OF CHARACTERS

Andrew Barrett was a Republican commissioner at the Federal Communications Commission from 1989 to 1996. He is currently a consultant in Washington, D.C.

Peggy Charren is the founder and former president of Action for Children's Television, based in Cambridge, Massachusetts. She is currently a visiting scholar at the Harvard University Graduate School of Education. She was awarded the Presidential Medal of Freedom in 1995.

Rachelle Chong was a commissioner at the FCC from 1994 to 1997. She is now a lawyer practicing in San Francisco.

Jackie Chorney worked at the FCC from 1992 to 1997. She was senior legal adviser to the chairman from 1996 to 1997. She is currently vice president in the Interaction Media Group of Discovery Communications, Inc.

Ruth Dancey has been at the FCC since 1993, serving as my confidential secretary from 1993 to 1997. She previously worked with me for seven years at Latham & Watkins.

Ira Fishman is currently a consultant on educational enterprises in Washington, D.C.

Julius Genachowski worked at the FCC from 1994 to 1997, and was chief counsel to the chairman from 1996 to 1997. He is now senior vice president, business affairs, general counsel, at USA Network, Inc.

Judy Harris was head of the Office of Legislative and Intergovernmental Affairs at the FCC from 1994 to 1996. She now practices law with the firm of Reed, Smith, Shaw, and McClay in Washington, D.C.

William Kennard has been chairman of the FCC since November 1997. He was general counsel from 1993 to 1997.

Karen Kornbluh joined the FCC from the staff of Senator John Kerry in 1994. She was head of the FCC Office of Legislative and Intergovernmental Affairs in 1997. In 1998 she was chief of technology policy in the Mass Media Bureau. She is currently deputy chief of staff at the Department of the Treasury.

Blair Levin and I met in 1975 when we both worked on the campaign for city council of Portland, Maine, of John O'Leary, my college roommate. Levin was chief of staff of the FCC from 1993 to 1997. Previously he was a lawyer in Raleigh, North Carolina. He is now a consultant in Washington, D.C.

Roy Neel is the president of the United States Telephone Association. He was deputy chief of staff to President Clinton and chief of staff to Vice President Gore during the first term of the Clinton Administration. He served on Al Gore's House and Senate staffs from 1977 to 1992.

Susan Ness has been an FCC commissioner since 1994. She was previously a banker and also has a law degree. She lives in Bethesda, Maryland.

James Quello was a commissioner of the FCC from 1974 to 1997, the longest tenure of any commissioner in history. In 1993 he was chairman. Previously he was an executive at a broadcast company in Michigan. He was a captain in World War II. He is presently writing his memoirs.

Paul Taylor is the executive director of the Free TV for Straight Talk Coalition, a nonprofit foundation in Washington, D.C. Previously he was a reporter at the *Washington Post*.

Such figures as Warren Buffett, Bill Clinton, Barry Diller, Richard Dreyfuss, Clint Eastwood, Mike Eisner, Bill Gates, Newt Gingrich, Al Gore, Sharon Lawrence, John Malone, Mike Ovitz, Bob Reich, Ray Smith, Steven Spielberg, and Sharon Stone need no identification here.

PART 1 **Experience Keeps a Dear School**

One **Coincidence**

Good government, independent thinking, the love of the fight for the right thing

ought to begin here—the enthusiasm of it all. Hang it, I can't express it; but the

idea is immense, and no one sees it.

Owen Johnson, Stover at Yale

Under the stage of Madison Square Garden, I stood in a conga line behind Mike Dukakis. The foot-stomping event above me was the Democratic National Convention of 1992. I was on my way to dance on television, along with hundreds of others, in honor of the party's nominees for the only two nationally elected offices in our democracy. The line began a rapid shuffle upstairs. I worried about tripping and falling on the former Democratic presidential candidate. I hoped my wife, Betsy, was watching on television back home in Bethesda. I wondered if the cameras would single me out. Perhaps I should have worn a funny hat; but that had not worked well for Dukakis.

We broke into the noise. Dukakis was swept up a level on the stage; I was shunted toward the bottom. Strobes played over our ranks. "Don't stop thinking about tomorrow," sang Fleetwood Mac. "Yesterday's gone. Yesterday's gone."

Yesterday—and if I wanted, tomorrow and all the days thereafter until retirement—I was a lawyer at Latham & Watkins, a successful national law firm. Long hours, hard work, good money, seventeen years of seniority so far. But in the Garden, I was a jiggling prop reeled onstage by the convention choreographers, third dancing line down from the top, stepping left and then right, left and then right, through innumerable renditions of the same song.

Above the dance lines, on the highest level of the stage, stood a fel-

3

low I had gone to high school with and another I knew from law school. The former, brown-haired, hazel-eyed, shy, strong, smiling. The latter, taller by a couple of inches, gray-to-blond bushy hair not much shorter than it had been when I met him in Admiralty class in 1972, seeming to greet everyone in America by his or her first name as he beamed at the distant camera. The former, Al Gore; the latter, Bill Clinton. They held uplifted hands. They believed they were on the way to the White House.

I started thinking about tomorrow, as Fleetwood Mac insisted. If my friends won the general election, I would be, according to my research, the only person in American history to have gone to high school with the Vice President and to law school with the President. Such syzygy of coincidence should not be under-utilized. If yesterday was gone, I had better make a plan for the future.

The day after the November 1992 election, Al Gore's closest advisers sat in attendance on the Vice President–elect in his modest suite at the Colonial Hotel in Little Rock. Al grinned at us and said, "Now we're running the White House. This is going to be fun."

We all laughed. Government would be fun. We would slay enemies, reward friends, celebrate victories, and find out what the Navy stewards served at the White House mess.

Al proceeded down a list of things to do, assigning everyone some task. He asked me to serve on Bob Reich's economic policy planning team. I had been at law school with not only the President-elect but also Professor Reich of Harvard, as well as Hillary Clinton and other members of Bill Clinton's team. I would be a good bridge between the Clinton and Gore camps.

Al would stake out both the environment and communications as his domestic policy specialties. Reich assigned me the job of outlining the Administration's agenda for the environment. I would work with Al's congressional aide, Carol Browner (destined to be head of the Environmental Protection Agency), and another of his aides, Katie McGinty (eventually head of the Council on Environmental Quality).

For the purpose of carrying out Al's vision for the information highway, the most important presidential appointment was chairman of the Federal Communications Commission. Inside the Beltway, the FCC drew a great deal of contempt from lawyers and lobbyists. I did not understand the reasons, but the private sector generally disparaged the Commission's methods and accomplishments. Partly for this reason, the FCC chairmanship was somewhat obscure and none of the President's many close friends sought the post. Nor did Al have a particular candidate from his own circle.

I had long wanted the opportunity of public service. Al's interest in promoting new technologies meant that it could be interesting and even important to be the chairman of the Federal Communications Commission. If the Vice President–elect wanted to cause change in this part of the economy, he needed someone dependable at the FCC. I decided to seek the post.

To broach the subject of my ambition, I had lunch with Roy Neel, designated to be Gore's chief of staff. In the clatter of the cheap silverware and heavy china of the Excelsior Hotel coffee room in Little Rock, open to the lobby where other office seekers could see us, I could not hear what Roy was saying. I asked him to repeat.

He said, "It's kind of cold in Little Rock in November, isn't it? I was freezing at the election party. Did you think Al went on too long? It didn't seem to bother Clinton. They sure make a great couple of families."

Roy continued, "I wish we could move back to Washington right away. Have to wait for inauguration, I suppose; that's traditional. So Al will have to stay at the Colonial at least through Christmas. Then he's going to have to move from Arlington. He won't like that. Loves his neighborhood, and I hear the Vice President's mansion is a rat trap, wind blowing through the clapboard."

He explored his soup with his spoon. "Now who do you think should be secretary of Education or Labor or HHS?" he asked. "The Governor, or President-elect—whichever we're supposed to call him—asked Al this morning."

Ignoring his question, I made my move, "Roy, I would like to be chairman of the Federal Communications Commission."

I explained that as Al's lieutenant at the most important communications agency, I could effectively implement his agenda. And, I added, from the work of Bob Reich's committee I could tell that the new Administration would want to promote investment by pushing a pro-competition agenda. In that event, an antitrust lawyer like me would be the right sort of person for the job.

"What's your second choice?" asked Roy, as he brought the bisque up from the bowl.

"There isn't one."

He took a sip of iced tea and said, "Well, I'll see what Al thinks. Did I tell you that the Clintons gave me golf balls and a golf shirt for my birthday? Wasn't that thoughtful?"

Everyone in Washington knew that Roy would rather play golf than do anything else in the world. But how did Bill Clinton know? Bill Clinton knew everything about everyone.

Several weeks later, Al said to me, "You've got to understand distance learning. I need you to study the impact of the media on families. We have to see the world through the eyes of a child. And we have to get the economy going through private investment instead of public spending, because we're going to balance the federal budget." When the meeting was over, Roy explained that Al had promised he would do what he could to get me the FCC job.

What could be more aggressively named than Renaissance Weekend, with its suggestion that the work of several centuries could be re-created in a couple of days at a resort? This annual gathering in Hilton Head of mostly modestly accomplished folks for easy-going seminars and a very staid New Year's Eve celebration was elevated in 1992 by the election of one of its own to the presidency. Suppressing the embarrassment of demonstrating ambition, I attended. I looked everywhere for the President-elect, but I found him nowhere.

Then, out running on the beach one morning, I encountered a hoard of bicyclists. Leading the pack like a tame, suburban version of Marlon Brando in *The Wild One* was Bill Clinton. I had seen him twice in the two decades since law school. As he passed, he called out, "Hello, Reed!"

Possibly he had studied the weekend guest list. Possibly he recalled that I had loaned him notes from tax class. But my heart skipped a beat at the hope that Al Gore had sold him on my candidacy.

However, the weeks passed, and rumors about the FCC were discouraging. In politics, all rumors are true. Another person was offered the FCC nomination. Miraculously, she declined the post. Then, in March, as I was leaning back in the chair in my law firm office, pondering questions I would ask at a deposition the next day, the phone rang.

"Hello, Reed? This is Al."

"Hello," I said, pulling my feet off the desk as if the Vice President had just walked through the door.

"The President is going to nominate you to be the chairman of the FCC."

For almost six months I had dreamed of this moment, and when it arrived I almost fell out of my chair, literally.

"Did you hear me?" asked Al.

Sitting up straight, I said, "I'm so grateful. I won't let you down. Or the President."

"Just do the best you can for the country," said the Vice President. He paused, and added, "Don't forget, public service is a privilege."

He hung up, and I realized my career had suddenly changed in a rare way. The President makes only about 500 Senate-confirmed appointments at the beginning of an Administration. I owed the job to Al Gore, of course. Indeed, I had never even been interviewed for the FCC chairmanship.

My duty, as I saw it, would be to fulfill Al's vision for the information highway. We would cause the new technologies of communications to spread across the country. We would not use public spending; the deficit precluded new spending. Instead, the Democratic Congress would rewrite the 1934 Communications Act to replace monopoly with competition, in accordance with Al Gore's wishes. Academics had long argued for this policy. It followed logically from the 1984 breakup of AT&T into a long distance company and the seven separate local telephone company monopolies called the Baby Bells. After this divestiture, competition had flourished in the long distance telephone market. Now it was time to introduce competition in the local markets. The technical regulatory challenges, I believed, were within the competencies I had developed in 17 years of litigating in antitrust and communications. From the White House, Vice President Gore would negotiate the new law with Congress, and at the FCC I would handle the fascinating details of issuing the regulations that put any necessary law into specific meaning and effect.

Upon announcement as the President's choice on June 29, 1993, I contracted laryngitis—a metaphor for the speechlessness urged by White House handlers on all nominees pending Senate confirmation. Cindy Skrzycki, poison-penned gossip columnist for the *Washington Post*, phoned me at home.

"What is your agenda?" she rasped.

"I can't talk to you," I croaked.

"That's what they tell you, isn't it?" she hissed. "Your handlers? Can't you give me any reason why you should be FCC chairman?"

"I can't talk to you."

"Not even one reason?"

"I really can't," I coughed.

She snapped, "That's ridiculous."

"No," I eked out of my throbbing throat, "I'm sick."

"Oh," she said, "that's a new excuse. You're faking, aren't you?"

Not really. If we could create the right marketplace conditions for investment in new technology, then private funds might build the information highway. But how exactly the Administration wanted Congress to rewrite the communications law, I did not know. And what, by the way, to do about violence on television, I had no idea. Not only did I have no new or old answers, I could scarcely describe the issues.

The White House staff assured me, however, that the confirmation process is when the nominee does *not* reveal the answer to any question. Everything is to be taken "under advisement." In the absence of information about my views, the industry magazine *Broadcasting & Cable* ran my photo on its cover under the label, "Mystery Chairman." A lobbyist for a public advocacy group told the press, "He looks splendid on paper and seems to have the right equipment—intelligence, understanding of the D.C. scene—but there are lingering doubts because he is an unknown quantity and has no track record."

Despite the dubiety, the Senate reviewed my financial statements, tolerated my "courtesy visits" to each of the Senators on the Commerce Committee (which had supervisory jurisdiction over the FCC), and held a committee hearing. Learning of my willingness to work with all the Senators on everything, the Senate Commerce Committee voted on me favorably, and I then began the wait for a full Senate vote. Meanwhile, as these steps in the process consumed the summer, Al Gore assembled a communications policy team, including Greg Simon from Al's staff; Commerce Secretary Ron Brown and his representatives Jonathan Sallett and Larry Irving; Gene Sperling from Bob Rubin's economic advisory team; Joe Stiglitz from the Council of Economic Advisers; Sally Katzen from the Office of Management and Budget; Anne Bingamann, head of the Antitrust Division of the Justice Department; and myself, albeit still as a private citizen. We began to design a complete revision of existing law.

A dozen of us met at least once every two weeks in Al's West Wing office, large by the standards of the White House, but small for our group's size. In each meeting, Al proceeded down a checklist of items. He heard discussion, asked questions, then resolved each matter with an explicit and prompt decision.

In order to promote economic growth, the group wanted to stimulate investment in new communications technologies. In order to produce consumer benefits, we wanted to promote competition. To these ends, Al and his team crafted a policy that reversed the century-old ordering of the information sector into separate monopolies, each tightly regulated by the FCC and local governments.

We wanted to permit the cable companies to compete in the telephone business, and the telephone companies to sell video, encouraging these industries to rebuild their networks to sell multimedia content against each other. We wanted to order the local Bell telephone companies to lease their phone lines to competitors. We planned to forbid the Bell companies from entering into the long distance business until competition actually existed in the local telephone market. And so forth, for months, the Gore team made dozens of separate decisions amounting to reform of almost every element of existing communications law.

At the end of one meeting, Al said, "Now we have to do something to connect the schoolgirl in Carthage, Tennessee, to the information highway."

We all grinned.

"I've used that expression before, have I?" he asked us.

Everyone continued to smile, and he deadpanned an earnest look. He had included the image of the Carthage schoolgirl rolling down the information highway in hundreds of speeches over the previous decade. "Should we put in the law a prohibition on that metaphor?"

"Whatever you say, Mr. Vice President," said an attention-seeker in the back of the room.

Al pretended to make a note in his pad. He often tried out his jokes to these friendly audiences. If we did not laugh, the press certainly would not. One of the requirements of public office in America is to be a stand-up comic, but the patter has to be self-deprecatory. Professional comedians rarely make jokes that put themselves down; another double standard.

"So what about education?" he asked.

"We need to build networks into schools," I said.

"Schools must already have telephone lines," said someone in the back.

"Telephone lines are surely in every school's principal's office," I said. "But if we want to make a difference in the way teachers teach and the way kids use technology, we have to build networks that connect to kids in their classrooms."

"This is a good thing," said the Vice President. No one disagreed. Not much more was said in those 1993 meetings about the reason to connect all classrooms to the information highway. Only later, for unforeseen reasons, did we develop a detailed explanation of the importance of this national mission.

In that first year of the Administration, our thinking on this topic was simple. Our agenda was stated in the campaign. We won. Now we had to fulfill the campaign promises. One was to use technology to improve education. Al Gore had long wanted this. And I wanted to do something for education from the FCC, based on my own difficult experience as a teacher in a public school after I graduated from college. I learned then that in public schools, America teaches inequality of opportunity to its next generation. The haves learn that they get everything the rich world can offer—more money spent per student, more athletic facilities, more art and more science, more, more, and more. The have-nots are taught that the country denies them an equal opportunity to learn: that is why their school buildings are decrepit and their books are old and their art classes are canceled and their sports equipment is second-hand. In our time, technology is a critical path to opportunity. Al Gore wanted it to be a benefit that was extended everywhere and to everyone on an equal basis. In that way we would improve not just the quality but also the equality of education.

In that long-ago year of 1993, Marc Andreesen and Netscape had not yet popularized the Web browser. Word of the universal addressing system called the World Wide Web (www), accessible through the footnoting technique known as hypertext markup language (html), had only begun to reach Washington. It was during our planning of the new communications law reform that Jon Sallett at the Commerce Department and Greg Simon, Al's chief domestic policy adviser, first showed me these "cool new tools" on their computers, and under Gore's leadership, the Administration quickly began putting government information on the Web. But in the Vice President's office, we did not talk about putting the Internet in classrooms; we did not know what specific technology would bring change to the education world. We only believed that government should guarantee that all necessary beneficial technologies were available equally to all students and all teachers.

Lines or pipes—the connections included in Al's term "the information highway"—were the physical links necessary to disseminate the new opportunities of technology to everyone. If these links were built to all classrooms, teachers, and students, then revolutionary change would come to education. The dimensions of the change were unforeseeable. But less than one percent of all spending in education was dedicated to technology. That amount would have to be doubled or tripled in order to link every classroom to the information highway. Cash-strapped public schools did not have the financial resources for this new spending; only schools for the well off would provide the new technologies to students. If the national government did not act to link all students to the information highway, then Gore's vision of the connection between any schoolchild and the world of knowledge would not be fulfilled.

As Al Gore formed the Administration's communications policy, the Senate and House Commerce Committees, led by Senator Ernest Hollings and Congressman Ed Markey, also moved forward with telecommunications reform bills. Negotiations among the Administration and these two powers produced a Democratic consensus that a new law should repeal the 1934 Communications Act's authorization of communications sector monopolies, subject to FCC regulation on the prices and services of the monopolies. Underlying this agreement was the desire of different industries (cable, local telephone, long distance telephone) to gain regulatory advantage against their rivals. Despite differences on the role of the Department of Justice, Democrats generally agreed that the FCC should be given the power to write rules that opened the local telephone, long distance, and cable markets to new competitors and that protected consumers from monopoly prices. As chairman of the FCC, I would have the interesting, technical, lawyerly job of doing that work.

Senator Bob Dole, Republican minority leader, extracted various prices from the White House before permitting my confirmation vote in the Senate. He demanded the right to pick one of the Republican members of the Federal Election Commission. Then he insisted on selecting a Republican commissioner for the FCC from a list submitted by the White House, which his staff said could only include "Real Republicans"—meaning they had not publicly supported Bill Clinton.

The FCC is an independent agency with five commissioners appointed by the President and confirmed by the Senate. The President selects one of the commissioners to be the chairman. Only three of the commissioners can be in the same political party as the President. The agency's rules and orders are enacted when a majority of commissioners votes for them. The Commission's authority to write detailed rules and specific orders comes from laws passed by Congress—that is why Congress regards the agency as its creature, whereas the White House prefers to think of it as related to the Administration.

The new President had only one Democratic seat to fill—the chairmanship. Incumbent Democratic commissioner Ervin Duggan was a Bush appointee, but I was told he was a friend of Bill Clinton's from Renaissance Weekend and would be helpful to me. Commissioner Jim Quello, 79—the chairman pending my confirmation—nominally filled a Democratic seat, but that was only a flag of convenience he had been asked to fly by Presidents Nixon, Ford, Reagan, and Bush each time they had appointed him. Republican commissioner Andrew Barrett's term ran until 1996. However, if Dole picked a "Real Republican" for the other Republican seat, then that appointee could join Barrett and Quello to form a majority against me.

On the other hand, if Democrats Jim Quello and Erv Duggan were with me, I would have the upper hand. Despite the closeness of these calculations, I believed that, regardless of party labels, we at the Commission would take our decisions judiciously, with a minimum of partisanship. In the high-minded atmosphere generated by legal and economic analysis, I assumed that, as a career advocate, I could persuade the others to adopt my point of view, such as it might be on a given issue.

While waiting on Dole to allow the confirmation vote, I persuaded a friend of nearly 20 years, Blair Levin, to become my chief of staff when I was confirmed. Upon my confirmation, he would leave his North Carolina law firm, and at the end of the school year move his wife and children to Washington. During the weeks before the Senate confirmation, commuting from North Carolina by car every Monday morning (a dawn ride through the tobacco fields), Blair joined me for confidential meetings with each part of the Commission.

The FCC career staffers swaddled us in details, acronyms, procedural requirements, legal prohibitions. They told us little of the Commission's inner workings. Their reticence suggested distrust. Or perhaps they anticipated a short term of office for Blair and me. That was not unusual for political appointees. If I stayed only a couple years, there would not be much reason for the career staff to teach me, much less to take any political risks for me. Or possibly they were only waiting to be told what I planned to do at the Commission.

I learned that the historical tradition of the Commission was that the chairman, working with the bureaus among which the Commission's jurisdictions were allocated, made the tentative decisions on major issues. The lobbying corps, press, and congressional staffs judged the chairman on whether he obtained majority votes for his recommended decisions. These expectations encouraged the chairman to compromise issues with other commissioners, so as to be sure of obtaining a majority. This process encouraged commissioners to run the agency by committee. During his interim chairmanship, Jim Quello created such a committee; it was his chance to run the agency in the way he had preferred in his nearly 20 years as a commissioner. If, as chairman, I adopted the same method of governance, Quello would retain enhanced power even upon return to the status of commissioner.

Each bureau and office of the Commission briefed me on its reason for being and explained the various "items"—proposed rules and orders— that it was preparing for Commission vote. In several thousand decisions per year (of which several hundred were voted by the commissioners and the rest made by bureau and office chiefs), the Commission determined the shape and the rules of the information sector of the economy. A feature of the Commission, as far as I could tell, was that in some respects it regulated too much, in others, too little. Some determinations were wildly wrong, in that the rules shrunk economic growth, limited jobs, increased prices to consumers, and minimized entrepreneurship. Other determinations were arguably useful to business and, occasionally, consumers; but these often appeared compromised, incomplete. Even as the staff taught me the substance of the Commission's work, the question of which rules were right and which were wrong was hardly discussed. It was as if the decisions emanated from an invisible and unalterable machine.

In sum, the FCC drew a blueprint for the most important economic activity of the country: the information sector. In this part of the economy, then about seven percent of the whole, five lanes of the information highway ran toward the future: broadcast, cable, wire, wireless, and satellite. Since the 1934 Communications Act, these were legally separate industries; for the most part none was permitted to compete with any other. Each was regulated so as to work well and to earn steady but unspectacular profits. FCC rules kept the monopolies intact, and drew the dividing lines between the lanes.

Over the decades, technologies evolved in ways that threatened the legal division between industries: different delivery mediums could deliver similar content and services. To maintain separateness, the FCC's rules grew increasingly complex and ridden with compromises. For example, I learned that under the rules, television broadcasters had a right to have their wares distributed on cable television channels, but they could not buy cable companies. Local telephone companies could not provide long distance service to consumers, but they could charge long distance companies an average of six cents per minute for originating and terminating long distance calls. Local television stations could not merge with local newspapers, but newspapers could buy television stations in cities in which they did not publish. By the 1990s, academic commentators had concluded that the hodgepodge of regulatory restrictions made no sense.

Technological advances permitted firms to enter new markets. Relaxing restrictions on the use of technologies could be pro-competitive. For example, the telephone companies could use new technologies to deliver video to the home and, even more readily, could offer long distance at new cheap prices. Consumers should enjoy the benefits of convergence of technologies and business organizations: specifically, consumers should have a choice of sellers, who would become both innovative and efficient in order to compete successfully.

Behind the existing rules, however, were two unwritten principles. First, by separating industries through regulation, government provided a balance of power in which each industry could be set against one another in order for elected figures to raise money from the different camps that sought advantageous regulation. Second, by protecting monopolies, the Commission could essentially guarantee that no communications businesses would fail. Repealing these implicit rules was a far less facile affair than promoting competition.

Between 1983 and 1993, for instance, the country had two cellular telephone companies in every geographic area. These companies did not compete vigorously on price or quality. They built the worst quality, most out-of-date cellular systems of any developed country in the world. But in this duopoly system, each cellular telephone company generated great value for investors.

The two-firm market was protected by the FCC's refusal to make more spectrum (or airwaves) available for cellular firms. But in the Omnibus Budget Reconciliation Act of 1993, passed by Al Gore's tie-breaking Senate vote, the Democratic Congress gave the FCC authority to dissolve this oligopoly by auctioning new licenses. Consumers, and the economy, would benefit hugely from the investment and innovation in wireless markets that followed, but existing companies reacted negatively to the threatened deterioration of their political alliances and the effects of new entry into their markets.

The Clinton Administration had the conviction that astute and sharp-edged rules could open markets to competitors not only in communications but in energy, environmental technology, health care, and other markets. In every market, some firms would succeed, others fail. But the competition would create choice for consumers, and the diversity of the competitors would weaken the political influence of the big, established (and typically Republican-leaning) firms. The new competitive markets would stimulate investment in new technologies and lead to fair prices for consumers. All five lanes of the information highway would converge in a race to tomorrow (which we would not stop thinking and talking about). If Congress passed the new telecommunications reform law that the Vice President wanted, I would then receive the delegated power to put the new convergence blueprint in place. In a couple of years, my job done, I could return to law practice, like Cincinnatus back to the farm.

As I waited through November for my Senate confirmation vote, I arranged to meet the popular Jim Quello for lunch at the Palm on 19th Street, across the street from the Commission building. Aware that I needed a voting ally and a mentor in the ways of the Commission, I assumed my place in Quello's "favorite booth," where Jim greeted a legion of well-wishing lobbyists under a huge cartoon painting of his cheery countenance.

He opened with what I hoped was the bottom line: "Kid, I'll support you all the way. I'm loyal. I know who got my mug on the wall." He referred not to the painting but to the addition of his photograph to those of the other FCC chairmen that were displayed on a wall in the Commission meeting room. That was by dint of President Clinton's selection of him as chairman while my nomination was under Senate consideration. He assured me that he knew Al Gore was responsible for picking him over the other incumbent Democratic commissioner, Erv Duggan. Knowing nothing about the facts of the matter, I nodded.

Quello continued over his corned beef hash, "But I've got some advice for you."

I leaned forward to listen.

Poking his chin at my sole, Quello said, "Kid, don't order the special."

He explained that the regular meals on the menu were less than ten dollars; the waiter's daily additions, always about twice as much. I got it. From time to time, he would take me to lunch at the Palm (meaning, he would teach me the Commission's ways) as long as I did not order the specials (there were limits to his support). I said I looked forward to regular lunches (I'd be his ally). Afterward, he commented to the Associated Press, "[Hundt] looks like a very solid guy. I'll help him."

Yet I was still not confirmed as the end-of-the-year congressional recess approached. Blair Levin had a friend at the White House fax us the Administration's list of choices for possible Republican nominees for commissioner, culled from letters sent to the President by a hodgepodge of interest groups and Congressmen. I found a reference to a lawyer from California, Rachelle Chong. Nothing in her file revealed a vote for Bill Clinton in November 1992. I put her on a list that, with a push from the Vice President, the White House sent to the Senate minority leader for his review. Predictably, Dole found "Real Republican" Chong's profile compelling and selected her. The White House promised that she would be nominated when the Senate returned in January. On this understanding, on November 20, 1993, a day before the Senate adjourned for the year, Senator Dole permitted me to be confirmed.

The Vice President swore me into public office on November 29, 1993. My family and Jim Quello met the Vice President in his glittering ceremonial office in the Old Executive Office Building and walked from there through the hallways to the high-vaulted, cacophonous Indian Treaty Room (the room where Native Americans had signed away their claims on the continent). In the classic triptych of our democracy, I raised my right hand while placing my left on the Bible (Old Testament only) that my wife Betsy held, and as I looked at Al, I repeated the oath after him (part of its magic), swearing with all my heart to protect and defend the Republic from all enemies foreign and domestic (and who would decide who they were?).

Then it was my turn to speak to the crowd, according to the custom.

I was amused to recall that when we debated in Government Club on Thursday nights in high school, I had never successfully silenced Al. But now I had him, the Vice President, in a captive audience.

I conceived of my job as calling for an opaque, judicial demeanor, but I knew the occasion called for something personal. As a compromise, I told the story of my father's childhood.

During the Depression, when my father was nine years old, his father died. His mother, my grandmother, was left jobless, living in an apartment in Milwaukee. She got a job as a switchboard operator—a new invention of the telephone industry. The communications revolution kept the mother and son going. My father went on to the University of Wisconsin, and after the war he got a law degree on the G.I. Bill. In turn, I explained, I received the education that had led to my wonderful opportunity to help build the information highway to all Americans.

"If by our work at the FCC, I can add only one job," I concluded, "I will call my family's account with history balanced."

A smattering of applause, not too long, but long enough in the echoing room. Al grabbed me by the arm and whispered to me briefly before trooping down the Secret Service–marked path to the elevator and the next event in his day of ceremonies and deliberations, experiences of pomp and exercises in persuasion. "Only one job," he said. "That's good. Best not set the bar too high."

The night I was sworn in, Betsy and I went to the White House— for the first time not as tourists—to a jazz concert hosted by Ameritech, the midwestern Bell telephone company. We sat with Jim Quello and his wife, Mary.

Quello leaned across his wife and said, as he had at the Palm, "I'll work with you. We need to knock those cable rates down. You can count on me." Then the President and the First Lady entered the room like gods descending to Ilium, unpredictably altering human destiny, immortal (at least through 1996). Ameritech's fate depended on how the Administration chose to rewrite the nation's communications laws. The company's corporate officers sat with the President. I was in the back of the room with Quello. The Commission had its place in the pecking order of Washington, and it was not that high. But from the quaint, edenic politics of friendship, I had won the job I wanted.

Two **Cockiness Goeth Before**

If you seek *yourself* outside yourself, then you will encounter disaster.

Harold Bloom, Omens of Millennium: The Gnosis of Angels,

Dreams and Resurrection

R uth Dancey, my administrative assistant at my law firm and now confidential secretary to the chairman, waited alone on the ground floor of the FCC's building to welcome me on day one of my public service: November 30, 1993. Someone had printed out a sign on ancient IBM computer paper and taped it above the elevator banks: "Welcome Chairman Hundt." The greeting drooped in the middle where the adhesive would not stick to the greasy wall. We passed apprehensively beneath the foreshadowing, and entered the ancient elevators. They groaned and shuddered, as if no return were possible, and deposited Ruth and me on the famous eighth floor where the commissioners' offices were set around the outer edge of the building. She led me through a maze of narrow beige-painted walls until we emerged into the low-ceilinged, dust-filled open space labeled the "Chairman's Office."

A battered desk, a sofa and chair setting, a large Formica table ringed by plastic swivel chairs. A sitcom studio setting, with one artifact: a globe denoting Manchukuo, the borders of Nazi Germany, and the blue and red swatches of colonized Africa. It was a thing willed down from chairman to chairman, through the eras of radio to television, analog to digital, terrestrial to satellite, narrowband copper to broadband cable.

Then I saw the wall.

The wall of the chairman's office. You wanted to touch it to learn what it was made of. Grass or sisal or straw, something that had once grown, or was perhaps still growing. And it was dusty. The dust had coated the room during the interregnum—the 11 months between the departure of the George Bush chairman and my arrival in his vast, dirty, ugly, grass-lined office.

"Ruth, they might have cleaned it," I said, surveying my quarters.

"I knew you would say that. I asked the staff already."

"And?"

"They wanted to see if you were confirmed. Then they ordered a cleaning crew."

"Maybe we should get a lawn care company," I said. "I think I'm allergic to this grass. Who put this cover on the wall?"

"I asked that."

"And?"

"A chairman's wife. They're not sure which chairman."

"Can we replace it?"

"I asked that too. Give me time to get things the way you want them."

Blair Levin entered stage left, walking past a decrepit, ancient coffee maker and a tiny refrigerator identifiable from a distance by a rancid milk smell. Heterogeneous chipped and salacious dishes were stacked in the nearby metal sink.

"Welcome, Mr. Chairman," he said.

From my arrival at the Commission, most people referred to me as "Mr. Chairman." It was a term used by some to show respect, by others to create distance, by Blair, ironically. Erv Duggan, the Bush-appointed Democratic commissioner, called me "Mr. Chairman" when I visited him on day one. Then he told me he was resigning to become the head of the Public Broadcasting System. Instantly, therefore, I needed pseudo-Democrat Jim Quello or holdover Republican commissioner Andrew Barrett to compose a majority for any decision. Later, the Administration would fill Duggan's seat with a Clinton Democrat, who would match up with Real Republican Chong. But before and after the two new commissioners arrived, Jim Quello would be the swing vote, capable of making a majority for the Clinton Democrats, or siding with a Dole Republican faction that might emerge. Either I would be an effective chair, or Quello-Chong-Barrett would be in charge.

Another revelation on day one was the omnipresence of congressional influence on the commission's work. On my desk were letters from several hundred Congressmen and Senators complaining that the Commission had blundered a few months earlier in its rules implementing the 1992 Cable Act. As Senate Commerce Committee Chairman Ernest Hollings, Democrat from South Carolina, stated in his letter, "the intent of Congress to protect consumers from unjustified rate increases is not being met. We're hearing about rate increases, complex formulas and outright evasion and mockery of the law by cable operators." The letter demanded a revision of the cable regulations Chairman Quello's FCC had written.

I learned quickly that the volume of lobbying defined the major issues before the agency. On questions like the price paid by long distance companies for connecting to the local telephone system, as many as 50 different teams of lobbyists pounded the linoleum halls of the Commission building for not hours but weeks, sometimes months. A single company might send soldiers from its regiments to the Commission as many as 100 times, visit or phone the chairman on a dozen occasions, call some member of the chairman's staff perhaps daily. Congressional staffers made tens of thousands of telephone calls to Commission staff. Congressmen wrote letters on behalf of different parties, up to 5,000 or more a year. Sometimes, when the members wanted a particular result they phoned the commissioners to solicit votes as they might call each other on the Hill. Smart and well-financed lobbyists also ran media strategies to persuade the Commission to write rules in their favor. Industries might spend millions of dollars on television advertising to influence a handful of commissioners.

Cable regulation was an important business and voter issue. The 1992 Cable Act was the only law passed over George Bush's veto. The lobbying over the FCC rulemaking that set the prices for cable had been very intense in 1993, and was equally pressured when I took another crack at the rules after I arrived at the Commission. The country has 16,000 separate cable franchisees. Choices abounded. Should the FCC lower prices for all franchisees in all markets by a percentage? Or by a fixed dollar amount? Or by a formula that reflected deviations from a national average or by costs of building a system in a particular place or by some other of hundreds of possible techniques?

Usually on communications issues, in its laws Congress punted the details to the FCC. Acting alone or in groups defined by co-signing letters to the FCC, Congressmen then pushed the Commission toward some interpretation of the law. The language of the law seemed merely the medium of debate, as opposed to the source of direction on how to write the rule at issue. Indeed, in the case of cable, and many other matters over time, upon examining the details of a rule one could only conclude that the lawmakers had expressed no transparent intent about the desired result. Hence the forceful, if conflicting, guidance from the members appeared justified, or at least relevant, to those concerned with maintaining good relations with the Hill.

The lobbyists for the cable industry reveled in the complexity of rate regulation and the ambiguity of the law, and listening to their arguments, before I arrived the Commission indeed had flummoxed its work. The FCC price regulation resulting from the Cable Act had two effects. First, no cable company lost revenue. Second, one-third of the country's cable consumers had their prices raised by government fiat. The newspapers and the consumer groups shrieked that prices were supposed to have gone down. It was my job to fix these failed rules.

Still another dimension of the real FCC materialized a few days later. I was taken down to the street to welcome the FCC's new $100,000 Ford, a vinyl and blackwalls job chockablock with antennae, tuners, and radar equipment worthy of a Tom Clancy novel. Its purpose was, in the words of an FCC enforcement agent, "to trace spurious emissions."

"Excuse me?"

"Yes, Mr. Chairman. Unauthorized use of the airwaves. Pirate radio. Spurious emissions."

I said, "Suppose we just let the emitters emit?"

"It's against the law. Pirate radios use unauthorized wavelengths for their broadcasts."

"Can we hear them?"

"If you tune in to them."

"What kind of formats do they favor?"

Ignoring my question as an attempt at humor on an inappropriate subject (crime), the agent demonstrated how the car could find the naughty signal and then drive to its source. The previous year, for example, a spurious emitter was found in Staten Island, sending a signal on a frequency band normally used by boats ("marine craft"). Someone was drowning! In the middle of Staten Island? In hot pursuit of the emission, a helicopter whipped overhead; the fantastically pricey Ford skidded up the suburban driveway. Airwave Police rappelled from the sky, others burst from the car. Frequency monitors clicked like machine guns. The government agents stormed into the garage. Their find: a motorboat up on wheels. Its shorted radio was fraudulently calling for help.

Notwithstanding this peculiar anecdote, the radio car driven up to the Commission did not have many miles on the odometer. Seems that we have a big country and it takes a long time to drive the car from one spurious emission to another; a longer time than the emissions continue. So the car was used primarily for demos.

Not just the agency's work but the agency's customs were curious. A week after I started, the thousand lawyers and lobbyists of the Federal Communications Bar Association (more than 200 of them for every member of my personal staff!) summoned me for the annual event known as the Chairman's Dinner. On this festive, near-holiday occasion, the private industry advocates oblige the chairman to do a stand-up comedy routine. The audience cannot lose: either they are amused by the jokes, or they are amused by the failure of the chairman to tell good jokes. Blair Levin, my friend Nick Allard, and I spent at least ten hours working on my ten-minute monologue. I was mildly entertaining, judging by the mild applause. The evening bespoke the existence of a complex FCC culture in which, by night as well as day, Mr. Chairman was expected to gratify the influential agents of private sector puissance.

In December 1993, John Malone—the number one cable executive in the world, chief of Tele-Communications, Inc., nicknamed "Darth Vader" (for his asserted hostility to cable consumers and municipal franchisers) by a youthful Senator Al Gore in the 1980s—invited Blair and me to dine in a private room, as if we had something to hide. We were joined by his Washington representative (the term denotes a cynic skilled in flattery), his lawyer (closely connected to the White House so as to suggest a message from my captains), and the president of Bell Atlantic, Jim Cullen.

Malone had agreed to sell the country's biggest cable company to Bell Atlantic, the mid-Atlantic regional telephone company. Although subject to the FCC's approval, it portended to be the largest merger in history. With small strong chopping gestures that shook his frail chair (the more expensive the restaurant, the less sturdy the furniture), he described the convergence of the nation's cable systems with the telephone networks. As Malone explained, Ray Smith, chairman of Bell Atlantic, and he would combine hundreds of billions of dollars of assets to give Americans pictures on their telephones and conversations on their televisions. All this would be possible, of course, only if Congress passed a new law dropping the legal barriers that kept the telephone and cable industries from competing against each other, and if the Administration permitted the combinations of capital necessary to finance the necessary overhaul of the infrastructure. If Bell Atlantic and TCI both lobbied for the law, surely Congress would pass it. Of course, if we at the FCC over-regulated cable, or did not bless the merger, we would create business havoc. The country would be denied the benefits of convergence. I understood that in this event not only would I be blamed, but the Vice President would be castigated as anti-business, given that I was his agent.

The next night, Blair and I dined with two visionaries—Nick Negroponte, head of MIT's Media Laboratory, and George Gilder, professional futurist and free marketeer. Glowering, self-confident Negroponte was the popularizer of the famed "Negroponte switch"—the theory that what traditionally goes over the air (such as broadcast television) would be transmitted on fiber optic or coaxial wires, whereas what normally travels by wire (such as voice telephony) would go wireless. The thesis was based on the low cost of transmission on wires, relative to wireless. It reflected a belief that in the future, technology and economics would match content with the appropriate conduit. Thus, because fiber optic cables naturally carried information more cheaply than did the airwaves, information-rich content, like video, should go on cables, and thin content, like voice communication, should go over the air.

George Gilder's words burst forth in clumps like (I was to learn in years to come) compressed data down fiber. He assured us that the elimination of a governmental role in communications was necessary to unleash boundless business energy and assure the country's safe homecoming at the Ithaca of the information age. The Bell Atlantic–TCI merger would be a boat to a new world where a single firm delivered massive bandwidth—a huge volume of information per second—for whatever price the market would bear. If government repealed all laws and regulations, then in time, through networks, consumers would buy and sell, teach and learn, give and receive education, health care, whatever. At fantastically low cost, pictures, words, numbers in infinite volume would sail from point to point, from person to person. Government could not stop this new world from taking shape, and in it, government would have scant purpose.

I loved their enthusiasm, and I agreed with their dismissal of the existing regime of pro-monopoly, anti-competitive regulation. But a corollary of the Negroponte-Gilder argument was that cable rate regulation was a disastrously bad idea, because lowering revenue from consumers would reduce investment in bandwidth. In other words, they were saying that consumers should pay more to build bandwidth. This vision did not appear to benefit all Americans of all income levels and ages. Moreover, under the Gilder-Negroponte thesis, I should repeal all FCC rules and close the agency. Instead, the Administration was bent on using the agency to promote investment, innovation, and the Carthage schoolgirl's incorporeal trips to the Library of Congress.

"You're at Royce Hall, University of California Los Angeles campus, with Barbra Streisand in the audience and Al Gore backstage. You're on national television. Don't be nervous," said Blair on a sunny day in January 1994. He walked away anxiously, then returned with more advice: "You need to be funny, but not funnier than the Vice President. He follows you." Blair was looking over my shoulder at the famous faces filling the Green Room: Barry Diller, Mike Eisner, Dick Cavett. (One purpose of my job, I was realizing, was to meet celebrities.)

The UCLA conference—with an audience of students, business and government leaders, assorted Hollywood figures, and the general public—was assembled by a Disney executive as a kind of indirect lobbying on the government's rewriting of the communications law. The purpose of the conference was to explain the convergence of technologies into the information highway: what it was and how it would be built.

I went on stage for the first of four years of warm-ups, set-ups, and intros for Al Gore. I explained to the gathering crowd (in California it is not fashionable to be on time for the preliminaries) that at the end of the 19th century Gustavus Swift invented the refrigerated railroad car. But the railroad cartel refused to let him ship meat from Chicago to New York. He beat the monopolists by running the cars over Canadian lines. But there was not in all industries a Canada available to bypass monopoly.

Behind this laborious anecdote was point one of my message: what we called "access." If you could get the meat to New York, the economy would grow. Message point two was "jobs" or "economic growth." Swift had employed people in Chicago. Point three was "reinventing government." I had *some* difficulty applying the Canadian story to the challenge of making the FCC smart and effective. No English-speaking place is more remote from Los Angeles than Canada. Perhaps that was the reason my message did not sell. When I finished, the skimpy applause drained my tiny store of confidence.

"Good work," said Blair when I returned from the podium, shaky and hoarse. "No risk of stealing the scene from Al."

Unveiling the Administration's policies (developed in those many hours in his West Wing office), the Vice President predicted that the communications revolution would transform education and health care and economic growth. In metaphors of parallel processing drawn from the computer industry, he envisioned the convergence of computers and communications. He outlined the basic principles of a policy revolution: the Administration would repudiate the embrace of monopoly by government and instead use the power of law to open all markets to innovation, competition, new investment, new entrepreneurs. Convergence meant that technologies like cable, telephone, wireless, and satellite would compete to offer choice to consumers. In addition, all Americans would benefit from government's funding of communications technology in classrooms.

Al is an idealist in the Emersonian sense—for him the idea and the plan take precedence over the story in the next day's newspaper. After he lost in the Democratic presidential primaries in 1988, Al decided to study in more detail the topics he felt were critical to reshaping Democratic Party policies: economics, international finance and trade, tax policy, the role of innovation and development in increasing productivity. Peter Knight, then Al's chief of staff, and I designed a course of seminars, one or two hours a week, and brought to Al's Senate office edgy thinkers and tested pundits— Nobel Prize–winning economist Kenneth Arrow from Stanford; Stanford's Brian Arthur, one of the earliest popularizers of the theory of network effects; chaos mathematician Per Bak; Richard Tedlow, one of the country's finest business historians, from Harvard Business School; and many others. The professors and the Senator developed insights that two years later would find their way into Al's famous book, *Earth in the Balance*. Later, the learning of the seminars found expression in his belief that a new communications policy could unleash vastly beneficial, technologically driven change in the economy and in society.

After Al spoke, I had my first meeting with Barry Diller, chairman of QVC Network, Inc., the shopping channel. Scalp shining, eyes blazing, Diller discussed his titanic bidding war with Sumner Redstone for control of the movie studio that used to employ Diller.

"Paramount," he said, in a rich baritone. "Some days I want it. Some days I wish he'd win the bidding. I can't make up my mind."

"In any event," he said, "your job is simple." He stared into my ignorant eyes. "Just get them to build two pipes into every home. Cable and telephone will each put a pipe in. That way I'll have a choice when I negotiate who will carry my content."

Like Gilder and Negroponte, Barry Diller apparently believed that pipes would efficiently carry voice and video communications. But unlike the two futurists, he feared a pipe monopolist would gouge him on the cost of carriage. Diller was a content-maker, and like Gus Swift, he wanted multiple channels to get to the consumer so that competition would drive his distribution costs down.

In another corner of the Green Room, Bell Atlantic chairman Ray Smith hovered off John Malone's elbow. Smith would run the combined Bell Atlantic–TCI, the company that would be created by the biggest corporate merger in history. Later that day, he explained to the audience that in his vision Bell Atlantic and TCI would together build the information highway to two-thirds of the homes of the country. As monopolies—cable in some markets and telephony in others—the two companies would earn enough profits to build the interactive, multimedia communications networks that his Bell Atlantic engineers were itching to construct. The cost would amount to more than $200 billion, but if joined, the twin monopolies could carry the weight of the expenditure.

Three problems were revealed only later. One, the Bell Atlantic engineers believed the cable network was technically unsuitable for their purposes. Two, the Bell Atlantic plan ignored the Internet. Three, Ray Smith's one-pipe monopoly would require government regulation in perpetuity, whereas our policy was to introduce competition and then to deregulate.

Blair asked the merger partners, "So what about classrooms?"

John Malone smiled thinly, as if looking down from his saddle at a sheepherder.

Blair continued, "Would this information highway built by TCI and Bell Atlantic run all the way into the classrooms?"

Some in Congress wanted a law that required the telephone companies to offer discounted prices to schools for local and long distance service. Behind this idea was the goal of promoting distance learning—meaning the delivery on live video of a particular lecture to a remote school that did not have that particular expertise on its payroll.

But Al Gore's goal of classroom access reflected a vision of community, not just distance learning. The Vice President's speech at UCLA spoke not just of access to *schools,* but access to *classrooms.* Teachers for a hundred years had been the most isolated workers in the economy. Networks in every classroom would end that isolation.

With access to classrooms, every parent would be able, by telephone and e-mail, to contact every teacher. Teachers would communicate with one another not just over coffee in the lounge, but on computer networks. They would exchange lesson plans, share information about students, and reduce administrative hierarchy as communications eliminated layers of management.

Malone turned to Smith, "What about it, boss?"

"Pardon?"

"What about the classrooms?"

"Sure. Schools. We already connect to schools," said Ray Smith. Telephone companies had for years promised state officials they would give preferential rates to schools as a quid pro quo in agreements to increase or at least not decrease the price of basic dial-tone service to residential consumers. Teachers in *classrooms,* however, were left unconnected.

"No," said Blair. "I said classrooms."

The difference was the billions of dollars necessary to put wire or wireless networks into the two million classrooms of 100,000 schools, as opposed to the few million dollars it would cost to give cheap rates for the telephone in the principal's office.

A year later, McKinsey and Company, the consulting firm, would estimate the total cost of networking every classroom in the United States at about $10 billion. That sum represented less than one percent of annual spending on education and even a smaller percentage of the annual revenue from the communications market. But it would be the largest single national program to aid elementary and secondary schools in the history of the country.

"How about it, Ray?" laughed Malone.

"Sure," Smith said. "If that's what they want, we will do every classroom." Paris is worth a mass, said the medieval king who converted to Catholicism to win the city. Smith would be a Gore person to get his deal approved.

We rode back to Washington on Air Force Two. The grandeur of the long silver jet that boldly announced itself as "The United States of America" and the magnitude of our decisions merged in my mind. This Administration was going places, and in high style.

Back in Washington, at the Commission, my law school classmate Judy Harris clattered on her tall heels across the linoleum toward me as I approached the chairman's office. I had been trying to enter stealthily. I hoped to escape a sighting by the lobbyists who trolled the narrow halls. I pulled her into the office, even as she began talking.

Judy's mind was a maze through which a powerful intellect drove to firm conclusions. No one could imitate her path of reasoning but all were intimidated by her consideration of an infinity of choices. When I first met Judy, she sat in an adjacent study carrel in the law school library. Her blonde hair hung down like Rapunzel's. Now, twenty-five years later, it was a mop of curls that she shook in agreement, then disagreement, with her various opinions.

Judy was one of several friends—from law school, college, high school—who joined me at the Commission. Judy, a Washington lawyer, and her husband, Norm Ornstein, a political commentator of wit and substance, knew everyone in town. She had agreed to run the Office of Legislative Affairs at the FCC.

Judy said as she followed me into my office, "You've got to get to know the Hill. John Dingell and Ed Markey are the keys." Dingell of Michigan was then chairman of the all-powerful House Energy and Commerce Committee; Markey was chairman of the Telecommunications Subcommittee.

"Ed will be a great friend," she continued, "but Big John is more complicated. You have no relationship with him. He can be impossible. The way you can be. If he gets to know you, it could backfire. It probably will. You could charm him. Anyone would know better than me how to do this. We'll have Tom Downey do it."

She offered me a chocolate from a large box of bonbons she carried everywhere like a talisman against political blunders. Her reference was to former congressman Downey, good friend of Al Gore, former compatriot of Big John Dingell. Shortly thereafter, Downey invited my wife and me to his row house on Capitol Hill for a diplomatic dinner with John and Debbie Dingell.

Big John was enormous, unsmiling, menacing as a bomb.

"Do you know what I learned when I first went into politics?" he asked me. The bomb appeared to be ticking.

He ignored any answer I might produce. The question—like all his questions, I would learn—was rhetorical.

"No," I said, hoping to forestall an explosion.

He resumed, "My father was a New Deal Democrat. Helped Roosevelt in everything. Never passed health care. That's my responsibility. My father's dream shall be fulfilled when I succeed. I promised Hillary Clinton on my father's grave that we shall pass a law that gives health care to every American, poor as well as rich."

Big John adjusted his bulk in Downey's easy chair. He began again, "My father died suddenly, in 1955. I was 29. I immediately gave some consideration to stepping into his shoes, not that they were small in any respect. I went to the editor of the major newspaper in the district. He had always supported Dad. I expected his assistance. I asked for his help. Do you know what he said?"

I shook my head. He smiled, as if pleased with the punch line he was about to deliver.

"He said, 'Son, you're going into politics. Here's my advice: Grow thick skin.'"

John glowered at me for effect, and added, "I thought he would say he'd help. I was angry. But it was the best advice I ever got. Man's a fool who can't take good advice."

I gathered that I too should aspire to grow thick skin. I did not realize then that in the fullness of time John Dingell himself, as a friend of the Bell companies, would remove my original layer.

After dinner, as he smoked an enormous cigar, John said, "I'll never tell you what to do. But I want no surprises. I don't want you to be like that sneaky guy Reagan sent over to the FCC. I don't recall his name. The sneaky one. The one who didn't do what I wanted."

I suggested he might be alluding to Mark Fowler. I neglected to mention that affable, conservative Fowler was not only Ronald Reagan's FCC chairman but also my friend and former law partner.

"That's the one. Don't be like him."

The next chapter of my introduction to the politics of the House was lunch with Ed Markey, Democratic chairman of the House Telecommunications Subcommittee and prince to King John Dingell of the full Energy and Commerce Committee.

Markey invited me to his private office in the Rayburn Building. Markey, a six-foot-two Baby Boomer shooting guard from a safely Democratic district outside Boston, was in favor of competition, deregulation, broadcasters showing children's television, lower cable prices, and satellite companies battling in the marketplace to deliver new products to the world. He was Al's best ally on the Hill for communications issues. Dingell and Markey disagreed about almost everything. Big John preferred monopolies, and light regulation of them. But Markey and Dingell had agreed about Fowler: the right wing was against the exercise of government power, and they were not.

Markey pointed to a battered chair and pushed a cardboard box at me.

"Chicken salad. Or ham. I think," he said. Ed opened the subject of cable regulation. He explained that people on limited incomes depended on cable for their entertainment. They noticed—and Ed said his father always telephoned—when the bill went up.

"These days I go on the elevator with other members," Markey said, "and listen to what I hear: 'Ed, my constituents are very unhappy about cable prices.' 'Ed, we're looking bad on cable.' 'We've got a cable problem, Ed.' This from guys who never talk to me. You have to fix this mess, Reed. I'm sure Al agrees."

I had only once talked to Al about the issue. The Vice President said, "You will get a lot of pressure on cable. Ignore it. Do what you think best." But I assumed Ed was telling me that he had talked to the Vice President. Everyone on the Hill, I was learning, spoke in code language.

At one point in his career, my lawyer father served as a judge at an administrative board in northern Virginia, presiding over disputes arising under defense contracts (bombs and billions). The work suited his style of communicating. "Good morning, Dad," I would say. "I'll be the judge of that," he would respond.

Perhaps by dint of family background, at the outset of my time as Mr. Chairman, I thought that I had a judge's job—discriminating, issue by issue, case by case, among competing legal arguments and factual assertions. Occasionally, I imagined, I would give a learned speech explicating my philosophy, but primarily my decisions would speak for themselves.

Listening to Congressmen Markey and Dingell, I suspected that perhaps, on occasion, politics—meaning the search for results that pleased a majority—might play a role in my decision making. But Dingell and Markey disagreed about cable regulation. The former liked the Commission's earlier decision; the latter disparaged it. Under these circumstances, I vowed indeed to make our cable decision a matter of principle. I would be a judge, adjudicating the claims of consumers and cable executives. I would get the answer right.

I hired a chief economist from Berkeley, Michael Katz, geographically and spiritually from so far outside the Beltway he indulged the view that he was above the considerations of politics. He wandered through the maze of the Commission building for 48-hour, sometimes 60-hour stretches, searching for mathematical models that described truth. He carried a Sony Walkman that pounded Smashing Pumpkins into his brain so that, he explained, he could "focus." He invented a multifactor polynomial that set prices equitably in every one of the fantastic variations of cable packages and prices that populated the market. Dazzled by the impenetrable brilliance of our economist, and oblivious to the risks of our formula's complexity, Blair and I sold this solution to Commissioners Quello and Barrett.

As a result of our new cable regulations, virtually every cable company charged less to every customer. In total, consumers spent on cable subscriptions in 1994 more than three billion dollars less than they would have but for our regulation. It was the largest consumer benefit created by the federal government in 20 years. The consumer groups praised me. And the firestorm of other criticism nearly destroyed my chairmanship.

Our cable decision was condemned by business page writers, Wall Street financial analysts, cable investors and executives. In addition, I appeared to have won my first congressional enemy. The ranking Republican on the House Telecommunications Subcommittee, Jack Fields of Texas, said of the rate regulation, "It's going to ignite a war."

The critics ridiculed our formulaic approach as governmental micromanagement. But their strongest argument was that by reducing the cable businesses' cash flow, rate regulation undercut the attractiveness of investment in cable systems. Yet if the telecommunications reform bill were passed as the Administration wanted, cable operators would need this investment to renovate their systems so as to offer two-way communication in competition with telephone companies. Notwithstanding Ray Smith's one-pipe vision, it seemed that, but for me, the cable industry had been prepared to build ubiquitously its half of Diller's two-pipe world. In effect, my interpretation of the 1992 Cable Act had discouraged the investment that the new telecommunications law was supposed to encourage. This appeared to be the snake of policy eating its own tail.

Cable companies had been granted monopoly status by the Cable Act of 1984. The 1992 Cable Act was passed to restrain abuses of the cable monopolies. The new policies of competition and convergence had not yet generated a choice for consumers. But now, in the confluence of cable regulation and the proposed telecommunications reform law, the twin concerns of constraining monopoly pricing power over consumers and encouraging investment in competitive technologies were at odds.

Three **On the Chin**

February 1994 – April 1994

Thou shalt not sit

With statisticians nor commit

A social science.

W. H. Auden, "Under Which Lyre: A Reactionary Tract for the Times"

The day after the Commission released its cable rate decision in February 1994, Bell Atlantic and Tele-Communications, Inc., announced that I had killed their merger plans. The companies explained that rate regulation had taken so much value from TCI that the companies would not be able to invest the billions needed to build two-way interactive video and voice pipes to two-thirds of American homes. Thanks to me, Ray Smith and John Malone could not build Al Gore's information highway. Smith told the *Washington Post* that "the unsettled regulatory climate made it too difficult for the parties to value the future today." Malone cited "regulatory uncertainties" as a major reason for the breakup.

Other cable companies also announced that harsh rate regulation would cause them to reduce their investment in two-way interactive services, like telephony or video-on-demand. They explained, and reporters reported, that I had sabotaged Gore's vision of an information superhighway. The *Wall Street Journal* ran an editorial awarding me their supreme insult: "French bureaucrat." In their cartoon I looked lobotomized.

The other commissioners' staffers told the press that I had wanted even harsher price cuts, but they had withheld their votes until I reduced my demands. Friends called but had nothing to say. A top White House aide said important people were unhappy. In merely two months I had lost my air of mystery. I was now known widely as an old friend of Al's who had let the Vice President down. I was someone who was in over his head. Better, the lobbyists whispered, to have picked a pro, someone who knew how to play the game. An unreported casualty was the Smith-Malone promise to connect every classroom to the information highway.

Hardly anyone in Congress supported me against the business community's criticism, although stalwart Ed Markey stood out as an exception. Loyal Al Gore issued a positive statement, but other White House staffers communicated to my staff, to reporters, and to the cable industry that I had gone too far. An oft-repeated story in the White House was that one cable CEO was angry because he had been obliged to wait a long time in a sitting room before being invited into my office. This piece of apocrypha was cited as proof of my obtuseness. For White House staffers, insult and injury are seamless concepts.

As a former litigator, I figured I had a right of rebuttal. I asked every reporter I could drag into my office why, if TCI was now cheaper, Bell Atlantic could no longer afford to buy it? John Malone's explanation was that his company was temporarily worth less, but he was so sure it would rise in value later that he wasn't willing to sell at the new low value caused by the cable rate decrease the FCC had ordered. Why then wouldn't Bell Atlantic take the same long view and pay the higher price Malone envisioned?

I was arguing as if the reporters were judges. I misunderstood: their job was to report not what they thought but what they heard. Besides, sharp-edged remarks make good quotes, and so a good reporter finds ways to exacerbate the natural human propensity to be unfair to someone with whom one disagrees. We also discovered that reporters must report what other press has reported lest their readers be left uninformed. This echo effect caused a wave of barely distinguishable critical comment to crash over me. One paper called me imperious. The next said I was tone-deaf. The third called me aloof and arrogant. (Of course, I consoled myself, if you're arrogant, you're doing people a favor by being aloof.)

Night after night Blair and I stayed late at the office, replaying events. We counted our mistakes. (1) We failed to let the industry know in advance where we were coming out on the rate regulation. (2) We neglected to ask congressional allies to support us publicly and we wrongly assumed that praise from consumer groups would defend us from political and media criticism. (3) We did not explain our decision in common-sense terms. (4) We had no plan for changing the subject.

Some think that actions speak louder than words; that you get the most accomplished if you let others take the credit; that you should speak softly and carry a big stick; that silence is golden. In the information age, these are dated, false aphorisms. Today, power comes from message coupled with audience. Message requires repetition. You can never stop making the same point over and over again (as my friend Greg Lawler never stopped telling me). When you've made the point so often you're bored, you've only made a first impression. When you've made it so often you're hoarse, you're only hitting your stride. And when you can't say it even one more time, that's when you're probably only finally getting it on television, where it is as if it were being said for the very first time. I learned from the cable brouhaha that I could compel an audience to pay attention. But before selling my message, I needed to assemble one.

One sour Monday, during the routine morning meeting of our team, Blair said, "The great thing about life in Chapel Hill is, when you're suffering through a bad football season, there's a simple solution."

"What's that?"

"Focus on basketball."

I looked at him dourly.

"What are you talking about, Blair?"

"I think you should accept Peggy Charren's invitation to speak at Harvard," he said. "We just got a letter from her."

Blair explained Peggy Charren to me.

Charren, a Boston liberal, had led citizens' campaigns against the television networks in the 1970s, creating a protest group called Action for Children's Television that decried the commercial character and non-educational content of television directed at children. She collected more than 400,000 signatures to petitions filed with the Carter Administration FCC. She persuaded President Carter's chairman, Charlie Ferris, to pursue a rulemaking under the 1934 Communications Act to require children's educational programming (kidvid) from each television station. Commissioner Jim Quello, however, successfully withstood Carter's effort to replace him with a commissioner chosen by a Democratic White House. Quello rewarded his Republican and broadcaster friends by casting the deciding vote against the proposed Ferris-Charren kidvid rule.

Even if Ferris and Charren had prevailed, the Reagan Administration's chairman, Mark Fowler, doubtless would have repealed any such kidvid rule. Indeed, Chairman Fowler's opinion was that the "public interest" obligation imposed on broadcasters by the 1934 Communications Act was met if broadcasters showed programs the "public" was "interested" in watching. This word game was meant to convey that the market, and not the government, should determine what broadcasters would transmit. By "the market" was meant the advertisers who paid for free over-the-air television.

To facilitate this pure market-based approach to the use of the public airwaves, Fowler's FCC rolled back regulatory constraints on the linkage between advertising and content of children's television. The result was a wave of cartoon shows synthesizing story lines with toy promotion and relying on violent imagery to attract audience. Although many parents and psychologists disapproved, broadcasters in the 1980s helped Baby Boomers raise their kids amid fictional video carnage: G.I. Joe, Mighty Morphin Power Rangers, Mortal Kombat, and Teenage Mutant Ninja Turtles.

In reaction, the Democratic Congress passed a Children's Television Act in 1988. Reagan vetoed it. Congress passed it again in 1990. George Bush refused to sign the bill but let it become law, fearing that a veto would incite parents and teachers to vote against him in the next election. But in 1991, the Bush Administration's FCC implemented the new law with regulations that in effect made it meaningless. Anything qualified as children's educational television under the FCC rules and any amount sufficed to meet a broadcaster's duty to serve the public interest. After more than 10 years of effort, Peggy Charren had been defeated on the eighth floor of the FCC. Now, with Democrats in the White House and a Democratic Congress and a "Real Democrat" as chairman for the first time in 13 years, she had invited me to Harvard so that she could argue her case one last time.

I was to speak to the Harvard Graduate School of Education. In the wake of the cable industry's unhappiness, I was exploring the possibility of amicable relations with cable's traditional opponents, the broadcasters. ("My enemy's enemy is my friend," recited Blair.) A rapport with broadcasters also could solidify my relationship with Commissioner Quello. To be thought trustworthy by broadcasters, in my speech I expressed the traditional lawyer's concern for the sanctity of the First Amendment. No matter how violent or prurient was television, was it not true that government should never intrude on the content of television programs?

Yet children's educational television was an exception to unfettered free speech—it was a modest concession that the broadcasters owed to the country in return for their licenses. Gliding hastily over the academic debate over the "public interest" definition, I moved on to discuss connecting all kids in all classrooms to the information highway. I reported that I had told Congress in January that the most important feature in Senator Ernest Hollings's version of the telecommunications reform bill in the Senate could be a parcel of language that would direct the FCC to promulgate rules that "enhance the availability of advanced telecommunications services to all public elementary and secondary school classrooms . . . and libraries." The Harvard audience was visibly uninterested (yawns, glimpses at watches) to hear about technology in classrooms, at that time a backwater topic for university education departments.

For my part, I was only mildly interested in children's television. I did not appreciate Peggy Charren's long struggle, and I thought the issue rather non-controversial. By my calculation, the Democratic House of Representatives would pressure the two newly appointed commissioners, Republican Rachelle Chong and the new Democratic commissioner, Susan Ness (a Renaissance Weekend friend of the Clintons), to vote with me for some form of requirement that broadcasters show educational television. Although Dole had believed her to be a "Real Republican," I knew that Commissioner Chong had promised to be free of partisanship when Al Gore had interviewed her before okaying her nomination. Despite Commissioner Quello's predictable opposition, Chong surely would recognize that a few hours a week—not more than a half-hour a day of good kidvid per station—was so modest that she would be embarrassed by a vote against imposing such an obligation on broadcasters. With reliable Ness and obtainable Chong, I'd have a new kidvid rule without controversy.

The week after speaking at Harvard, I was off to France.

"If you're in town," Madame Ambassador Pamela Harriman had said to me when she left Washington for Paris in 1993, "don't hesitate to visit." When I arrived in the City of Lights in March a year later, I received an invitation to dine at the American Embassy residence. Paris and Harriman were both ineffably charming, but I was out of place at her dinner for a host of reasons: bad French, poor conversationalist, unknown agency, bourgeois background. Everyone's focus, however, was on the honored guest, Bill Gates, the youngest self-made billionaire in history.

Gates and I were in Paris to address a conference on convergence, competition, computers, and communication. At this and many similar conferences, industry leaders and government types give speeches to one another, reporters, and investors. Big companies do big slide shows, have big sound systems. Government speakers have no *son et lumière,* and a basic skepticism to overcome. To woo the crowd I tried oddball jokes. They did not translate, and I still had scant message. The audience yawned, went out for demitasse, returned for Gates.

Gates had them in awe, perhaps more at the improbable conjunction of youth and wealth than his difficult, jargon-ridden speech. The AT&T telephone network was an "intelligent network" governed by a central brain, or a core mainframe, whose proprietary software determined the pathways, priorities, and nature of the data coursing through it. But Gates's slides described a "network of distributed intelligence." In Gates's vision, each PC was a node or individual brain that responded not to the commands of a central machine's core but to the wishes of the individual user. (Later, users would learn to direct Internet "browsers" to gather information and would send electronic mail and other information to other PCs, although existing networks were not sufficiently robust to deliver rich experiences.) Each PC provided a stand-alone experience to its user. Like a kaleidoscope, each machine offered a vantage point on a world inside a box. Each controlled the way the user communicated.

As Gates and Intel's CEO Andy Grove explained a few months later in a joint interview in *Fortune* magazine, the PC box provided "virtual" bandwidth, or the "illusion" of bandwidth. By "bandwidth" they meant a rate of delivering volumes of bits—the throughput of ones and zeros of software code that are translated by hardware into dazzling moving pictures, vast arrays of data, and communications. To compensate for the inadequate trickle of bits over the telephone network, Intel and Microsoft had collaborated on making and selling boxes that were the private libraries, screening rooms, and video arcades of the emerging information society.

That was the computer world. It regarded itself as utterly unlike the communications world, where firms were allegedly big, dull, and stupefied by interaction with government. It was true that when Theodore Vail had assembled the AT&T monopoly, he purposely sought government regulation. In return for price regulation AT&T obtained protection from competition and a guaranteed return on investment in construction and maintenance of the Public Switched Telephone Network (PSTN), the largest machine ever built. State and federal regulatory commissions were acolytes to this communications machine that carried the world's voice and fax traffic; they guaranteed that precisely the right amount of money oiled the gears. Hundreds of pages of regulation in each state and at the FCC memorialized this regulatory deal.

Just as the country's road system consists of driveways and roads that flow into multilane highways, so the phone system is built of copper lines, called loops, that carry communication into glass fibers (typically in pipes dug alongside interstates, railroads, pipelines) that carry millions of phone calls to any one of nearly 200 million other copper lines to which telephones (or computers) are attached. Stand in your driveway; look up; that wire from the side of a house to the telephone pole is a loop. More or less, the loops (and associated equipment) of America cost more than $100 billion.

When streets intersect, traffic lights, signs, or cloverleafs reroute the cars. For the phone system, when loops connect, the intersection points are called switches. The switches are computers that read the dialed phone number to route the communication—"Watson, come here, I need you!"—from an originating loop to its intended destination.

A voice communication is, of course, usually two-way. Watson is supposed to respond. In order to permit the parties to speak clearly and continuously to each other (unlike, for example, a cellular call), the network engineers create a discrete path from the caller to the party called. This route is called a circuit, as in the term "electrical circuit," which is a natural linguistic stretch, because the conversation is an exchange of electrical impulses. For a call, a circuit is open from a caller through one or more switches and the line called. Hence the great machine of the telephone network is "circuit-switched."

Through the circuit, electrons roll like waves toward the person talked to. The electromagnetic wave carries a reproduction of speech that is translated at the other end into a close facsimile of the speaker's voice. This is analog communication: the reproduction through electronics of a sound in the listener's ear that resembles closely the sound of the speaker's voice.

By contrast, the packet-switched network—some of which is now used by the Internet—is indiscriminate and deconstructed: post-modern, in literary terms. In packet-switched communication a phone message ("hello," for instance) is translated into a digital code language of ones and zeros, which are divided into packets, like trains on a railroad car. But instead of traveling down one open circuit or path from the originating point (say, my grandmother's house in Kalamazoo, Michigan) to the destination (my house in Bethesda, Maryland), the digital packets are divided into separate bundles (imagine the "hel" in "hello" as a separate bundle from the "lo") and the bundles are sent down whatever path might be available at a given instant. Perhaps the "hel" would go from Michigan to Maryland by way of Pennsylvania. But the "lo" would go south through Indiana, down to Kentucky, over to North Carolina, and up Virginia to Maryland. Just before reaching the end—my loop—software reads the labels (headers) on the packets and reassembles them as appropriate, so that I hear "hello" as opposed to "lo-hel."

Why deconstruct and then reconstruct the message? Because packet-switching is cheaper and more robust (if one pipe is down, another can be used) than circuit-switching. The reason is that packet-switching does not require an open circuit to stay unused even when Grandma has finished saying "hello" and is pausing to catch her breath before launching into the reason for her call. Packets can be jammed into the full capacity of a network, like a freeway traffic jam that nevertheless moves at top speed. By contrast, circuit-switching creates a single lane for every phone call, as if every car on the freeway had its own HOV lane.

If a machine runs at optimal capacity, it produces more units for the same cost. So if the machine of a telephone network runs optimally, it carries the maximum volume of messages at any given nanosecond. Then the cost of carriage per message is at its lowest.

For nearly a century, the cost of carrying a pound of anything anywhere on the globe—by truck, boat, plane, or fiber—has been dropping, as the machinery of transportation has become more efficient. (Containers fill vehicles more completely and quickly, just as packet-switching does networks.) Packet-switching greatly accelerates this trend for communications. Specifically, packet-switching will cut the cost of a long distance call by as much as 90 percent.

Starting in the 1970s, the business world began to use packet-switched systems to transfer data (for example, billing records) from place to place. Over time, the software companies that ran these new networks (Novell, Sun, Oracle) had little in common with BellLabs, the telephone companies' software designers. Cisco and Ascend made the parts that directed the packets: the servers and routers. On the other side, in the circuit-switched space, Western Electric for the United States and Northern Telecom for Canada made the switches.

The packet-switched and circuit-switched worlds collided when the invention of the World Wide Web, and later the browser, made the packet-switched network—in its manifestation as the Internet, a term that describes the software and hardware that uses packet-switching to communicate across multiple networks—a mass market phenomenon. Because packet-switching is much more efficient (cheaper per unit) than circuit-switching, it sends rich information like pictures, music, and text, just as Negroponte and Gilder described, over long distances at almost zero cost. The Internet is an irresistible experience for individuals, a playground for ideas, a hotbed of new ventures, and eventually will be the successor to the existing telephone network because it is cheaper, and it will combine text and pictures with voice.

A great breakthrough for the Internet was the invention of the World Wide Web by Tim Berners-Lee, the most successful cyber-inventor not to make big money from the Internet. The Web is an addressing system. In December 1990, Berners-Lee put it on the Internet and, in effect, everyone just decided to use it. (As Internet users pointed out, they had cobbled together this consensus in the absence of federal regulation. On the Net, they said, the government is not necessary. But of course the government—specifically the FCC—had promoted the Internet in multiple ways; the expectation of gratitude, author C. P. Snow wrote, is the worst of human emotions.)

Berners-Lee, a bookish individual, conceived that the infinite detail available on the Internet would best be accessed in a bibliographic manner. His means for linking all networked PCs was super footnoting: hypertext markup language (html). On the Web, everything you read or see invites you to plunge more deeply. With Web addressing, you click on a word or an icon and fall like Alice in Wonderland through the looking glass into another world of sights and sounds: one click makes you think larger, and one click makes you focus smaller. Web users experience the visuals as a stack of pages, some with images, and others mostly text.

As every PC in the world absorbed the Web by using software that adopted the Berners-Lee communications techniques, both the FCC's historic role and Gates's vision were made defunct. Through packet-switched, Web-based Internet communications, both the telephone industry's "intelligent network" and Gates's "network of distributed intelligence" would be supplanted by a network of multiple networks, in which intelligence would be created and would reside in many different locations.

But in Paris, in that spring in my first year in government, Gates did not discuss the Internet or the World Wide Web. I knew next to nothing of the implications of packet-switching for the FCC. I uncritically thought that his presentation was the most impressive speech I had ever heard from a businessperson: technical, visionary, impassioned. But if networks of intelligence were destined to penetrate into every home and business, then perhaps it was my duty to assure that they reached every classroom.

Returning to the United States, it was time to take to the international stage the Gore vision of economic growth through technologies of change. I suggested to the Vice President that he give the keynote address at the first convocation of the International Telecommunications Union Development Conference. The ITU, headquartered in Geneva, was the oldest international body in the world. It was founded in the mid-1800s for the purpose of assuring that telegraph lines heading across a national border would meet at the same point as telegraph lines emanating from the country on the other side of said border.

After Alexander Graham Bell conceived of the telephone, the ITU had a new but similar job. Busy with its diplomatic and engineering tasks through the 19th-century industrial revolution (steel/autos), the ITU had never set the goal of promoting economic growth or enhancing social benefits from communications. In recent years, as the latest industrial revolution (digitization/transistors) created still more wealth in developed countries, the ITU had begun to explore how communications technology could bridge the gap between the rich and the poor.

In the 20th century, more people are rich than ever before in history. Examples abound: the top one percent of Americans have more than doubled their income since 1977. More than eight million Americans are worth at least a million dollars, 250,000 in Silicon Valley alone. Yet a greater number of poor people are on Earth than ever before in history. Even in the United States, a fifth of children grow up in poverty. For every one person in a developed country, as the century closes there are five in the less developed world. If current trends continue, by the time my ten-year-old daughter Sara reaches my age, that proportion will be one to ten.

Previous industrial revolutions (coal and steam, iron and railroads, oil and roads) had benefited countries that enjoy access to natural resources. By contrast, the communications revolution depends on fiber made from sand and communication made from intangible code. The new low costs óf production created by this revolution can stimulate the economy of any country that makes a commitment to competition, capitalism, and investment. In brief, the American way of thinking, championed by Al Gore, was that competitive communications markets could generate widespread, equitable economic growth. Advocacy of this vision, the Vice President agreed, was worth his time.

The ITU meeting was in Buenos Aires. Al called in his staff and asked, "What do you say, shall we go to Argentina?"

The staff recommended against the trip. He needed to focus on health care and congressional relations. No time for overseas trips.

He said, "And on the way I want to stop in Bolivia and Brazil."

They groaned. South America meant at least two overnight flights. Most of the seats on Air Force Two did not recline far enough for a good sleep. But they dutifully set about the complex business of negotiating the invitations from foreign leaders, and several weeks later the White House schedulers confirmed the trip.

The ITU convention was the same week as the National Association of Broadcasters' annual convention in Las Vegas. I had agreed to make the keynote speech to the broadcasters, just as all FCC chairmen had done since television was invented. But I could not bear to miss going with the Vice President on the trip I had suggested that he take. I assumed the NAB would understand, and told Blair to cancel my appearance. The broadcasters' chief lobbyist, Eddie Fritts, called to complain, but I explained the circumstances. Then he had friends of mine call to change my mind, but I told them the country's foreign policy was more important than a largely ceremonial appearance before broadcasters.

On the evening of our departure the Vice President entertained a white tie and tails crowd at the Gridiron Dinner in Washington. At the ritual dinners of the capital city, fame and public office can get a ticket, but wealth cannot. The diners rarely stay seated at the crowded tables. In the narrow aisles, they ceaselessly schmooze, clutching hands, elbows, shoulders, grinning, laughing, trading information, negotiating. Doing my part, I took the occasion to urge Ray Smith, Bell Atlantic's chairman, to encourage Congress to pass the telecommunications reform bill then being negotiated in the Senate. He made little reference to his failed merger, asked genially for my opinion about the congressional timetable, and gave no hint of what time revealed was his real purpose: to defeat the Democratic Congress's telecommunications reform bills.

Al Gore, the white of his tie and shirt shining bright against his black suit, body rigid as a board, had himself wheeled onto the Gridiron Dinner stage on a forklift. Huge laughter. After the sight gag, he japed verbally at his image: "Every time I hear another joke about how wooden I am, I always say, 'Very funny, Tipper.'" Everyone admired his ability to laugh at himself; the applause was large.

As soon as he was finished, I raced to find my vehicle. When the President or Vice President hits his car, the motorcade guns off. If you're not then in your assigned car, you do not make it to Andrews Air Force Base in time for the flight. Across town in the dark of night, on the tarmac, and in the air. At dawn Air Force Two landed on a high plain in Bolivia. A band struck up a greeting that blew away soundlessly in the thin Andes air.

Bolivia had one of the world's most advanced telecommunications systems, but it was possessed by drug cartels. Public switched traffic was relegated to a skimpy, outmoded network that did not reach most rural villages. To dramatize the potential of the communications revolution, the Vice President led an automobile caravan across Bolivia's llama-strewn plain to Lake Titicaca. There, Bolivia's Vice President welcomed us to Huatajata, his home village. With our fingers we ate chunks of grilled salmon, chicken, and numerous kinds of potatoes while discussing the impact of technology on universal economic growth.

Late in leaving for Buenos Aires, we were behind schedule and still working on Gore's ITU speech. On the flight, one of Al's staff members and I finished our suggested draft of the speech. Al called ahead to Argentina's president, Carlos Saúl Menem, who held up the banquet until we arrived at the president's mansion. We landed close to one in the morning. At Menem's we sat at a long, narrow table that almost filled its room: Americans on one side, Argentineans on the other, matched according to rank and jurisdiction (I believe I sat across from the communications minister). Only the President and Vice President (and interpreters) talked. They exchanged views, point after point, across the range of issues (trade, patent infringement, pharmaceuticals, and so on) on the agenda. I wondered when Al would look at the final draft of his ITU speech. By 3:30 A.M. the dinner was over, and I went to bed. Four hours later, his staff and I gathered in a small sitting room at the American ambassador's beaux-arts mansion to discover that Al had spent the rest of the night rewriting the entire draft. As he read the new speech aloud, one of us typed on a laptop; the final version for the teleprompter was finished a half-hour before delivery.

To the ITU, Gore traced the impact of the telegraph and its successor technologies on global development. He described a new communications revolution driven by the export of three American ideas: competition instead of monopoly, the rule of law, and the connection of networks to existing networks at a fair price. (These were the tenets of his UCLA speech, turned into our country's foreign policy.) He said that half the people of the world had never made a phone call, yet all had a right to participate in the information age. More than 100 years earlier, Nathaniel Hawthorne had written of a world wrapped in a "great nerve of intelligence." Hawthorne referred to the telegraph, but digital networks would fulfill his vision. Gore brought the thousand delegates of the world's communications industries and government ministries to their feet in applause.

Al and I descended in the freight elevator. (Our highest ranking officials always go out the back way.) He said, "It was a little long."

"If we had more time we could have written a shorter speech," I said. "But it went over very well."

As it turned out, Gore's speech defined the agenda for the next three years of American trade advocacy, which culminated in a 1997 agreement among 69 countries to eliminate monopolies, open all markets to competition under transparent regulatory regimes, and guarantee fair interconnection between new and existing networks.

Showing no signs of sleeplessness, Al went to the American Embassy for a meeting with American industry. After the Vice President's remarks, the first question was, "How come your friend the FCC chairman over here killed the Bell Atlantic–TCI merger? Wasn't that inconsistent with your plan to build the information highway?" Al defended me, but plainly my failure to reconcile cable rate regulation with our pro-investment goal had hurt my reputation in the press.

Meanwhile, in Las Vegas, a lowbrow pleasure dome of kitsch and iced drinks, more than 60,000 broadcasters gathered for the NAB convention. No visit to the NAB was more important for an FCC chair than his first, and no visiting chairman was more likely to be watched closely in that first visit than a Democrat. I would be suspected of believing that television owed something to the public that it had not delivered. My absence increased doubts about my intentions.

But broadcast television was of modest interest to my agenda. Indeed, I was sure that foreign policy deserved more of my attention than domestic television. To be conciliatory to broadcasters, however, I agreed to "appear" at the NAB on the last day of the convention by way of a satellite feed from Buenos Aires.

The delay from the satellite bounce made my jokes come off poorly. (Thesecretofhumoristiming.) Perhaps in closing I should not have said, "Hasta la vista, baby" to the chief industry lobbyist. I had forgotten that when Arnold Schwarzenegger used this phrase in the movie *Terminator 2,* he then executed his interlocutor. But location, not termination, was my big gaffe.

Headlines in the trade press announced that by not attending the NAB convention, I had snubbed the country's most powerful political lobby, the 1,500 local television stations of America. Lobbyists all agreed that I had made a serious mistake. I had found a new way to hurt Al Gore. Advancing the Administration's international communications agenda in Buenos Aires was not an excuse. It was only proof that I did not understand American politics, where television was more important than global economic development.

Eli Noam, director of Columbia University's Institute for Tele-Information, had said when I entered office, "The honeymoon won't last long. There are more toes to step on here than at a centipede convention." His prediction had come true. By the April azalea season, the press covering the FCC beat had firmly concluded that the new chairman was off to a terrible start. New winner of the award for worst ever, wrote one columnist. Curse of Yale Law School, opined another. Reporters described me with the dread doubled trait: if controversial, I must be also unbending; if opinionated, then also arrogant; if disliked, then ineffectual.

Like anyone, I believed what I read in the paper. I hated the person with my name who was depicted in the press. The staff delivered the newspaper articles to me by 8:00 A.M. and postponed the staff meeting to 8:30 so that I would have at least a half-hour to rage alone in my office. But we needed more of a plan than that. Blair suggested I ask Jim Quello to be my emissary to the powers that shaped an inside-the-Beltway reputation. I swallowed the pill of humility, and asked Jim to arrange a lunch with the broadcasters' chief lobbyist, Eddie Fritts.

At the Palm, naturally, we dined in the back room where Jim's face is painted on the wall.

"You've got a lot of learning to do," said Jim, offering advice as I had requested. "You have to remember those guys who put us here. Pay attention to them."

He was referring to the United States Senate, not the White House. Senator Dole had recently spoken against me on the Senate floor, mocking me for destroying Al's information highway. I assumed Jim was alluding to the minority leader's unusually personal remarks. The industry lobbyists used their Hill allies to push the FCC around through public criticism, questions at hearings, and, later, investigations. I had harbored a lawyer's idea that Congress would conduct itself more dispassionately, but only some members approached elective office in that way.

Eddie Fritts took the conversation to his issue: "It's too bad that you couldn't attend our trade association meeting." I knew he had complained to the President about my failure to attend the NAB convention. Presidential staff had eagerly reported the NAB's ire to my staff, thereby lending a flavor of endorsement to the criticism. Al's Buenos Aires speech was a success in trade diplomacy, but irrelevant to domestic politics.

"I hope you'll be at the convention next year," Fritts said.

This was a business lunch: I understood that the NAB meant business. In politics, if you are going to dip the knee, do it quickly. I said, "Certainly. I know how important television is to the country."

"It's important to everyone," he said.

"It's the national drug," I said, even after having promised Blair I would not go for the glib.

"Too bad about that Southwestern Bell merger," said Eddie Fritts, ignoring my remark. He referred to SBC's cancellation of its merger with Cox Cable as a result of my rate regulation: another set of markets where the information highway would not be built because of me.

"And Jerry was tough on you, wasn't he?" Fritts added.

He referred to the speech Time Warner's CEO Jerry Levin had given the previous week. Levin said our rate regulation echoed the style of the Soviet Union. I had not liked being called, as I saw it, a Communist, but that perhaps was too personal an interpretation. Besides, it was open season on Mr. Chairman.

Avuncular Jim Quello said, "Listen, you'll find the broadcasters easy to work with. You just have to tell them where you're coming from. I know. I'm one of them." (Jim was a retired broadcaster when the industry persuaded Nixon to appoint him in 1973.)

Jim Quello's view was that every commissioner was on the side of one or more special interests. A commissioner should not be an impartial and remote judge; every commissioner needed friends. He made sense, but other than Al Gore and Ed Markey I seemed to have no friends.

"You know," said Jim, offering an illustration of the lessons of friendship, "in 1978 I voted to take away a license. I'm never doing that again. There's nothing serious enough to take away a broadcaster's license."

"That's right," said the NAB lobbyist.

Under the 1934 Communications Act, before renewing a television station's license the FCC was supposed to consider whether the television station had served the "public interest, convenience, and necessity." Jim believed broadcasters always served the public interest simply by broadcasting for free. For him, the "public interest" standard of the Act meant nothing, because no broadcaster could ever be in breach of its obligation.

Jim had a second, constitutional string to his argument. "I'm not a lawyer," he said, "but I have learned a lot from lawyers. It's against the First Amendment to require broadcasters to run a particular kind of show. Besides, broadcasters are good corporate citizens. They give a great deal to their local communities." Quello, I understood, would never support Peggy Charren's kidvid rule requiring educational shows.

My father, a lawyer of high technique and equal dudgeon, had never shown me how to go along and get along. He confronted, challenged, and often came away defeated by the powers that dominated the business world in which he worked. As with every man, my father's personality surfaced, like a chain of islands above the sea, in multiple aspects of my character. To succeed in the capital city, I was being taught, it would be wise to shroud the difficult outcroppings of myself in the Washington fog of politically useful friendships.

"I hope you will let my wife and me throw a little party for you on the occasion of your 80th, Mr. Chairman," I said, bowing to Jim.

"I'll ask Mary. That would be fine, I'm sure. I'll ask her."

"And I know we'll work together well," I said to Fritts. He touched my outstretched hand briefly and nodded at the possibility that we might agree on some things.

Four **Learning the Ropes**

It's not what you do. . . . It's who you know and the smile on your face!

Willy Loman in Arthur Miller, Death of a Salesman

A s I was driven in the chairman's official Buick to the *Washington Post,* I saw flowering in the street-side gardens of April the pink and many-petaled peonies that suggest optimism. My host and the newspaper's chief owner, Katharine Graham, the grandest figure in Washington, explained that it was the *Post*'s tradition at these "newsmaker" lunches to serve a fine meal to the dozen writers and the target guest, but not to give the guest time to eat. All at the table laughed at this oft-told tale. I assumed Mrs. Graham was kidding, but as I took knife and fork to my plate, a business page writer opened fire:

"There's no doubt you've tremendously hurt the market value of the cable industry just when the businesses needed to raise tremendous sums to compete with the telephone industry. Wouldn't you say the 1992 Cable Act was misguided and that you made it worse by taking this extra bite out of cable prices?"

Possibly because I was hungry, I felt rising in me an unstoppable will to argue—always a dreadful mistake with the print media. I said that cable was not as bad off as cable said, for three reasons.

"First," I said, "there's an inflation price increase in September so the rate reduction is half as bad as you say. Second, because of our regulations, consumers are much happier with cable service quality than ever before. Third, with lower prices, cable is getting more subscribers and making more money from increased penetration."

In the wake of the "lunch" meeting, the *Post* reported that I said cable should be "grateful" for rate reduction. Even I thought the quote made me look like a fool. At the 8:30 A.M. staff meeting, with the miserable story in hand, I asked Blair to write a correction letter.

"Sure, boss," he said, "I'll just ask them to print that cable shouldn't be grateful to you."

Later that week the reporter from *Broadcasting & Cable* magazine asked if I knew anything about business.

"I understand business better than any chairman this agency has had, probably ever," was my response.

This they printed in large type.

I asked Judy Harris to write a correction letter to be printed in the magazine.

"Sure," she said. "I'll just write that you don't know anything about business."

Blair said, "The White House is buzzing over these quotes." A chief of staff introduces bad news by talking about what others are saying.

"What are you saying?" I asked.

"I think we may be getting some visitors."

A legion of long-time Democratic operatives, moderate Republicans, former office holders, not-on-deadline reporters, came to counsel me. Blair spread the word that I was prepared to listen. More friendly advisers visited. All explained that I was distant, stubborn, and disagreeable, although all flayed my thin skin most solicitously.

The best and kindest visitor was Barry Diller. I had not seen him since Al's UCLA speech. His bid to buy Paramount had failed, but now, I was told by intermediaries, he hoped to persuade me to support a clarification of our cable regulations that would encourage cable companies to carry QVC, his shopping channel. I invited him to lunch with Blair and me in my office.

"I can't believe it," said Barry Diller as we sat down. "They always do this."

"Is something wrong?" I asked.

"This is what happens when you have a public image," said Diller sonorously. The fluorescent lights of the chairman's office glistened on his pate.

"I am, you see, well known for some things. People believe they know what I like." And here he chuckled, a sound like sea waves retreating from a breakwater, "People are so dumb."

The intimate tone of his voice implied that the term "people" meant everyone outside the room.

Then the denouement. "Once someone wrote that I liked egg salad sandwiches. Now wherever I go, that's what I get for lunch," he said, chewing on the word "lunch" as if it were a piece of lettuce inserted along with the egg. "It's boring," he added. How many hours, I wondered, had others devoted to apprehending Barry's desires for food?

"I had dinner with the President," he continued. "The President asked for my views on the proposed new telecommunications bill. I wrote him a memo. I do almost all my own writing. It takes time. I have to get it down in a way that I'm comfortable with." His voice grew very low, as if he were saddened by the difficulty of the creative process.

Diller told us how David Geffen and Jeffrey Katzenberg and Steven Spielberg were advising the White House, using their creative skills to help define a new kind of presidency. Diller was pulling back a curtain on a world of opinion-shaping and decision-influencing. In our tumbledown offices at the Commission, we tingled at any news from 1600 Pennsylvania Avenue, three blocks east, five blocks south, and a vast political distance from our dumb sandwiches. I hoped, as I listened to Diller's tales from the great world, that he might tell his friends in the White House that I was not as impossible as described in the press.

Then Diller swooped down, with eagle eyes, on his issue. "I can't believe anyone except an idiot would interpret the Cable Act any other way than the way we see it," he said. "Obviously a shopping channel can share its revenue with the cable operator without violating your cable rules. Audiences need a clarification of your cable rules in order to get QVC on their cable systems. We get a channel by sharing sales revenue with the operators. If operators have to subtract our payment from its subscription rates because of the workings of your rate regulation formula," he waved his hand at the silly workings of the formula, "they won't carry the shopping channel. That's a crazy result."

I was totally persuaded. It would be crazy to write a rule that had such effect. The previous Commission had interpreted the Cable Act as mandating that the Commission's rules should discourage cable operators from carrying shopping channels. This attitude seemed to violate the First Amendment and it was snobbism as well, although it did demonstrate the power of FCC regulations to shape markets. Our rate regulation had unintentionally perpetuated this policy. I decided to correct the error.

Diller's visit marked the first time that a major industry executive had made a persuasive argument that had changed my mind. Perhaps I could listen; perhaps this was the way "Mr. Chairman" was supposed to do his job. Since the creation of administrative agencies to write detailed rules, Congress has routinely passed general laws that contain ambiguous and often contradictory provisions. In its rulemakings, the FCC dealt with the hard details that Congress had delegated away in the law. Indeed, it was as if we were Congress, only far more obscure and not elected. It was right and proper, then, for me to try to bargain with industry leaders on these hard details, not like a judge, but rather like a legislator.

In such negotiations, any agency has the opportunity to turn a poorly written law into a good piece of legislation. Or it can strip even a fine law of significance. The commissioners of the agency can do the right thing without fear of political retribution, because they face no elections, need not raise money from business to buy advertising time. Or they can do the wrong thing with little risk of attracting attention from the public. Most surprising to me, they decide right and wrong primarily by their own standards.

The next day, I read Diller's assessment of me in the *Washington Post:* "He's getting crucified. I think he's much more sensible than he's been given credit for. I say give him time. Let's see if he can balance the intentions of Congress [and] the muddled voice of the [Clinton] Administration into a coherent regulatory agenda." The lunch had gone well.

But Diller's comment only briefly interrupted my streak of bad press. *Business Week* reported that I was "Clinton's lightning rod." I flipped the magazine into the wastebasket and plodded, reluctant as a man headed to court for sentencing, down the hall to the elevator. I was bound for New Orleans that May, the site of the annual convention of the National Cable Television Association.

That evening Blair and I dined with the cable industry's leaders: avuncular Amos Hostetter of Continental, soft-spoken Brian Roberts of Comcast (the company's founder, Ralph Roberts, was his father), subtle Decker Anstrom, one of the few Washington lobbyists who always showed that he understood the listener's perspective. (Indeed, he often figured out my point of view better than I did.) They brought their investment banker and their commercial lender. Each explained that I had killed private investment in the information highway and—surely without malice, or even thought aforethought—wrecked the Administration's communications policy.

The next day, I addressed at breakfast the top 150 executives in the industry. Feeling the chill of disdain in the air, I tried joking my way into rapport. "I hope the rolls are nailed to the table." "Is it true that everyone else is also wearing Kevlar?" "I'm coming to praise cable, not to worry it." The substance of my speech was not threatening, although not apologetic.

The rustle of napkins, the tinkle of an occasional fork against glass in the hushed room, small suspicious laughter, composed the response. But the questions from the audience, although not friendly, were not hostile. After the speech, I walked the gantlet of the convention floor. Programmers explained that they could not get carriage on cable systems because rate cuts caused operators to cut back plans to expand the number of channels. None were happy with me, but all talked to me. I inferred that the most important fact about the cable convention was that I had attended. I had given an unhappy constituency a chance to petition its government. No one expected me to backtrack, but all felt I owed them a personal appearance, and they got it.

In summer 1994, the cool thing in the information sector was to get interviewed in *Wired* magazine. How could John Malone, the president of Tele-Communications, Inc., turn down the chance to be on the front page of the July issue pictured with his grinning face on the body of Mel Gibson's character from *The Road Warrior*? As he was always prone to do, Malone let it rip in the interview. When asked by *Wired* what would be the best way to get the information highway built, Malone verbally threw out a hip in John Wayne style and said, "Shoot Hundt."

Standing in my office, holding the magazine in my hand, I said, "This is strong stuff. How do you think he meant it?"

"I have an idea," said Blair, who, like all chiefs of staff, treated most of my questions as purely rhetorical.

Blair told the wire services about the printed threat made on the life of the chairman, guaranteeing that the *Wired* story was reported in all the press. Reporters from the major newspapers asked if Malone had called to apologize. Blair responded sorrowfully in the negative. This led to fairly widespread coverage of TCI's failure to express regret. Malone's Washington representative called to say he regretted his boss's statement. Blair explained that he could not necessarily stop an inquiry into the seriousness of the threat, although he was sure Malone was guilty only of a poor choice of words. The FBI, he suggested, might not take lightly threats against the life of a government official. He said that the chairman would be pleased to hear from Mr. Malone directly.

I received a letter from TCI's Washington representative that reflected careful crafting to avoid a quotable expression of remorse. Blair told reporters that Malone had still not called. They raced to ask TCI if the company was intentionally insulting the chairman.

Pressured by the reporters, and doubtless advised by his lobbyists that he had lost this media skirmish, Malone at last called me.

Affable and direct, he said, "I went too far. I need to apologize."

"I accept," I said.

I told Malone I would have to tell reporters that he had called. I suppose so, he acknowledged. After the story of his apology went over the wire, one reporter said that this was universally regarded as the first expression of public regret ever voiced by John Malone. Proving that I could listen was one lesson, but learning to fight a p.r. battle was also a necessary part of my training.

The next month Blair and I had lunch with Malone, Barry Diller, Sumner Redstone of Viacom, Ray Smith of Bell Atlantic, Ralph Roberts of Comcast Cable, and Craig McCaw of McCaw Cellular Communications. The all-star cast was assembled by a college friend, Steve Schwarzman, the founder of a prodigiously successful merchant-banking firm, the Blackstone Group. Steve reasoned that if important business leaders knew me on a personal level—as in a meeting where large policy directions were on the table—they might conclude that I was a reasonable person, contrary to reports in the press or from lobbyists.

Before we sat down, Barry Diller whispered to me, "This will be my first meeting with Sumner since I cost him so much more for Paramount." In light of the widespread view that Redstone had overpaid in the bidding for the studio, Diller had won by losing the auction.

After we took our chairs around the circular table, Diller looked across at Redstone. He asked politely, "How are you, Sumner?"

"Pretty good considering you made me pay a couple extra billion," said Redstone, with only faint asperity.

"Congratulations," said Diller. Redstone had paid him the compliment of acknowledging the infliction of pain.

The conversation turned to the status of investment in the so-called information highway. A public failure to close a deal often casts a cloud over an executive, but Ray Smith was irrepressible. "It is too expensive to build two or more routes to the household," he pronounced. "One lane on the information highway with multiple channels. That's the only cost effective way to connect the pipe to every home. We have the engineers. We have the switches and the intelligent network. We will build it." (In Smith's view, convergence meant new combinations of capital.)

Ralph Roberts, proprietor of the cable systems that occupied the mid-Atlantic heart of Smith's Bell Atlantic system, asked modestly, "I wonder if cable has a place in your vision. What happens to our network?"

"Forget about it," said Smith buoyantly, "it's cheaper to let us carry your channels for you." Roberts raised his eyebrows, as if Smith had elected to eat the delicate Blackstone lunch with his fingers. Roberts responded, "I would prefer to carry my own programs on my own network." (For him, convergence meant the combination of content and conduit under one corporate roof.)

Diller watched the conversation intently. Owning the content, he wanted a choice of distribution channels. He wanted to compel cable and telephone companies to compete to offer him low-price delivery of his programs to the audience.

I caught a glimpse of what would have been the purpose of the Bell Atlantic–TCI merger: in two-thirds of the country the new company would be the dominant monopoly proprietor of the information highway. The consumers of cable programs and telephone services would pay a great deal to the TCI–Bell Atlantic monopoly in order to fund its investment needs. Smaller rivals, like Comcast, would have been brushed away by the capital-raising power of the Smith-Malone firm. The merger would have realized the George Gilder–Nick Negroponte vision.

The Administration and the Democratic Congress sought instead to create competition and choice, benefiting sellers like Diller and buyers such as residential consumers. But if competition reduced profits, perhaps it would discourage investment. Then no one would build the new networks that could deliver both video and voice. It was a conundrum.

Turning to John Malone, I asked, "Is your business doing well?"

"I'm getting more involved again," he answered. "Thought I wouldn't have to work again when I thought I was selling the company."

A pause, during which I privately rejected as absurd the idea that I should feel guilty that rate regulation had delayed John Malone's early retirement.

He recommenced, "Sorry I fired my mouth off at you in that magazine. Sometimes I should keep my powder dry."

"Sometimes it's a matter of choice of metaphor," I said.

He continued, "I just shoot from the hip sometimes."

"Please stop," I said. "Your armory of phrases is being exhausted."

I thought I was pretty witty in my punning but the conversation
withered. Nevertheless, the lunch was another demonstration that I was
willing to attend on the moguls and show them the deference of listening
to their views. Steve Schwarzman's plan had worked. As the people's representative (the privilege of public office), I was in an "in" group, where great
matters were discussed personably and directly. The question then was
what to do with that access.

The cable rate regulation battle had left me with an enhanced fear
of failure, and caused me to revise my thinking about regulating retail
prices to benefit consumers. The gains from price regulation were small
for each beneficiary; the losses huge for the regulated. Cable regulation
meant so little to the former (perhaps a hamburger a month) and so much
to the latter (a difference of billions in foregone capital expenditure) that
inevitably the regulator was buried under a mountain of resentment from
an industry and its financiers, while mere pebbles of gratitude were prof-
fered from the consumer advocacy groups. Most Americans, indeed,
never knew that their cable bill had been lowered by, say, a dollar a month,
making it about 3 to 5 percent less than what it might have been. Much
of the savings went to buy an additional premium channel, or a cable out-
let in the basement or a kids' room. What indeed was the point of the regulation if the beneficiaries were neither thankful nor economically better off?

By late 1994, I was convinced instead that worthwhile government
action lay primarily in increasing investment in entrepreneurship in order
to stimulate competition against monopolies. Competition would generate new choices for consumers, who in turn would spend more on media
and communications, and get more for their money. The expanding size
of the market would attract more investment, and more competitive enterprises would be funded. After competition emerged, ideally before the
November 1996 election, we would happily deregulate the newly competitive telephone and video markets. The purpose of pro-competitive
rulemaking ultimately would be the elimination of rules. As a first step
down the path to such sunny days, we needed the Democratic Congress to

pass the telecommunications reform bill before the end of the 1994 legislative session. Then in 1995 I could get to work on the implementing regulations, which would repair my reputation among academics, investors, and businesspersons.

Andy Grove, chief executive officer of Intel, fabricator of the miraculous microprocessors that can inject intelligence into every object in the man-made world, is one of the most well regarded businessmen in America. When he invited me to dinner in July 1994, I felt I was being offered an entrée to the "in" crowd of Silicon Valley, the other coast's equivalent to lunch at the Blackstone. Apple, Sun, and others came with Andy Grove to dinner at the Stanford Park Hotel in Palo Alto. The subject was the convergence of computing and communications.

By 1994, Grove and the other Valley chiefs understood that digital personal computers were destined to be devices for communicating in competition with and through the Public Switched Telephone Network. In the past, almost to the date of our dinner, anyone possessing a PC could operate as an autarkic entity, generating in the home office or on the workplace desk essays, graphic presentations, income tax returns, business models, and high scores on video games. (A revealing metric was that revenues from software games had surpassed revenues from movie tickets.) But in the future, users would use their PCs primarily to communicate with the information on the Net and over the Net to other PC users. Silicon Valley, therefore, had to enter the communications world in order to realize its business future. They dreaded two things about this old world: its regulations, and the bias of the incumbent businesses toward analog and voice communications as opposed to digital and data.

None of us at dinner could predict how the telecommunications law being written in Congress would affect the convergence of computing and communications, or the delivery of data over parts of the national voice network. But this much was certain: Grove and the Silicon Valley business leaders did not want the government to shape the convergence of the new computer world and the old communications world. Yet unless the government intervened, the owners of the Public Switched Telephone Network—principally the Baby Bells—would charge high prices for carrying data on their networks, especially over local phone lines, thus reducing Internet access and thwarting the growth of the new data networks. This outcome was a danger of Ray Smith's "one-pipe" vision.

I assured the Valley executives that FCC should never stand for Federal Computing Commission, but that the government's competition goal was the answer to their fear of high charges on data transport by the telephone monopoly. (They were allies of Diller's two-pipe dream, although they wanted data, instead of television programs, to have multiple conduits.) And I argued that the convergence of computing and communication gave rise to the quintessential social goal for Silicon Valley (and Al Gore): to connect all children to the new data networks through PCs in every classroom. They appeared pleased, although still suspicious.

Over the sea bass, I pressed my education argument. I said that the Valley would lack for trained employees if technology education lagged behind business growth. Over the gooey chocolate dessert, I said that the children of the 21st century should learn with and about the communications and computer convergence that defined our economy. Over decaf cappuccino, I begged that the Valley join us in trying to get the telecommunications legislation moving through Congress.

When the table was cleared and I had paid my minutely calculated share of the bill (industry could not buy me, I meant to communicate by my accounting), Andy Grove, with a half-smile and a glitter in his eye, said, "This was the best meeting I've ever had with anyone from government." The praise bubbled in my head like a glass of champagne.

"Because," he said, "you didn't ask us for money."

The next week, the Democratic House passed a telecommunications reform bill that comported with the White House agenda crafted in Al Gore's office. Among other things, its provisions gave the FCC great discretion to encourage competition in all voice and video markets and to promote various social goals. It called for the FCC to order reduced rates for telecommunications use by schools. Contrary to Republican wishes, it did not permit significant concentration in radio or television markets. A disappointment was that it would not necessarily let the FCC fund the connection of every classroom to the information highway, but its language was fuzzy enough to pave the way for an amendment to this effect in the conference committee negotiations that would reconcile the House and Senate versions of the bill. Of course, Senator Fritz Hollings first needed to pass the Senate version of the bill.

While political powers mobilized for the Senate fight, I went to Atlanta to pay court to cable tycoon Ted Turner. He welcomed me into his office in the CNN tower high above the city. "Lead, follow, or get out of the way," read the famous sign on his desk. An artifact. An artful fact.

"This is the building built by an idea," Turner said. "A global, round-the-clock news station. They said I was crazy. I used to sleep here. Right in the office." He pointed to a wall where he had installed a Murphy bed. (Romance is found everywhere.)

Walking purposefully around the room like a newly caged animal, he continued, "Jane and I were going to give a billion dollars to your friend Gore. Not to him, but to those environmental causes he cares about. I agree with him. I'm the only one who agrees with him."

He raised his voice: "Gore's right. But you'll never hear it on the network news. I should own a broadcast network. I'd make a difference. Balance the Fox network with a liberal one. Pollution is writing the death warrant for the planet."

Then Ted lowered his voice and said slowly, sadly, like a television newscaster reporting on a funeral, "I can't give the money away now. It's gone. You took it away. You killed Al's foundation when you lowered cable rates."

Then he said gently, "I don't blame you. You did what Congress asked you to do. Cost the environment a billion dollars, though."

I had no words. "What are you trying to do at that FCC?" he asked. "What are you trying to accomplish?"

"We're focusing on education," I said lamely, and thought to myself that I had hardly justified cable rate regulation with that answer.

"Well," he said, "here's my advice: your dreams need to be worth your time."

Returning from Atlanta, I was summoned to the Vice President's office for a one-on-one meeting. His staff would not inform me about its purpose: a bad sign.

Al showed me a new photograph that nearly filled a wall in his office: the first complete photograph of Earth, assembled from a sequence of satellite shots. I recalled Turner's scuttled foundation, and sat down on the couch.

Al pulled his wing-backed chair close to me and asked, "Have you heard about the man who invented a new kind of dog food?"

"No."

"He studied the chemical composition of all the dog foods on the market. Then he combined all the formulas to create the new brand. He contracted with the grocery stores and put the new product on the shelves. He analyzed everything perfectly. Do you know what happened?"

"No."

"He went out of business."

Silence.

"The dogs didn't like the dog food."

When I returned to the Commission, I repeated this story to Judy and Blair.

Judy said, "That's the kindest way of giving advice I've ever heard."

"What do you mean?" I asked.

"You get it," she said.

"He's saying inputs don't matter; outputs do," said Blair. "And the key output is convincing people our policies make sense." We went to work on the redesign and selling of the dog food. We decided that two or three times a week, sandwiched between 10 and 15 hours of meetings with staff in my office, I would speak to the outside world about my objectives as chairman.

I lined up meetings with business leaders and speeches to groups of 50 or 100. Working with speechwriters, we prepared a standard stump speech. I did not like to read other people's words. It was like using someone else's toothbrush. And I could not determine what I wanted to say without writing the important paragraphs myself. But I did not have clear enough views about my agenda to write a clear speech myself.

The ideal was to speak without notes. Although I was afraid to discuss the details of communications policy without a text, I could manage an opening in the conventional self-deprecatory style.

"A lot of people think I was named FCC chair because I went to high school with the Vice President. Just a coincidence. [Laughter.] Or because I went to law school with the President. [More laughter.] And the First Lady. [Ditto.] And the Secretary of Labor, Comptroller of the Currency, Deputy Administrator of the EPA, and the United States Attorney for San Diego. [Laughter fading as the extent of the personal network knits a few brows.] All coincidences! [Laughter renewed.] The truth is I got the job because I have the same birthday as Alexander Graham Bell. [Ha ha!] Why did you think the President picked me?"

But then what to say? The majority of Americans approved of the information highway, although only a third knew what it was. Fewer still had heard of the FCC. What was its purpose? Was the FCC designing, funding, or getting out of the way of the information highway? Were we for regulation or deregulation; big government or small; one technology or another, mergers or breakups? Al Gore's agenda was clearly to promote competition, stimulate investment and innovation, and guarantee social benefits. The Democratic Congress had compromised among different industries, but focused on protecting consumers from monopoly prices. The details were left to the FCC. I gained nothing from discussing the specifics of regulation before Congress passed the new law. No one had asked the FCC to articulate a philosophy of the role of government in the information age.

One day, as we drove to an auditorium on the campus of Georgia Tech University for a conference on education technology, Blair looked at my draft speech. It was a bag of nostrums about competition and technology.

"You should throw this away," he said, "and talk to them about what you care about."

I told Blair a true story, as he directed the car to circle the building. After college I got a job as a schoolteacher in Philadelphia. I taught seventh-grade social studies. On average, in the three years at my school a child would fall two years behind in reading skills. Only half of my seventh graders would graduate from junior high school, and only half of them from high school. The best way out was physically to get out: to be permitted to enroll in one of the city's magnet schools.

I had three students out of 150 who started seventh grade reading well enough to give them a chance to be admitted to a magnet school in eighth grade. Every Saturday for several months I tutored them on how to pass the entrance exam. The day of the exam came. All my students failed the test.

In my government job, I wanted to make sure that schoolchildren today have better ways to escape poverty. I wanted teachers to have better tools than I did. I wanted to make recompense for my own failings as a teacher.

Blair said, "Right now everyone thinks you're just trying to deliver a kind of politically acceptable package on behalf of Al and the Democratic Congress. But this story about the kids and how you feel, that gets across to people. You have to make your job be about yourself."

"Because then it's worth my time," I said, thinking of Ted Turner.

"As long as no one asks why, if you care so much, you are not at the Department of Education," said deflating Blair.

But, as he wished, I told the story of my teaching experience to the curious crowd. The applause had a quality of sympathy I had never heard before. It appeared that as Mr. Chairman, I was obliged to put at stake not only my career but also myself. Public office required not thick skin, but no skin at all.

Five **On a Roll**

July 1994 – October 1994

British policy for four hundred years has been to oppose the strongest power in Europe by weaving together a combination of other countries strong enough to face the bully.

Winston Churchill

n the 1980s, Japan had brought together its broadcast and manufacturing industries to invent an exquisitely sharp high-definition television picture. Using analog transmission technology, Japanese television makers would take the world market from American manufacturers. The high-definition televisions (HDTVs) they invented were too expensive for consumers to buy, at about ten times the price of a traditional television. But other Asian countries with lower wage scales took the traditional market from American manufacturers anyway.

In response to the Japanese HDTV threat, however, in 1987, American broadcasters persuaded the FCC to give each local television station a second channel (or additional six megahertz of spectrum) for high-definition, along with a standard-definition broadcast in analog. In theory, broadcasters would simultaneously transmit a high-definition version of their signals. When viewers compared the sharp image of a show with its normal image, they would replace their old sets with new, high-definition home theaters. It would be like color's rapid replacement of black-and-white televisions. When all 100 million households had swung over to HDTV, the local stations would shut off the old standard-definition broadcast channels and return the spectrum to the government. It was an insanely complex scheme. Its unraveling, however, came not from its complexity, but from the source of so much other change: digitization.

In the course of development of HDTV in the United States, as if by accident, engineers applied the new magic of digital technology, rather

63

than analog, to over-the-air broadcast. They found that by sending packets of digital information, coded in bits in the frequency of the wave transmitted over the air, they could communicate much more information than in analog broadcast. The big point of the crucial new discovery was that by digitizing and compressing the signals, over a single channel's worth of spectrum the broadcasters could deliver not just one but a total of six simultaneous programs in traditional or standard definition. As a result, ten broadcasters in a city could deliver over the air a 60-channel video package that competed with cable. (Still later, digitization meant the so-called second channel could be used to transmit anything from the Internet over the air to PCs and televisions.) Consequently, federal cable rate regulation could be rescinded, and competition from digital broadcasters would keep prices down.

Apprehending this possibility, the cable industry insisted that the government should forbid broadcasters from using the second channel for anything other than a single high-definition show. Cable knew that consumers would not buy expensive HDTVs for such a skimpy enhancement of the viewing experience. Choice trumped quality (also a lesson taught by the proliferation of cellular telephones, despite poor service quality); and cable would face no competitive threat.

Alternatively, with the extra carrying capacity that digital technology enabled, the FCC could order whole new channels to be dedicated to such public purposes as educational television. From the cornucopia of new digital broadcasting channels, political figures could be given free time for addressing voters: we could reform the campaign finance process.

But creating dozens of new digital broadcast programs would be expensive and risky for local broadcast affiliates to fund. Meanwhile, networks were moving hot new shows to cable, where they could charge for the shows as well as sell advertising time. As Gilder and Negroponte had forecast, video was moving to wire and away from wireless. Under these circumstances, local broadcasters did not know what to do with the second channel or digital technology. Nonetheless, they and the networks decided that their lobbying group, the NAB, would seek the spectrum, primarily to keep anyone else from getting it. The NAB told Congress that the industry was only borrowing the second channel and would use it chiefly for high-definition. After everyone in the United States had bought a high-definition television, they said, the broadcasters would return to the government the analog channels they currently used.

I never met anyone who truly believed that the broadcasters would give back the analog channels. In the foreseeable future, Americans were not about to throw away their 200 million analog televisions, so broadcasters would not stop sending signals to them. Nor did anyone truly think high-definition televisions would supplement analog televisions—not at several thousand dollars a set to watch the exact same shows available on existing televisions, albeit in a sharper resolution. We had inherited a crazy policy.

Ironically, the spectrum was intrinsically valuable for mobile communications, if not digital television broadcast. It could be auctioned for billions if Congress did not limit its use. But Congress, broadcasters, and previous Commissions were bent on giving analog television station license holders the gift of the so-called second channel. This would be the largest grant of government largesse since the 19th-century donation of 10 percent of the public land in the West to three dozen railroad companies in order to persuade them to build transcontinental railroads. Yet unlike the railroads the recipients had no plausible business plans for using the boon from Washington.

The right answer was to auction the licenses, and let the auction winners use the airwaves as they wished. But in the surreal debate over digital television, realistic policies and reasonable expectations had never been publicly discussed. Instead, folks praised demonstrations of high-resolution pictures, and let the dazzle of the images' precision substitute for clarity of analysis.

On a torpid day in July 1994, Judy, Blair, and I went to see the latest HDTV demonstration in a studio somewhere in the trackless reaches of northern Virginia. The technicians and lobbyists running the demonstration would not let me sit in the back. Nor was I permitted to sit in the front, although all the seats were empty. They wanted me 12 to 14 feet from the screen. Why? Because only at that distance could one appreciate the vividness of the "high-definition" picture on the huge screen before us.

"How many Americans put their couches 14 feet from the TV screen?" Blair asked the broadcasters' representative.

"An increasing number," said the lobbyist, with practiced certainty. The lobbyist's assistant pointed out various visual features of the test trailer scenes, the opening Olympic Parade from the Norwegian Winter Games: light reflecting on ice, the brightness of flags waving against azure skies. His observations about the absence of artifacts and other technical successes seemed to be comments about the emperor's new clothes. Basically, the movie was only a little sharper than a perfect cable picture, except that the screen was enormous and the film's production values high.

When the demonstration ended and we were on the way back to the Commission, Blair said, "This spectrum giveaway could be the biggest disgrace of your chairmanship."

"That is saying something," said Judy, as she briefly opened the window to test the heat.

"But we could auction the licenses instead," said Blair.

"When the Senate passes the new telecommunications law," said Judy, "Congress will stick you with the giveaway. If they pass it."

"Why wouldn't it pass?" I asked.

"You never know. Could go one way or the other," said vacillating Judy as she rolled up the window.

As she intimated, partisan hostility to the telecommunications reform bill erupted in the Senate. Senator John McCain on the Republican side, an ally of Bob Dole, criticized the Senate bill authored by Democratic Commerce Committee chairman Fritz Hollings of South Carolina for delegating too much power to the FCC and for not relaxing existing regulations.

"Give more power to Reed Hundt?" McCain asked. "That's not what's in the best interests of society."

McCain's criticism signaled that Dole might not let the Hollings bill pass. Eager for a deal, Democratic staff members offered compromises to Minority Leader Dole. The Bell companies, long-time allies of Dole, wanted the Senate's version of the telecommunications bill stopped, because it would open the historically closed local telephone markets to competition long before permitting the Bell companies to enter the long distance business. (To this end the law would repeal pro-monopoly state laws without simultaneously lifting restrictions on the Bells imposed in a court order at the time of the AT&T breakup in 1984.) Ray Smith of Bell Atlantic and other telephone company executives bet that the Republicans would take at least the Senate in the upcoming election. The collapse of the Administration's health care effort had made this switch more likely. In the next Congress's rewriting of the telecommunications bill, the Bells believed they would obtain quicker entry into the long distance market and retain greater capability to defend their local telephone monopolies. Between the long distance and local telephone companies, the law was a zero-sum game, a matter of shifting market value from one industry to another. The Bells believed the Democratic Congress's bill would move value to the long distance side; they counted on a Republican Congress to move it the other way in the next year's writing of the bill. After days and nights of proffering concessions to Dole, Hollings ended the game. The Senate bill was dead; the already passed House companion bill would not become law.

As Congress failed to give me my big chance in 1994, I studied the art of running a deep-inside-the-Beltway regulatory agency. The agency was like a compass that pointed due south. I concluded that if I figured out where the FCC had been heading in the past, then the right course was the exact opposite. An example was the Commission's method of writing its decisions. Sensible exposition would have been to state a new rule, then to explain the reasoning for the rule and its relationship to the law that authorized the passage of the rule. The conclusion would be a statement of the rule's desired effects. An appendix would include a rejection or approval of each of the arguments made by the parties to the Commission.

The Commission's method was the opposite. It opened its rulemaking decisions with a laborious and generally uncritical recitation of the filings at the Commission. Then followed a comparatively brief explanation of the Commission's reaction to the filings. Attached to the decision was the rule, the details of which were often not clearly discussed in the writing itself. In practice, the Commission concealed its logic, avoided clear rejection of arguments before it, and left fundamentally ambiguous the reasons for the rulemaking.

On review, the courts of appeals rejected about 50 percent of the Commission's rules as inconsistent with congressional intent or inherently illogical. If, in lieu of thinking, the Commission had flipped coins to make its decisions, it would have had the same probability of being upheld in the appellate courts.

In fact, the Commission flipped not coins but points of view, compromising in different parts of its decisions among different business interests championed by commissioners. Each commissioner typically represented several of these interests; horses were traded, logs were rolled, deals done often until a majority cohered in the wee hours before a public vote; then in a public meeting all commissioners declared victory. Indeed, a Commission custom, I learned, was to compromise enough to obtain unanimous votes, thus making sure that no commissioner's favorite special interests were unattended.

The plentitude of compromises, however, often deprived the staff of the ability to write a persuasive rationale to explain the outcome. After all, no systematic logic of economics or law had controlled the result. Hence the structure of the item: the only section that the staff could write in advance was the summary of arguments. The reasoning was cobbled together by floating groups of commissioners' representatives who obliged despairing bureau experts to tailor the document to the hodgepodge eighth-floor process. Even less time and attention was spent on the rule itself.

Weeks later, the interested parties appealed to the courts. During the judiciary's ruminations the relevant technologies and business conditions often changed, mooting the rule. Moreover, if the courts reversed the Commission, they often did not indicate exactly what they thought Congress had intended in the usually ambiguous statute that required the rule to be written in the first place. Without clear appellate court guidance, the Commission's process then repeated itself. The second go-around on the rule writing often took so long—sometimes more than a year—that the courts would issue orders demanding that the Commission do its work.

Laziness was not the explanation for the Commission's recalcitrance. Instead, the make-up of the Commission changed over time, and the congressional (and agency) impulse for action faded as key members lost elections or businesses pursued new interests. In short, the will to make the hard decision was never strong, and then it dissipated. The original midnight compromises on the eighth floor proved ephemeral as midnight words and deeds of all sorts.

The new technological revolution, however, was based on microprocessors that went from first sale to close-out discounting in nine months, software that passed from beta to out-of-date in six months, next big things every quarter. As the digital and data revolution welled up like a huge wave heading for the rocky coast of regulation—as computing converged with communications—the Commission could either change, or be damned for denying the human species the actualization of its possibilities. That was how one could put the matter, if theatrically inclined. To fulfill destiny, we needed Congress to reform the old telecommunications law. And we needed the votes and talent at the FCC to write clear, sustainable, meaningful rules to implement the reform. For that, we needed to find new staff and liberate the existing employees from the historic constraints of the process.

Blair and I discovered that as employees retired, their "slots" opened up. As long as certain procedural forms were properly followed, under these circumstances we could hire whom we wanted. Andy Grove and the CEO of Sony, Mickey Schulhof, sent software and hardware experts. Harvard Business School professor Richard Tedlow (also my college classmate) sent us two first-rate MBAs. Our general counsel Bill Kennard hired the best lawyers ever employed at the agency, including several former clerks to Supreme Court justices, who helped increase the Commission's winning percentage in the court of appeals from 55 percent to 95 percent. Gina Keeney and Richard Metzger drove new thinking in the crucial Common Carrier Bureau. We hired trusted friends and acquaintances to create new bureaus. Our Smashing Pumpkins–loving economist tripled the number of economists on staff. By the end of my tour, we had brought into the agency about 200 new, able, energetic, multitalented people—10 percent of the workforce, about 50 percent of the policy ranks.

In the past, many of the FCC's decisions were not grounded in the law; few took into account even the most basic rules of economics. Blair and I invented a motto: "Read the Law. Study the Economics. Do the Right Thing." We put the motto on T-shirts, distributed them like decorations to warriors, and told the career staff not to tell us what they thought the other commissioners wanted done on items. Traditionally, the bureaus and offices shaped a consensus among the commissioners by developing recommended decisions with the staffs of the various commissioners. This process generated recommendations that reflected the views of various businesses instead of the staff's own views about the right course of action. Solving problems was up to them; politics was up to us—so we said to the staff.

As Andy Grove said, "There are two kinds of businesses: those that use e-mail and those that do not." We chose to become the former, and we created a networked culture at the FCC. We obtained new money from Congress. We had found the agency with a clumsy mainframe and no personal computers. We used the new money to wire the agency, provide computers for everyone on the agency's internal e-mail network, and put the agency on-line for outsiders to use the Internet to get our published decisions.

Our internal network became the principal way we worked. Our productivity went up as the staff worked nights and weekends, doing the agency's work both from the office and from home, on the agency intranet.

Anyone who did not use e-mail did not know what was going on. One employee came to tell me that she had been functionally blind, and had needed memos read to her in order to participate in work. Now, with a super-size computer screen on the agency network, at last she felt like a full member of the agency.

To teach e-mail to everyone on staff we conducted a campaign to rename the agency. Like Dilbert cartoons posted in a Silicon Valley cubicle, the name game also encouraged iconoclasm. My two favorite entries for FCC were "Frightened Cowering Commissioners" and "Funneling Cash to Congress."

Changing methods was only part of the re-education of the agency. We still needed to change the substance of agency thinking. For that, I needed to explain our purpose, in general and in detail. In an information business, explanation is leadership. To this end, I needed to know what to say and how to say it.

One day in August, Judy Harris poked her head in my door. She said, "We've reorganized the way we work, but I wonder if you've figured out the job yet. You might have. But probably you haven't. You may make decisions, but you need to have a message to lead. And you haven't figured out yet that nothing in your litigation background is in any way useful for that."

"Nothing? Not the contentiousness? The attention to picayune detail? The insistence on telling everyone what to say?"

"Right."

"What about the personal stories?"

"That's a start," she said. "But there's more to message than a personable style." Borrowing from the Ronald Reagan success story, we recruited a former actor to help us articulate an agenda. A graduate of the Yale Drama School, Michael Sheehan gave advice to the President and the First Lady. He was an expert in the New Age of Advocacy: the airwave war. The thespian's specialty was cogent television appearances. But he also shaped message.

I waited in Sheehan's consulting office on K Street. Blowing through the door like Kramer in *Seinfeld,* the actor demonstrated the importance of entrance.

"Let's get started," he said, as if I had been holding him up. "Now, TV rules. You can give all the speeches or write all the articles you want. That's somewhat important. But always try to get on TV. In fact, always act as if you're on TV. If you believe, they'll believe."

I nodded.

"What to wear?" he asked. Then he answered, "Bright tie on white shirt. Preferably bright red, any non-weird design."

I fingered the green, vaguely art deco tie I had unwisely selected.

"Second, dark blue or charcoal suit. Makes you look younger and on top of the game. And dark suits and white shirts emphasize forthrightness and integrity. TV doesn't reward a compromising appearance."

With the green tie I had coupled a light gray pinstripe.

"Third, you can make three or four points. Not more. Your message must be written in a triangle or a diamond."

"Can you give an example?"

"What's your biggest goal?" asked Sheehan.

"We want to put communications technology in every classroom," I said. I had never thought clearly about the answer to Sheehan's question. I believed I had a duty to do the right thing on every subject, and had resisted any narrowing of focus. But nothing else synthesized the power of technology and the power of positive government like connecting classrooms. I began to explain the policy.

"I've got it," said the actor, shutting me off.

He went to the board and drew a diamond. At each of its four points he put a phrase:

- A hand up, not a hand out.
- Put the future in the present.
- Connect parents, teachers, and kids: We are family.
- Equal chances for all.

I had the baseball fan's feeling of admiration when watching a home run sail over the fence.

"Axioms, puns, specific facts, and common terms are good," Sheehan said. "Abstractions and acronyms are bad. Now, go for it."

On a weekly basis, Blair and I met for an hour to develop our three or four points of message for the next week. We called magazine reporters on Wednesday or Thursday in order to get into their weekly stories, which were usually written by Friday. We prepared lists of puns, pithy statements, and well-honed facts. Then we meted out these verbal goodies to the reporters at Commission meetings or in one-on-one interviews that we routinely scheduled. Each reporter got a quotable phrase, and all got the message.

Judy Harris then gave lessons in congressional diplomacy. Most congressional inquiries to the FCC—tens of thousands a year—are on behalf of constituents: cab companies with dispatch systems that need extra frequencies, telephone companies upset about a reallocation of telephone numbers, people who receive radio signals through their teeth, hundreds of thousands of people made unhappy in the range of fifty cents to a few dollars each by a bill received from some communications company. Congressmen needed our help to respond to their complaining voters. Without it, they would punish us with hostile comments in the press. But if we could help, we might make them happy enough to give us the trust necessary for us to do our jobs well.

We had inherited a backlog of thousands of unanswered letters, and the failure to respond was inciting Congress to criticism. Cleaning up the Augean stable of letters, Judy developed procedures for each bureau and office to respond rapidly and usefully to every congressional inquiry, whether from Democrat or Republican. Judy also took me routinely to visit all the Senators and Congressmen on the Senate and House Commerce Committees. Usually we were able to do what the different members wanted; the requests were typically modest—a television station wanted to move a tower, for instance. When we could not cooperate, we explained in detail to the members the reasons. I was learning courtesy, getting along, going along, showing deference to elective office, giving public praise of the powers that be, privately accommodating the way things were. Of course my diplomacy was easier by reason of not voicing my qualms about HDTV, or other controversial subjects, since the cable imbroglio.

During the summer of 1994, my broadcast team, including a brilliant former Supreme Court law clerk, Julius Genachowski, assembled our network-friendly broadcast policy. In an effort to find compromise between the networks and the public interest advocates, the team proposed to require three hours of educational television per week. Peggy Charren wanted five, but we were trying to be moderate. I could not imagine that this humble request would be rejected, especially given that we also proposed to eliminate unnecessary regulations on commercial matters. Through commercial deregulation, the networks would become much more valuable and much more attractive as acquisition targets. By satisfying their public interest duties, they would bolster their standing with their social critics and perhaps create new programming to attract kids back to broadcast and away from cable. A win-win deal.

After Labor Day, I went to New York to explain our approach to the three Manhattan network CEOs. (Rupert Murdoch of Fox Television was in Los Angeles; I had met him after my UCLA speech.) Larry Tisch of CBS welcomed me into a small office where he and his famous programmer, Howard Stringer, listened affably to the outline of our policies. Everyone said Tisch had put CBS on the auction block. The rumor appeared to be true, as he showed no interest in discussing the medium.

When he graciously showed me to the elevator, Tisch said he was worried about the Administration's declining popularity. An invasion of Haiti would destroy the President, Tisch said. He asked me to warn the President not to send troops to quell the unrest there. Did he think the President asked for my foreign policy advice, or was he goofing on me?

Bob Wright of NBC was more engaged with the topic of television. He was delighted that I intended to eliminate the prime-time access rule, which forced networks to let their affiliates buy independent programming, instead of showing the network feed, for a half-hour during the optimal viewing hours. This governmental intrusion into television programming had produced only a plethora of game shows generated by independent programmers. In my team's view, the "public interest" of the 1934 Communications Act was not served by *Jeopardy*, not that any one of us found the show objectionable. By voiding the rule, the FCC would enable the networks to distribute an extra show per night and add hundreds of millions of dollars to their value. But later, when I moved to eliminate the rule, NBC only intensified its opposition to our children's television rule. It seemed that my broadcast decisions typically infuriated some of those concerned and left the rest ungrateful.

Wright wanted more than the elimination of the prime-time access rule. He wanted me to take away Fox's television licenses, and destroy Rupert Murdoch's American television business. In 1985, Murdoch had abandoned his Australian citizenship and become an American in order to persuade Ronald Reagan's FCC to let him buy television stations. If Murdoch had really acquired the stations not with his own money but with the borrowing power of his Australian media company, News Corporation, then the FCC had erred by allowing foreign ownership of television licenses. Moreover, if the Commission concluded that Murdoch had defrauded the government in 1985, then the punishment might be that he would be stripped of ownership of the Fox stations. An investigation of these old events would bring on me a firestorm of Republican wrath and convince many that I was simply a Democratic Party hack. Republicans, after all, prized Murdoch's network for countering the "liberalism" of the Big Three, and relished his blatant personal conservatism.

Yet NBC's allegations that Fox Television was foreign-owned in violation of United States law were plainly serious, even if self-interested. Years of litigation had left me highly dubious that the well-lawyered Murdoch had lied to the Commission when he applied for permission to buy the Fox stations. Nor could I imagine that a just punishment could consist of dismantling a major broadcast network, especially when such a step would appear to reflect partisan politics instead of common sense. Nevertheless, I believed that a self-respecting FCC had a duty to investigate all plausible charges.

In the months after the Wright meeting, I had the career staff seek Fox's documents and take depositions of Fox employees, including Murdoch himself. Murdoch was furious. One Sunday he personally wrote a screed against me and faxed it to the *Wall Street Journal,* which dutifully reprinted the vitriol for the reading pleasure of America's business community on Monday morning. (First cable, now this!) A sad irony was that only Murdoch among the network heads was willing to support a new children's television rule: he figured he could beat the others in the youth market and did not scruple over meeting quantifiable public interest obligations. Congressional Republicans condemned me for looking into the allegations. NBC, meanwhile, dropped its charges upon reaching a commercial arrangement with Murdoch on some forgettable joint venture. As a result, they spent not a cent of political capital to defend me from the Republican onslaught. But these developments unfolded in the politically chilly winter. In the fall I believed without foreboding that I could sell my agenda, like other new chairmen had believed, to the nets.

I left Bob Wright in the humming beehive of the General Electric empire and went to the last of the Big Three. Tom Murphy of ABC greeted me with a big smile. He looked hugely prosperous in a blue and white striped shirt with burgundy tie. Tall, red-faced Murphy had been a broadcaster for 40 years. He always called me "Mr. Chairman," as if I were respectable but untutored in the real world, like an academic or a priest.

Murphy, however, did want something from my jurisdiction: rapid elimination of the financial interest and syndication rule. Under this rule, a network could not control the syndication rights of its first-run shows. In other words, by government order, the studios that produced the shows, rather than the networks that aired them, controlled the reruns of those shows. As a result, if Disney bought ABC, it would have to give up its profits from the sale of syndicated programming because it would become both the network and the studio. This rule had kept Hollywood from buying the networks, and vice versa. But in line with convergence, studios and networks might merge. So the financial syndication rule had to go. As history records, the Commission did later eliminate financial syndication. Thus I made possible Disney's acquisition of ABC, which in turn inaugurated a new era of declining share price for the buyer and a new intransigence on children's television by ABC.

After my visits, someone told the industry magazine *Broadcasting & Cable* that I had offered the networks a quid pro quo: I would relax some rules in return for commitments on children's television. The trade reporters criticized my would-be wheeling and dealing. In fact, I had not made such a proposal, and no network agreed to provide more children's television. Each only urged rule changes that increased their value.

In any event, I would never persuade the networks to announce that they favored a rule requiring public interest programming. That was an article of religion for them as capitalists, because kidvid subtracted from the bottom line. Moreover, they knew I would vote to eliminate the offensive rules if I had integrity, because all reasonable people knew the referenced rules had no useful effects. Indeed, voting to reject those rules was the only way to show I was guided by principle, and that in turn was the best means by which I could demonstrate I was serious about kidvid. Listening to the networks was important, but voting in a way that displayed my values was more useful.

Clear purpose on my part also encouraged Commissioner Chong to send positive signals on children's educational television. She announced that on a trip to Australia she had discovered that the regulators there ordered broadcasters to educate children. From her new learning she had developed a new plan and would be urging me to support it. For the most part, her proposal was happily indistinguishable from my team's old proposal for extracting kidvid from the networks.

Adding to the pressure, Peggy Charren got trade press coverage with the statement that Commissioner Andrew Barrett should not be reappointed when his term expired in 1995 unless he voted for the new kidvid rule. Commissioner Barrett responded by saying he was open to compromise, reversing his adamant opposition to any specific requirement for kids' television. With Chong and Barrett joining Commissioner Ness and me in support of a revised kidvid rule, we would overcome Commissioner Quello's opposition, and change the FCC's record of failing to extract quantifiable public interest programming from the broadcast industry.

My team believed we were entering a phase of accomplishment at the FCC. We had learned to be concrete and insistent, within a range of reasonable requests. The defeat of the telecommunications bill in Congress had blocked our plan to connect classrooms to the information highway. But we could think of other means to this end. Airwave spectrum auctions could generate the money to connect classrooms. Or we could give incentives to the cable industry to build the education networks. For instance, we could relax cable rate regulations—only a tad—in return for commitments to connect classrooms.

We put these proposals to Brian Roberts, not only the new CEO of Comcast Cable in Philadelphia but also the incoming head of the cable industry trade association. He publicly announced that he favored using spectrum auction revenue to pay for putting communications in classrooms. Auction winners would pay for the spectrum. The proceeds would go to school districts. Then cable would submit winning bids to school districts to build the networks into classrooms. My staff anticipated raising billions in the round of auctions that would start that winter. When the new Democratic Congress convened in the new year, the House could initiate the appropriations bill that would spend this money on kids.

After a speech in Berkeley in September, Blair and I headed north across the Golden Gate Bridge to the headquarters of the great multimedia teacher of our time—George Lucas. Not far into Marin County, we turned down a road and drove through a gate where we were greeted by blue-uniformed Skywalker Ranch firemen.

Lucasfilm was headquartered in a white Victorian mansion, known as the Main House of the ranch. In glass cupboards along a wide central hall were tiny sculptures—the famous nonhuman characters of *Star Wars*. As I studied the icons, I felt a slight breeze, perhaps the ruffle of a force field, and turned to see that Lucas himself had materialized in the room.

He ushered us into the dining room. Lucas discussed mythology, and the director's, producer's, and writer's block that was holding up his progress on the first prequel to the *Star Wars* trilogy. Blair was awestruck, I, dumbstruck.

We readily agreed with Lucas—perhaps telepathically (I don't recall anyone trifling with humdrum expressions of assent)—that there were three grand events in the history of communications: the invention of writing, the printing press, and electronic communication. The latter was exploding in scale and scope. The world would soon be wrapped in continuous high-speed transmissions of voices, texts, pictures, and moving images. Lucas wove a spectacular vision in which artists of teaching would use broadband technology (which meant full-motion, movie-quality video) to impart education through stories that would inspire the unique imaginations of every individual child. This, he said, was why we had to connect every classroom to communications networks. Over these networks we would teach children and ourselves to teach, learn, and think anew.

I saw that my greatest quest was to build those networks. They would be, among many other things, the vessels not only of Al Gore's vision, but of Lucasfilm's imagination. I asked for his help. He could testify in Washington; by waving the wand of his fame he could persuade Congress of the importance of networked education. George Lucas passed his small hand over his almost untouched lunch, as if dismissing from consideration the mechanics of political action.

"The only real power I have is the power of ideas," he said.

In late October, Senator Dole's communications staff person told the press that the FCC should not take any new actions until the election determined who was in charge of Congress. A spiteful comment, I thought. I was sure that Senator Dole had no power to thwart my plans (and Gore's). He could not stop the Democratic telecommunications reform law from passing in the next year. He could not stop me from fulfilling Al Gore's goals for reshaping the country's policies for the information age. After the November election left New Democrats in charge of at least the House and the White House, we would put our policies in place. We would stimulate private investment and create new public benefits. I would punch a checklist of achievements that would draw praise from the business community and public interest advocates alike. We needed only the return of the routine Democratic majority in the House that all the Washington insiders predicted.

PART 2   **Changes and Choices**

Six **On the Floor**

November 1994 – February 1995

Sing to me of the man, Muse, the man of twists and turns

Driven time and again off course.

Homer, The Odyssey, Translated by Robert Fagles

At the Commission, the day after Election Day, none of my team knew what would happen to us. The Republicans had seized control of both houses of Congress for the first time in 50 years, for the first time in my lifetime. Voters had not merely punished Democrats; they had virtually exiled the party. The election had not set back Bill Clinton; it had repudiated him.

The health care industry's paid television advertising, coordinated with the Republicans' strategic decision to resist any solution to the problem of the uninsured, had savaged the White House. The President's staff had discovered too late that in information age politics, private money could effectively sell such powerful negative images that no President could survive without himself conducting a continuous airwave war against his adversaries.

The White House had erred also in rejecting Al Gore's advice to concentrate on welfare reform instead of health care and in not responding to Newt Gingrich's "Contract with America"—which Gore dubbed the "Contract on America." The media age favors the counter-puncher, the critic, the defender. In today's politics, an adversary is essential, but in 1994, because Democrats controlled both houses of Congress, they had only themselves to blame for falling short of voters' expectations.

At the Commission, one of the outer planets of the Washington solar system, we feared that we would freeze to death as the light faded at the White House. Then the Gingrich Deathstar filled the sky, and our apprehension turned to horror. The Speaker, Newt, the New Man, instantly eclipsed old Dole and all the other dim icons of the Republican Party. Some thought we could do business with Gingrich, but I read the books he lectured the country to read. The military works: Sun-Tzu, *The Art of War;* Musashi Miyamoto, *A Book of Five Rings: The Classic Guide to Strategy;* General Heinz Guderian, *Panzer Achtung.* The futurism and sci-fi: Alvin Toffler, *The Third Wave;* Isaac Asimov, *The Foundation Trilogy.* Based on the amalgam of aggression and grandiosity in this material, I was not surprised when he offhandedly explained his intent to liquidate the FCC. It was no comfort that we were but one of his targets, along with the Department of Commerce and the Department of Education. In Gingrich's opinion, national government was unnecessary in most respects, and evil in many.

Newt Gingrich was pervasive, ubiquitous; he was high-speed communications. He opined 24 hours a day, seven days a week, about everything on his mind. Surrounding his ultimatums, apothegms, axioms, and precepts was a cloud of a new communications philosophy. Deregulate monopolies and let mergers build enormous television, radio, newspaper, cable, and telephone conglomerates, the Speaker declared—he pumped the one-pipe vision of Gilder and Negroponte into a great balloon of the idea that American information monopolies would teach our ways to the world. The previous Congress had not wanted to give up control over the information sector, or to permit media mergers that aggregated great political as well as economic power. But Gingrich spoke of an ungoverned and ungovernable communications economy, in which bigness was good in business and bad in government.

The Speaker's animadversion to government action led him to argue for elimination of the Public Broadcasting System. His eager equation of wealth and the right to govern led him to call for increasing the amount of money poured into political advertising instead of creating free access for underfinanced candidates. He agreed with Gore that technology could create prosperity, but cheerily assumed away any need to provide the tools of technology to the next generation: someone, he said, would give laptop computers to children. For his part, he would stop the government from providing networks or even electrical outlets in classrooms. The have-nots, apparently, were meant to enroll in the School of Hard Knocks, whereas the haves would obtain the opportunities for learning and advancement that the happy accident of fortunate birth had earned for them.

The Speaker despised governmental altruism. Charity should begin and end with the impulses of rich individuals and wealthy non-governmental organizations. Taxpayers should not be mulcted for support of public life. If roads, schools, and parks fell into disrepair, local communities bore the responsibility. If the community was too poor to address its problems, the Republican doctrine of personal responsibility excused the rest of the country from the burden of compassion.

Gingrich summoned to Capitol Hill the leading executives of the information sector. No small companies; no entrepreneurs; no software or hardware companies; no consumer groups were invited. Broadcast, cable, satellite, wired and wireless telephony—all five lanes of the information highway—gathered in a closed-door session to tell the House leadership what the CEOs wanted in the new telecommunications reform law. The Speaker asked who preferred total deregulation of the information sector, open season on mergers and price increases, and—the bonus prize—elimination of the FCC. Many hands went up.

Because Washington lawyers and lobbyists charge money for reporting rumors in Washington, the gossip circulates at record velocity. Immediately after the meeting, I was told that Jerry Levin, the CEO of Time Warner, had asked the Speaker to agree that government should never regulate the media. Gingrich supposedly responded with a tirade about the coloring of his *Time* magazine cover photograph. He complained about *Time*'s description of his mother. He demanded better visual and verbal coverage of himself in the future, starting with more flattering pictures. Then he left the room. Next up was the House Republicans' chief fundraiser. Everyone at the meeting understood that access to the new Republican Congress went through the "green door."

Harry McPherson, a familiar Washington lobbyist who had worked in the Johnson Administration, argued in his memoir, *A Political Education: A Washington Memoir,* that money is so freely available to politicians that they all feel it comes with no strings attached. His thesis was that if everyone is drunk, no one is under the influence. McPherson's view pertained, if at all, only to the Democrats who ran Congress in the era covered in his book. When Democrats took money from business lobbyists, they were receiving from sources whose interests ran counter to Democratic constituencies. For instance, the milk industry lobby might give the Democrats money whereas the milkmen gave them votes. In this tension Democrats obtained some freedom to act for the employees and not the employers.

In the Republican Congress, however, the milkmen had no sway with the majority. The country had elected a Congress exquisitely responsive to money. (This was the principal reason for the Republican insistence on a tax cut in 1999 rather than paying down the national debt. The taxes cut would not be those of the milkmen.)

An innovation of the Gingrich Congress was to permit business lobbyists to draft legislation in committee rooms, as if they were staff to the member. Indeed, many of the new Republican members acted like staff to the business lobbies. Some new Republican Congressmen demanded, from me, rulings "on behalf of" a particular business—a locution that appeared to dispense with the traditional assumption in our Republic that elected officials represent voters, not corporations.

No one outside Washington seemed to know about the new deal for moneyed interests. The reason for national ignorance of this stealthy scandal was that the degradation of the legislative process by money was not on television. It did not meet the requirement of television news. Nothing is broadcast unless it sparks at least one of four basic emotional reactions— regret, bathos, horror, prurient interest. (The Monica chord hit all four keys!) But in American politics nothing matters unless it is on television. As a practical matter, the new degree of money's corruption of politics was an illustration of the famous non-event of philosophy: when no one hears a tree falling in the forest, then it has not fallen.

The chief aide to Larry Pressler, the new Republican chairman of the Senate Commerce Committee, visited my office. Senator Dole's aide also attended, confirming rumors that the majority leader and prospective presidential candidate wanted to supervise reform of this information sector so generous in campaign donations. As a show of respect and humility I had my top staff greet the congressional conquerors.

The Pressler aide explained that the Republicans would write a very different telecommunications reform law from the Democratic versions of the previous Congress. In the new law, the FCC would have a very limited and transitory role. Years earlier the aide had worked in a lowly job at the FCC. Now in a grand reversal of role that is characteristic of revolutions, he would rule the bureaucracy that had been blind to his skills. The only purpose of the agency, he explained, was to rubber-stamp licenses given out to businesses according to the wishes of Congress. Nothing else.

The aide went on. The new telecommunications law written by Senator Pressler and the new Republican head of the House Telecommunications Subcommittee, Jack Fields of Texas, would not interfere with the marketplace. This Congress would free communications and media companies from the shackles of regulation. Industries like radio and television historically had been fractionated by rules into small companies in order to promote local control and to dissipate the political power of the media. Now these companies could merge. That the proposed new media monopolies would be pro-Republican hardly needed saying. Existing monopolies such as the Bells would not be opened for competition by sharp-edged FCC rules. Nor should government pay for or order anyone to provide public benefits from the communications revolution. Markets would generate everything people wanted. Government had to be smaller to this end, and in light of its imminent desuetude, the FCC could be phased out of existence.

Next, Judy Harris reported that Jack Fields wanted to see me. Fields had joined Ed Markey to co-author the telecommunications reform bill that had sailed through the Democratic House in 1994. Now, as I had been informed, the Speaker had him writing a very different bill. The policies the Vice President had outlined at UCLA and described to the world in Buenos Aires had no sway with the Gingrich Congress. All our efforts had been wasted.

Fields's staffer showed us into his office. From behind his large, regal desk, Fields explained that he was writing a deregulatory telecommunications law in accord with the new Republican vision. As Fields spoke, I had a vision. In order to build a case for eliminating the FCC, Fields would conduct public hearings to prove I had overspent on software for auctions or lost my temper at some staff member or otherwise demonstrated unfitness. The House Commerce Committee would join with the two Republican commissioners and quasi-Republican Jim Quello to wrest the FCC from my control. In concert with Congress, the gang of three commissioners would dismember the agency, bureau by bureau, driving out the members of my team, eviscerating my authority, mocking Gore's goals. The press would cackle at my collapse: from cable to catastrophe.

The Congressman said I should not have created the new International, Wireless, or Cable Bureaus. I came out of my reverie. The FCC should not be enforcing equal employment opportunity laws on broadcasters. My educational television ideas were too regulatory. Broadcast networks served the country well by providing free television, and should not be asked to do more. Cable had adequate children's programming.

Moreover, I had gone too far in doing what Gore wanted on cable regulation.

"Gore didn't insist on our cable rate regulation. Congress did," I snapped.

"This Congress will fix that mistake," said Jack bluntly. "We will deregulate cable. Al won't like it. But he will have to accept it."

When Judy and I escaped into the marble hallway where the lobbyists stepped happily from one Republican office to another, hearing good news everywhere, I said, "Here's what I heard: the Gingrich Congress is against competition, minority rights, the satellite industry, kids, and consumers. For starters."

Judy responded, "Here's what I felt: Republicans are sexy now."

"What?"

"Sex. Power. You're a male. You don't get it. He was just telling you who's in charge."

I shuddered at the shame of a Democratic presidential appointee taking orders from one of Newt Gingrich's subalterns. This was not in accord with my concept of an independent administrative agency, or the purpose of my public service.

"One thing for sure," Judy patiently explained, "is that they won't be writing the new communications law the way Gore and you want."

Your dreams should be worth your time, Ted Turner had said. But what was a nightmare worth?

Back at the Commission, my staff brought the news that Commissioner Chong had taken down her photograph of Bill Clinton. All presidential nominees keep on their wall a photograph of the President who nominated them. Chong had done so, but now she had replaced the President's photograph with one of Bob Dole. On it, the new majority leader had inscribed a message for her in a Washington gesture of reciprocal loyalty. I understood the symbolism: Chong's loyalty was not to the President who made her a commissioner, but to the man she thought would be the President who would make her the chair.

The Republican Congress would want the agency to be independent of the White House and the President who nominated the commissioners. They would wish it to be dependent on the whims and wishes of the new congressional leadership. To this end, they could pass laws, shrink our budget, abuse us in hearings, conduct investigations, berate us in public. Even if Congress passed a new telecommunications law delegating powers to the agency, the Gore agenda could get short shrift in the implementing rule-makings. The Congress had vast powers to influence the commission, and I feared that the members of what might become the Commission's Gang of Three would be eager to throw themselves at the feet of the new congressional majority.

I visited the Vice President to report my assessment of the impact of the election on the Commission. I told how Commissioner Chong had replaced the President's photograph with Dole's. Al had personally interviewed Chong for the job. She had assured him of her sympathy to his agenda and given a guarantee that she would not play politics. Many in public life believe they are loyal to people and principles, but they excuse disloyalty to some people on the ground of principle, and disloyalty to some principles on the ground of personal ties. There is always an out. Al shook his head at Chong's apostasy.

The Vice President was hearing similar stories from other political battlefields. Republicans were assaulting his environmental and education policies. Republicans were cutting funds for basic science research, biotech, education, NASA. Republicans did not want government to be smarter and more efficient; they wanted it reduced or eliminated.

I suggested that the White House could block Chong from assembling a Gang of Three by cultivating Jim Quello (invitations to White House dinners and so forth). Al smiled indulgently. I realized from his reaction that these stratagems would fail. Al had a better idea.

"I'm going to invite Pressler and Fields over here," he said.

"Old friends of yours."

"We've known each other since we were in the House together. Almost 20 years ago. I'm going to tell them what the basic elements of the new communications law must be. Opening monopolized markets; interconnecting new and old networks at fair prices; the classrooms program. You know the elements."

"Jack Fields wasn't in a compromising mood when I visited him last week," I said.

"I'm going to tell them what I want in the new law," replied Al.

I had the word. He wanted to fight. Al got up to show me to the door. A courier was waiting outside with another battle report.

Al pulled his collar away from his neck with his forefinger and said, "I don't mind telling you that this is the tensest time we've had around here."

"I bet," I said.

"Everyone should remember that we have the veto," he said, forecasting the legislative battle at the end of 1995.

A few days later, the Vice President met with Larry Pressler and Jack Fields. He read them a list of items that had to be in the telecommunications legislation they were writing: real powers for the FCC to create competition; connecting all classrooms to the Internet; no monopolies in television; no deregulation of the cable monopolies until competition emerged. Texan Jack Fields pungently said that Congress would decide the contents of the new law. Soft-spoken Larry Pressler agreed.

Al told them that the White House would veto any bill that did not meet his demands. Fields said that he doubted the threat. Fields did not believe the President had the political will to challenge the Republicans and the powerful business constituencies they represented in the information sector. The meeting ended with an exchange of confrontational remarks.

During a long and famous night in August 1969, I sat, and occasionally slept, on the damp earth in a crowd of a half-million youths. In the wee hours of the day, a pale light suffused the clouds that surged over Max Yasgur's farm. On a tiny stage, surrounded by scaffolding, at the bottom of the natural bowl of the pasture, stood a single figure whose hair enveloped his head like a black nimbus. As a single pink ray of sunrise sliced through the lowering skies, the man said in a soft voice that was amplified directly into the ears of each of us: "I see we meet again."

Then Jimi Hendrix started into his jangled, jumping "Star-Spangled Banner." His rendition of the "dawn's early light" awoke the distinctive patriotism of my youth: the country belonged to us, not our parents. If he could play the national anthem his way, we could change the world our way. We could rewrite the rules.

I forgive our arrogance, our unwillingness to seek consensus. After all, in those days everyone was emotional—families, friends, national leaders. No debate was civil. Violent language filled the newspapers and violent imagery filled the nightly television news. Even those of us headed for law school rejected lawyerly logic; we believed in a higher, natural law that dictated various acts of revolution.

But the Gingrich Revolution was not what anyone at Woodstock had contemplated in those halcyon days. The Gingrich dream was half a vision of a future in which transforming technology made everyone self-sufficient and half a memory of isolated, change-resistant, rural society. The combination of change and constancy amounted to meaningless contradiction. Under the hallucinatory spell of the Speaker's speaking, some anticipated boons like tax cuts for the rich. Others yearned for lost privileges. Still others responded to what they thought was expression of their view that certain ethnic groups had been given undeserved assistance by government. All his enthusiasts heard what they wanted.

At Woodstock in 1969 we had thought the government was the enemy. Yet as the New Year of 1995 approached, no one in America more vigorously and violently asserted that the government was the enemy than Newt Gingrich. The army at Woodstock in 1969 and the legions of Gingrich Revolutionaries each believed that government threatened personal freedom. This coincidence masked reversal: the irony was that most who in the 1960s had chanted "Power to the People" now in the 1990s wanted government to do the people's business, and those who had supported the Old World Order 30 years ago now wanted Gingrich's government to roll back change in the 1990s.

When Gingrich said the FCC had to be extinguished for the betterment of the information economy, he was at least correct that the right end of a competition agenda was deregulation. But Gingrich's agenda did not promote entrepreneurial activity. Deregulating monopolies and encouraging new monopolies was no way to stimulate private investment in new companies built around technologies (digital wireless, packet-switching, wave division multiplexing, servers, routers, and so on) that were weapons against the defending incumbents. Nor could Gingrich's sunniest talk belie the mean consequences of his rejection of altruistic, communal effort through government. Lincoln had said that the purpose of government was to do what needed doing but could not be done except through government. Gingrich was the anti-Lincoln. For him, if government was the only way to accomplish something, then by definition the thing was not worth doing.

The Speaker's new Congress would empower monopolies and mark for slow death by budget cuts and role reduction one of the public's watchdog agencies, the FCC. I would be denied authority to promote competition, or to accomplish the change-causing connection of every classroom to the information highway, or to create any other public benefit from the communications revolution. The logical extension of the Gingrich Revolution would be businesses so powerful that individuals counted for nothing, and democracy so feeble that the many would be controlled by the few.

As Christmas approached, our NBC-inspired investigation of Rupert Murdoch's ownership of the Fox network led to taking depositions from Fox's top officers and interviewing FCC officials involved in the 1985 decision to approve the Fox Television station acquisitions. At this point, Senator Pressler moved to block the inquiry. Pressler announced that our confidential treatment of the investigation (a normal step to deter coordinated testimony and political pressure) was a violation of the First Amendment. He described it as a "draconian measure" and said the FCC presented "no compelling rationale for arbitrarily slapping such an egregious limitation on free speech."

The Senator's comments plainly had been coordinated with Commissioner Quello. When I complained about Quello's leaks of confidential investigatory material, Senator Pressler criticized me for having "an almost paranoid level of concern over commission matters being examined and covered by the press and others." He demanded that I close the inquiry and threatened numerous retaliations if I did not obey.

The congressional bludgeoning inspired a new forcefulness among lobbyists. One of them told Blair that if I did not do what the lobbyist's client wanted, I would "never work in a suit again." It was a very buttoned-down East Coast threat, but ominous nonetheless. Backing down in the face of Pressler's demands, however, would destroy my credibility with the Commission staff and the television networks I had visited in the fall. I also felt it was inconsistent with the attitude the Vice President had tried to convey in his meeting with Pressler and Fields. Moreover, I wanted to prove that the agency had integrity and was independent of Congress. Principle also was a weapon against the new Congress.

I ordered the staff to continue the Fox investigation. Commissioner Quello objected. I told him we could have a public vote of commissioners on whether to continue, and I would debate the issue with him in front of the press. In the 1980s he had voted to let Fox buy the television stations, and he knew I would publicly accuse him of covering up what had happened. Given that other television networks supported the inquiry, Quello feared for his reputation for fairness in the closed community of broadcasters. Fox's frequent employment of Quello's friends and departing aides created an additional possibility of embarrassment. He relented. But I worried that I was encouraging Quello to create a Gang of Three.

Weeks later our inquiry discovered, as we expected, that Murdoch and his representatives had not lied to the Commission when he bought the Fox stations, but that he had indeed used Australian funds in a way that constituted foreign ownership of American television stations. The allegations had been partially true. The evidence also showed that Murdoch had not lied about his financial structure. Rather, in its zeal to encourage a new network the FCC in 1985 had not asked probing questions. We ordered Murdoch to restructure his ownership to comply with the law, which he easily did.

We had forced Fox to comply with the agency's rules, despite the pressure against us. No one applauded the agency's courage. Instead, the other networks said we had given Fox a whitewash, reminding me again of the impossibility of gratifying the Big Three. Inside the agency, however, I sensed support among the career staff. Not many chairmen had been this stubborn—even if I had accomplished nothing much. And I had backed up the staff investigators' efforts. If I would be as committed—or obtuse—in the future, then the staffers would be able to count on support from my office for their own initiatives, for their own attempts to do the right thing.

The Republican criticism of government would be validated—at least in the communications area—if the Commission bungled the upcoming auction of new spectrum for mobile telephone use (the so-called PCS, or personal communications services). The rights for sale were licenses to broadcast an electromagnetic wave through what in pre-Einsteinian physics had sometimes been called the ether—a term used to describe the nothingness that frequencies occupy.

In 1993, the Democratic Congress had passed the law that ultimately balanced the budget for the first time in 30 years. Al Gore's tie-breaking vote passed it through the Senate. The Republicans, who did not vote for it (the foreshadowing of the disappearance of consensus that marked the Clinton Administration and limited its possibilities), derided this law so successfully that they took over both House and Senate in 1994. But as part of its effort to close the budget deficit, the 1993 law gave the FCC the authority to auction the right to use the public's airwaves for mobile telephone service.

An FCC team assembled by former McKinsey and Company consultant Don Gips had developed an innovative spectrum plan (the licenses to use the airwaves that were to be sold) and auction methodology (how the licenses would be sold). The plan was to stage a simultaneously inter-dependent auction of two PCS licenses in many geographic markets. An auction failure could force me to resign and might doom the agency. A suc-cessful auction would be a triumph of free market ideology and smart gov-ernment, sweetened by the failure of any Republican to vote in favor of the auction legislation in 1993.

In the late 1970s AT&T had told the Commission that mobile phone service was an uncertain and expensive technology. At most, it would at-tract a million customers by the end of the century. In order to reduce com-petition and increase profits for this risky experiment, the Commission had created only two analog cellular licenses for using spectrum for mobile tele-phony in each geographic area. It gave one to each Bell company that emerged from the breakup of AT&T and awarded the other by lottery.

Although customers presumably would want to travel with mobile telephones (hence the name), the Commission bizarrely decided to divide the country into about 500 postage-stamp-sized markets. Serendipitous investors (often, inexplicably, dentists) won each lotteried market, sold the license to speculators, who then sold at a higher price to entrepreneurs, who after a few years sold to bigger companies. As sales prices escalated along the chain, thousands became "cellionaires." But the duopoly system pro-duced little rivalry between the cellionaires and the local Bell telephone companies' wireless affiliates.

With the Commission's connivance, the local telephone company meanwhile charged huge prices for connecting wireless calls to the existing network. Lack of competition and these high interconnection charges raised prices for mobile service to about ten times higher per minute than for wire-based service. Cellular phones therefore were primarily for the well off.

The United States wireless industry then marched down a path of high, anti-competitive prices that gave America by the early 1990s the worst cellular system of any developed country in the world. The FCC had served its characteristic if unwitting historical purpose: it had precluded vigorous competition, discouraged innovation, handed out wealth to a few, denied price competition to the many, hampered the creation of national businesses, and guaranteed that the United States would lag in promoting a new technology.

The 1993 legislation authorizing auctions was passed by the Senate and House Budget Committees over the protests of the Commerce Committees, which resented the usurpation of their jurisdiction. The Commerce Committees perceived no problems with the cellular duopoly. The Commerce Committees enjoyed their traditional privilege of presiding over, through the FCC, the giveaway of hundreds of thousands of narrowly defined communications licenses (satellite, broadcast, mobile telephony, taxicab dispatch, or boat radios) free to assorted special interests. (Every day can be Christmas at the FCC!)

An auction earned government only the admiration of editorial page writers and the approval of free market ideologues. Worse, in the opinion of the existing cellular and wire-based telephone industry, an auction would put into the market so many licenses of such ample dimension that deep-pocketed capitalists could assemble a handful of national wireless firms. Ruinous price competition might break out.

Our team was enamored of these possibilities. If the Commission conducted the auctions efficiently and designed the method rationally, wireless investment would soar. The new firms would hire hundreds of thousands of people. They would offer radically lower prices to get customers. Eventually the new companies would steal voice traffic from the fixed-wire phone network. When cellular and wire competed with each other, the FCC could preempt all state-level retail price regulation of fixed-wire phone service—assuming that Congress gave us the authority to deregulate so broadly.

In the next stage of wireless entrepreneurship, laptop computers and other hand-held devices would have wireless capability so that mobile Internet access would be commonplace. As the wireless dimension of the communications revolution unfolded, the planet would be unwired. Economies and social structures would be based on a network of three billion interconnected mobile devices: laptops, cell phones, pagers, toys, e-mailers, automobiles. All this would come from an auction success. If the auctions failed—not raising enough money to please the budget hawks in Congress or suffering a system breakdown that proved the FCC's incompetence—then the tradition of restricting access and use of spectrum might again gain the upper hand. Then the exciting future of wireless might be fulfilled in Finland, or some other innovative country, but denied in America.

Another threat was that the incumbent cellular telephone companies wanted an auction licensing plan that produced little competition, excessively high prices, and skimpy investment. Under their influence, Commissioner Quello began issuing press releases criticizing me for failing to adopt his original plan (which all lobbyists told me privately was a disaster) and for slowing the start of the auctions. Beset by criticism before our decision, we went to the country's leading cellular telephone maker, Motorola, for support. That company had an interest in a robust competitive market because lower service prices meant higher market penetration and thus more cell phone sales. The company's motives and political clout, coupled with our team's analytical strength, produced a Commission vote for a license allocation plan that won widespread praise. Even existing cellular telephone companies appreciated the opportunity to expand their businesses to national scope. This was a far cry from the way cable regulation had been received.

Over months of preparation in 1994 my team studied auction theory in search of the best possible system. No one had conducted an auction like ours, and there was neither time nor money to conduct a test run. Nevertheless, I arranged for Al Gore to kick off the auction. If Gore was to be castigated in the event that our software or the auction methodology failed, then he might as well get in position to take the credit he deserved on the chance that we would succeed. On December 5, the Vice President stood on a makeshift podium in the former bag room of the main United States Post Office in Washington, D.C., adjacent to Union Station, now turned into our auction site. He announced our experiment in reinventing government: The auction would be conducted on-line, through computers, an innovation necessary in light of the expectation that the auction would last several months. The duration of the auction was designed to mimic the stock market's search for a fair price, which is best reflected not in a day but in a moving average or trading range—in other words, it lasts for weeks, as bidders in effect search for the efficient price.

Al said that the auctions would lead to radically lower prices for cellular service because of the new competition (which proved true). He predicted with a laugh that people would use mobile phones so much that they would be working "all the time" (which also proved true). Then, as we had persuaded the White House staff to let the Vice President say, he proposed that the revenues from the auction ought to be targeted for connecting classrooms to the Internet, as Brian Roberts of Comcast Cable had previously suggested. We would not relinquish our goal of connecting the Carthage schoolgirl to the Library of Congress just because the Congress was now Republican. Congressman Ed Markey, next on the podium, upped the ante. The auction revenues, he said, would be large enough also to fund public broadcasting in perpetuity.

Senator Larry Pressler, invited to the event as a bipartisan gesture, followed with a sputtering rejection of the Gore and Markey initiatives. He said he did not like the idea of targeting auction revenue for kids or classrooms. The budget had to be balanced. Spending had to be cut. Later his staff told reporters that Gore had overstepped his bounds; the Republicans and not the White House would decide the country's priorities. With this eruption of controversy, Al Gore gaveled into motion the biggest auction of anything in history.

Auctions are typically held to raise the maximum amount of money. But our staff had designed an auction that, if successful, would obtain the *minimum* fair price for every license. Our auction method would sell all licenses at an efficient price: that is, a carefully considered price that reflected what everyone in the bidding believed the licenses were worth. My team wanted a guilt-free auction—no buyer's remorse—because our goal was to help the winners attract the capital necessary to invest in building their businesses as quickly as possible. An efficient, market-set price would encourage investors to loan the money to the winning bidders, both to pay the government for the license and to build the new networks. The result would be huge capital expenditure stimulating the economy, creating hundreds of thousands of new jobs, and lowering the price of cellular phone calls through competition instead of retail price regulation.

Starting that December day, the auction of the airwaves ran for about two months of daily bidding. In boardrooms across the country, executives plotted their moves. In Kansas City, Sprint's CEO Bill Esrey had wheedled into his consortium the captains of the cable industry: TCI, Comcast, Cox Communications. Sprint intended to buy enough licenses to create a national wireless business that would complement its long distance brand name. (Later, this decision made Sprint a very desirable acquisition by WorldCom, which had no wireless arm.) AT&T and others would also be bidding.

Bob Allen, AT&T's statesmanlike CEO, had not waited for our auction to begin before planting his stake in the wireless business. (He told me a year later that he did not think the FCC would get the auctions rolling as soon as it did.) In September 1994 he paid more than $10 billion to buy McCaw Cellular Communications, Inc., the largest wireless company in America, assembled by Craig McCaw in the early 1980s. Now, McCaw's team, led by Wayne Perry, pushed AT&T to buy more licenses in the auction so as to complete their national footprint in the wireless business and permit them to compete against Sprint and the Bell wireless companies. A half-dozen years later, under new CEO Mike Armstrong, AT&T found that the licenses won in the auction were an essential part of the armory for battling the local Bell companies for customers.

AirTouch was another big bidder in our auction. In 1992, Pacific Bell's CEO Sam Ginn had seen that the company had a limited future in wireless. The California Public Utilities Commission would never let Pacific Bell spend the money necessary to build an international wireless business. To pursue his wireless dream, Ginn spun out Pacific Bell's cellular business to a new company called AirTouch. Then he quit Pacific Bell and became AirTouch's CEO. This new company borrowed billions of dollars and began acquiring wireless licenses all over the world. Now it also bid to fill out its national footprint. Dozens of other companies also won licenses. The auction was the single biggest promotion of entrepreneurship in FCC history.

The FCC team had done a masterful job—they had planned and executed an enormously complicated auction that, all told, raised $7.7 billion in cold cash for the Treasury. The team blew up a huge check in this amount to give the President. The picture ran in newspapers across the country. The FCC went into the *Guinness Book of World Records* for conducting the largest auction in history. I gave the head of the FCC auction team the highest bonus possible for a civil servant: $40,000, or one two-hundred-thousandth of the money raised. I told the press that the FCC had raised more money than its total budget for its 61-year history. We were, I said, the most profitable American business in terms of return on equity. The Vice President awarded the auction team the Hammer Award for excellence in reinventing government. The award was named after the hammer he had used on Jay Leno's *Tonight Show* to break an ashtray in the officially required manner that symbolized dumb government rules.

"Auctions are a lesson in comeback politics," said Blair after we returned from the award ceremony in the Vice President's office, the same place I had taken my family for the swearing-in a political eon earlier.

"What do you mean?" I asked.

"Auctions are great government: pro-market, fair for the taxpayer, pro-competitive. No Republican voted for the 1993 budget law that gave us this power. Now we force them to acknowledge our side did the right thing. That undercuts their argument that the FCC cannot be trusted to reshape the communications sector."

Even as the auction was going well, my wife and I went to the White House for a Christmas season dinner of Yale Law School graduates who had helped the President in some way. In the East Room where Betsy and I had attended the Ameritech-sponsored concert the day I was confirmed a year earlier, the President was holding a diminished court, like Bonnie Prince Charlie in a Paris chateau. He plowed again and again the same ground: what had the congressional election really meant, where did the country want to go, where might he find political success. A crowd gathered around him, like a freeway traffic jam of rubber-neckers ogling a crash scene. The President continued his monologue for more than an hour. His verbal wandering for a way to counter the Republican Revolution added to my gloom: I realized the President did not yet have answers.

Toward the end of his life, my father, who had died only weeks after Bill Clinton was elected, told me that the members of his generation had fought for identity against impersonal forces. His thought paralleled Franklin D. Roosevelt's statement (inscribed on the wall at his memorial near the Tidal Basin in Washington) that Americans rejected "the regimentation of the individual by the commanding forces of a government of the few." In my father's view, his generation had defeated authoritarian government, but had met its match against the great concentrations of capital. From this perspective, the Gingrich Revolution strengthened the hand of the strong and diminished the power that a democracy can grant individuals.

Public office, like a mountain climb or a golf match, is measured by the quality of the experience in the moment and also by the inescapable after-the-fact judgment: did you succeed or fail, win or lose? It has its amusements: comic scenes aplenty, the curiousness of seeing one's name in print, learning what the rich and famous were "really" like (if 15 minutes could impart that insight), the constant attention from relative strangers. But if the public official has no chance to succeed, the quotidian attractions of the job are slight and far outweighed by the potential embarrassment of public failure.

The Gingrich Revolution would prove to define the nature of my public service: whether I could learn to fight and what to fight for, whether I could be loyal in deed as well as thought. The Speaker taught my team and me the line between necessary and gratuitous compromises. Some compromises are necessary to accomplish any practical goal. But other acquiescences to the wishes of the new majority would in truth serve no purpose other than easing the daily difficulties of my job or making me a serviceable deliverer of professional advice in some post-government career. How to choose where to give in and where never to give up was the lesson of leadership that I was taught consciously by Al Gore, and unwittingly by Newt Gingrich, in the months that followed.

In January 1995, Blair and I pondered how we could both attack the FCC's historic mistakes and defend its future mission. As we rethought our ends and means, he and I drew the diamond—four points in tension—that our drama school coach had endorsed.

(1) Deregulation: by auctioning spectrum with no rules attached and preempting all state regulation, we had totally deregulated the wireless industry. We would do the same wherever we could create competition.

(2) Trim down and beef up the FCC: we would privatize many functions and provide expertise appropriate to create competition in formerly monopolized markets. The net result would be a much different agency but one about the same size as the year before.

(3) New technology, new jobs, and new companies: we wanted Congress to pass a pro-competition telecommunications law so that under our new rules for sharing monopoly power with entrepreneurs, the communications revolution could jump-start economic growth and job creation. The new companies would compete to build the information highway, providing perhaps even more than the two pipes to consumers that Barry Diller thought were necessary.

(4) Commitments to kids: educational television (something from the old media), and classrooms connected to the Internet (something from the new media).

Even shorter: smaller and smarter government, pro-competitive rules and pro-kid rules. Shortest: we were for private competition in and public benefits from the communications revolution. We had our big picture, our sound bites, material for the road, and the guiding principles for our hundreds of necessary decisions.

We also had concluded that in some respects our agenda could benefit from the Republican Revolution. Where the Republicans were right and the old Democrats were wrong, the change in control of Congress could permit us to do what we thought best. Auction spectrum. Shrink the agency. Fight for free trade in communications services. Change the law to allow foreign investment in communications companies in the United States. That would be the Republican part of our agenda. And on the Democratic side, we could battle for true competition and concrete public benefits against visible and voluble opponents.

The liberating aspect of the Gingrich Revolution was that we could be more principled than Congress—more Catholic than the Pope, in a political sense—without offending Democrats. Going along with the Republican Congress would have been regarded as quisling behavior. Drawing attention to the contradictions between sound conservative ideology and Republican legislative behavior, on the other hand, was only fair political counterattack.

For example, I was more hawkishly in favor of auctions than anyone in Congress, except for the strange grouping of free market stalwart John McCain and anti-handout liberal Barney Frank. One day in early 1995 I related my enthusiasm for auctions to a Democratic Senator from the South. The Senator thought a bit, and said, "You all actually sell those licenses to the highest bidder?"

"I'd like to auction all licenses," I said.

"You mean for TV too?"

"Yes, sir," I answered. "We could sell TV licenses at auction."

He grinned and slapped his knee. "Well, that's not how Lyndon got his," he said.

He laughed long at his memory of Senator Lyndon Johnson's wife's good luck at receiving from the FCC the first television license for Austin, Texas. Indeed, for many years, the FCC granted no other television station licenses in that city. All the license grants in the 1940s, '50s, and '60s were free money, but the LBJ station was a particularly lucrative cash cow.

Auctions ran counter, of course, to the history of broadcast television and to the future digital television spectrum giveaway. The failed Democratic communications reform bills of the 1993–94 Congress had ordered the FCC to give the bonanza of new digital television licenses to the existing television broadcasters and had forbidden us from holding an auction. The new Republican Congress would be even more committed to the giveaway, in light of the historic closeness between the owners of television licenses and the Republicans. (Rounding off, and permitting exceptions, Hollywood creative people lean to Democrats, while television network and group owners favor Republicans. This division of alliances promotes a stable bipartisan system. It also means the Democratic National Convention has better celebrities and a lower average age: not a bad argument for being a Democrat.)

Ten years earlier my former law partner Mark Fowler, the same FCC chairman of whom John Dingell had not approved, had written a law review article saying that spectrum licenses should be auctioned. He had been exactly right. As we were proving, auctions produced efficient outcomes, put the licenses in the hands of those who valued them the most, and promoted investment, job creation, and competition. But we would do best if we had a notorious Gingrich sympathizer to champion the cause of auctioning the digital television licenses. Even if the effort failed, it could only strengthen our argument that, in return for the handout, the broadcasters owed the public such concessions as educational television or free time for political debate.

Mark Fowler had left Washington to become a successful entrepreneur in Florida. I needed someone in town who had influence in the Republican right. I needed an incongruous intellectual ally. Ideally, that person would be William Safire. His *New York Times* columns instructed and admonished Republicans, appalled and discouraged Democrats, and plausibly could materially aid my shaky fortunes if only I could persuade him to argue for my policy goals. I had a chance. A print guy, Safire had no love for the broadcast lobby. He enjoyed injecting backbone into congressional conservatives. I was presenting a truly deregulatory thesis. When I reported to Safire that Speaker Gingrich had said that the broadcasters should have to pay for the spectrum but that Congress would not have the courage to make them pay, I closed the sale.

Safire wrote that the high-definition giveaway was unconscionable. Blair showed his column to the staffers for Bob Dole and Larry Pressler. I buttonholed John Kasich, Republican Congressman from Ohio and chairman of the House Budget Committee, at a party and related the content of the article to him. We faxed Safire's piece to reporters to help them prepare for interviews with Gingrich.

Blair and I explained to everyone in the press that in the 1994 telecommunications bill passed under Democrat Ed Markey's leadership and now scuttled by Gingrich and his House lieutenants, the broadcasters had to give back various commitments in return for the digital licenses, including binding promises to serve the public. By contrast, Gingrich wanted to abandon the idea that the people could expect to receive some public service programming from the recipients of the handout. One goal of my advocacy was an open debate, so that later no one could say the public had been hoodwinked. We also hoped that the publicity about the magnitude of the giveaway without any giveback to the public would build support for our children's television rule, and perhaps give the public a clear appreciation of why they did not want Republicans to control both Congress and the White House (a theme for 2000 as well as 1996).

Meanwhile, in each of its chambers, Congress was writing telecommunications bills that gratified lobbyists from the cable, telephone, and broadcast industries. The Speaker was eager to reduce regulatory barriers to consolidation and loath to authorize the FCC to enact market-opening rules. But I was confident that Al Gore had not been bluffing when he said he would use the veto threat to force compromises. If a compromise bill emerged from Congress, then it inevitably would confer great power for rule writing on the Commission. While the FCC shaped the rules of the communications revolution, Congress would hardly be able to eliminate the agency. If I ran my agency independent of this Congress and synchronized with the White House's politics, then Al Gore's policies would shape the communications revolution.

One problem, however, could be insurmountable. I still faced a majority against me at the Commission in the form of the Gang of Three. To combat the possibility of coordinated action by my colleagues, Blair and I decided we would make our arguments to the public, outside the Commission's confining walls and its world of watching lobbyists. Like a drummer carrying sample cases of New Democratic policies, I would put on my traveling shoes, speaking everywhere to everyone until I grew hoarse with repeating the message, as I tried to choose the battles that would define my public service.

Steve Spielberg and the *Lost World* dinosaur were part of the ensemble cast lobbying the Federal Communications Commission to mandate that all television sets be wide enough to display movies in the dimensions found in cinema theaters.

Blair Levin and I wrap ourselves in the flag.

I present the President and Vice President a ceremonial check for $7.7 billion, representing the money raised for taxpayers by our auction of spectrum for wireless telephony.

Judy Harris made sure
I stood up to Congress,
in a nice way, and
generally kept my head
screwed on right, as
a true friend will try
to do.

Blair and I congratulate Karen Kornbluh on the 1996 children's television
rulemaking, and on the first visit to the Commission of her son Sam Halpert,
born August 20, 1997.

Al Gore dictates final changes to his speech at the International Telecommunications Union Development Conference, in the residence of the American ambassador to Argentina, in Buenos Aires, March 1994.

The Vice President, United States Trade Representative Charlene Barshefsky, and I enjoy the prospect of a successful conclusion to the telecommunications agreement in the World Trade Organization, which occurred in January 1997. (Photos, Callie Shell, Office of the Vice President)

I make appropriately positive remarks about my high school classmate, the Vice President of the United States. (Photo, Callie Shell, Office of the Vice President)

Although I pull myself to full height, I discover that Clint Eastwood is still taller, among other differences between us; he came to inquire about the possibility of obtaining a radio license for Carmel, California.

Commissioner Rachelle Chong and I examine a large snake with Jack Hanna of the popular television show *Jack Hanna's Animal Adventures*. Whether the program qualified as educational television was one of many issues the commissioner and I debated.

One of the lineups of the chairman's team: (*left to right*) Brian Browdie, Tom Boasberg, Gretchen Rubin, Blair Levin, Jackie Chorney, Julius Genachowski, Karen Kornbluh (with Sam), and Bob Pepper.

Seven **Finding a Way**

March 1995 – September 1995

To reform a world, to reform a nation, no wise man will undertake; all but foolish

men know, that the only solid, though a far slower reformation, is what each

begins and perfects in himself.

Thomas Carlyle, Signs of the Times

ull skies; dull decor. Low narrow buildings arrayed on the damp land like the grid of a chipboard, all perpendicular turns, electric, heartless. Redmond. A bland fortress for one of the two greatest business leaders in the intertwined history of capitalism and invention. The other, Ford, built a belching, bustling, industrial city as much dependent on workers as Redmond is on thinkers. Microsoft's headquarters, by contrast, were silent, odorless, at the edge of the country, in a suburb of Seattle.

There 95 percent of all personal computers—the world-shaping devices that extend in orders of magnitude all previous information technologies—are given sensation. Assembled in antiseptic, robotic factories around the globe, the PCs sit, like inert creatures, awaiting the Creator's life-giving directions. The Creator is, of course, operating system software, sprung from the heads of Bill Gates and his school friend Paul Allen.

Gates and Allen started their first company, Traf-O-Data, in 1971. Its business model was stretching wires across roads in order to count passing cars. ("Like the Internet backbone, only shorter," said Blair.) In 1971, only two years after Woodstock, square in the middle of the Nixonization of the Vietnam War, my generation thought of technology as the generator of the tools of war, not as a way for the young to change the world. My crowd then lived in the present. The founders of Traf-O-Data, the company that later changed its name to Microsoft, were decades ahead of us.

Twenty-four years later, in March 1995, Blair and I went to Seattle to meet Gates and his team. Our Baby Boomer politics was on the defensive in the other Washington, whereas Bill Gates and other PC revolutionaries had become the new powers of American business. My immodest goal was to persuade Gates to align his corporate interests and the public good, and then exercise political as well as business leadership. Specifically, Blair and I wanted Microsoft to block the high-definition television channel giveaway and to break the grip of broadcast television on the country's politics.

By the beginning of 1995, Bill Gates had decided to make his own face the picture of his industry. Joking on Letterman and present in every form of media, Gates propelled Windows 95 and himself into the country's consciousness. He became one of the most admired people in the country (perhaps the reason why he could not fathom the motives of the Department of Justice in suing his company), and his new software cemented and extended Microsoft's monopoly. The perception of Microsoft's indomitability became the key to his company's fabulous success on Wall Street as well as the reason for its historic clash with the government and its Silicon Valley rivals. Our purpose in Redmond was to entice Gates into aiming Microsoft's vast power at the television screen.

If Gates led the software industry into battle with the broadcast lobby, then it was possible that the FCC could escape from the hopeless congressional plan of creating by regulation a national high-definition television market. With the power that would come from the wealth of the software industry, Gates's celebrity, and the installed base of personal computers, we might be able to persuade Congress to let the FCC write rules promoting instead a national over-the-air Internet access network—ubiquitous, rich with both entertainment and educational content, perhaps even, like broadcast television, free.

The audience for this network could buy products that merged the features of PCs and televisions. They could pick and choose a personal menu from the smorgasbord of the media. Individuals (the deadened audience of analog television) would at last talk back to television. This interactivity would defeat the seductive power of broadcast.

In the new data-networked world, the old broadcast networks would lose power. Americans would gain the power to choose, to build political communities on the Net, and to control the television screen and influence society in the way that unseen forces had previously shaped these matters.

Blair and I had gone to Redmond to seek an ally for this crusade, the best of all possible allies, the Henry Ford of the information age.

Pale, anonymous acolytes escorted Blair and me down unadorned hallways, past gray windows opening on a verdigris landscape, past cubicles flickering with pale green computer light. Then a door opened on a tiny room, the navel of the New Economy. Slight, bespectacled Gates greeted us with a quick, shy smile. His lawyer Bill Neukom, later televised repeatedly on the steps of the United States District Courthouse for the District of Columbia (the venue for political prosecutions), nodded distantly from the corner of the room. Nathan Myhrvold, Gates's jolly sidekick on the high plains of intellect, beamed and chuckled at us. All three were taking a break from what one in retrospect can speculate was the analysis of the litigation risks of the Microsoft Internet Explorer's attack against Netscape's monopoly share of the browser market. Or perhaps Myhrvold had been analyzing the destructive effect of the Internet on the PC's success at selling what Gates and Andy Grove had called "virtual bandwidth." Or it may be that he had been reporting on his hobby—calculating with arrays of parallel processing computers the speed at which dinosaurs cracked their tails. In any event, due to the intense heat of his brilliant ramblings into realms of past and future beyond the vision of others, or because of the vapor rising from the hot food sitting untouched on a side table against the wall, Myhrvold's glasses were befogged.

The staff of six that arranged my trips turned down a dozen meetings for every one held. They negotiated time, place, and agenda for the agreed-upon events. Gates had at least as many go-betweens. For me to come face-to-face with a business leader was like Stanley discovering Livingstone after bushwhacking through a jungle of disparaging lobbyists, problem-generating lawyers, personality-disguising public relations advisers. But discovered in the clearing of the small, plain office, and at last left to his own inclinations, Gates was affable, engaged. Myhrvold and Neukom were involved, but Gates was in charge.

"Those auctions were successful, weren't they?" he said politely. Everyone in business was impressed that the Federal Communications Commission had become a profit center. I thanked Gates for the compliment and pulled out the stack of diagrammed pages, called "slides" in the business world, for our presentation.

We had come to appeal to Gates's self-interest. As everyone on the West Coast knew, computing was headed directly toward communications. Relying upon technology, wealth, and genius, software armies were marching toward the regulated kingdom of communications. With Gates as commander-in-chief, the entrepreneurs could win a lobbying war even against the powerful broadcasters. Raggedy programmers in Birkenstocks stepping on the Gucci-shoed toes of Italian-suited network television lobbyists; pale plump chip designers besting the bullies from cable; woolly code-writing anarchists imposing Internet Protocol over congressional protocol—the possible pairings delighted us. And not only did we wish to incite rebellion against the suzerainty of the new Republican Congress; we also were pitching the American Dream. We wanted Gates to embrace our vision of a new politics that used technology to equalize opportunity and to elevate the choices of the individual over the dictates of business or government.

Our Redmond meeting preceded Gates's determination to study politics, as he felt the increasing impact of the Department of Justice on his company. About a year later he said to me, "I've found the people in politics to be surprisingly able and the systems surprisingly complex." But in our meeting, Microsoft's knowledge of government was in the early innings.

I wanted Gates to go after the spectrum, because the auction was such a pure and sensible goal. Later, depending on how the meeting went, we would ask for his help in connecting every classroom to the information highway. I had seen Mosaic, Marc Andreesen's Internet browser. In effect, it made the Net experience pictorial. Teachers then could transform education by drawing on the new graphics of the Net for their resources. So George Lucas had explained to me. Digital broadcast television fused with the Internet and running into classrooms was a large idea—as big in its way as Microsoft's market capitalization.

Blair and I laid out bar graphs, pie charts, and revenue forecasts that showed that the airwaves Congress would force us to give to the broadcasters were worth perhaps $10 or $20 billion if used by entrepreneurs to broadcast voice, video, and data in digital formats that were compatible with the new data networks. But they were perhaps worthless if used for broadcasting high-definition signals, one per channel, for big-screen televisions that would cost so much that less than one percent of Americans would buy them.

If those who bought the spectrum at an open auction could ignore the networks' deal with Congress and abandon high-definition television, they could transmit digital information to PCs. Already Americans spent more money on PCs ($2,000 each) than televisions (average price $300), and soon even PC unit sales, not just revenue, would surpass television sales. Not only was the world going digital, it was heading toward computerization and broadband. Capturing the value of these trends, a continuous local digital stream—to PCs, cable head ends, telephone company central offices, dishes on residential rooftops—could engender dozens of entrepreneurial business plans. As for traditional analog television—the medium that dominated Baby Boomers' childhood memories, and 50 years of advertising and politics—our proposal was to let it alone. I suspected that many digital media, especially cable, would steal its audience, but the best government policy would be to allow the attackers to take their chances, while giving no handouts (like the digital television spectrum) to the incumbent defenders.

Gates rocked in his chair. His eyes magnified by his glasses, he stared at me, and asked urgently, "Does anyone else know about this?"

Only a thousand lobbyists, I thought. But I reported, accurately, "The digital television giveaway is not the subject of national discussion."

Then Gates explained with brilliant clarity the half-dozen reasons why he agreed that the broadcasters would never make a successful business from digital television despite the spectrum gift: extra cost, no new advertising revenue, insufficient bandwidth per licensee for downloading software, lack of vertical integration, no two-way communication. His reasoning was far more compelling than our presentation. I believed at least we had his interest.

"But you could turn this mess into a good opportunity," I said.

He leaned forward and glanced at Myhrvold, who nodded.

"We'll have to look into this," he said. That was enough of a day's work, I thought. I did not raise the goal of connecting classrooms.

When we emerged from the Microsoft maze, Blair and I swam in the optimism that the richest man in the world might mount a political advocacy campaign for our ends.

Karen Kornbluh reported that the Senate Commerce Committee was preparing to debate the telecommunications bill. Predictably, Senator Pressler had not inserted the classroom connection initiative in the draft. Karen had stumbled upon an obscure coalition of computer and education groups who were focused on extracting from Congress a tiny appropriation for technology programs at the Department of Education. She explained to them that the concept of universal service—affordable phone service for rural Americans—could be stretched into affordable communications technology for teachers and students. Senator Jay Rockefeller and other Democrats were inclined to agree, and of course Al Gore's White House aides advocated that the new communications bill include a provision empowering the FCC to guarantee communications in classrooms. But the ranking Democratic member on the Commerce Committee, Senator Fritz Hollings, could not make the provision one of his top items. He was focused on making sure that the Bell companies, the tightest of allies with Majority Leader Dole and well-entrenched with most of the other Senators, did not roll over the long distance companies in the campaign for competitive advantage through law.

Long distance was an artificial and transitory industry, created by the separation of AT&T's long-lines business from the local telephone companies in the government-ordered divestiture of Ma Bell in 1984. The customer does not desire to make a call of a certain distance, but only wants to "reach out and touch someone." Advertising and regulation (not consumer preference) created long distance. Nevertheless, because history divided them, the mammoth local and long distance industries, each with revenues of about $100 billion a year, lobbied brutally against each other.

Such conflict can create an opportunity for Congress to follow good policy, like walking safely along a tightrope as a result of being balanced both on one side and the other. Gingrich's deregulatory impulse and the motives of key industries provided momentum for some bill. But to alter the legislative direction, rivers of money were poured over the Commerce Committees in both houses of Congress. Millions in political contributions and lobbying fees were as nothing when billions of dollars in value were at stake.

The Bells sought a share of the $100 billion long distance market. The new law would repeal the famous court order of 1984 that had broken up AT&T and created a separate long distance company and seven local Baby Bells. As part of the breakup, the Bells were precluded by court order from entering the long distance market, where they could use their local monopolies to obtain unfair competitive advantage. Almost no price was too high for the Bells to pay in return for a legislative repeal of the court order.

A few Democrats—principally Fritz Hollings and Bob Kerrey in the Senate, and Ed Markey in the House—wanted to give the FCC the power to create actual competition in the local telephone market. That was good policy. It also meant a share of the $100 billion local telephone market for AT&T, MCI, and the other new entrants. These companies would not have had the motive and influence to pass a new law, but if Congress intended to legislate, no price was too high for the long distance companies to pay in order to escape being crushed by the advantages Congress might grant the Bells.

Cable valued deregulation of its own industry as worth as much as $3 billion to $5 billion a year in light of the certainty that, in the absence of competition, the industry would then raise prices to consumers. This industry too was willing to spend staggering sums on campaign contributions and lobbyists in order to accomplish its legislative goal.

The radio and television industries desired to effect mergers and acquisitions worth billions. They too clamored for a new communications law. In short, the communications and media industries believed the new Congress was willing to write a law that would generate new value for their businesses. Consumers were on the paying side of the equation, and, not surprisingly, the consumer advocacy groups were not pushing for a new law. But the Bells had hundreds of thousands of employees, located in almost every congressional district in the country. The labor support for a reform law provided critical support on the Democratic side of congressional aisles. Bills would pass both houses. The question was who would get legal and regulatory competitive advantages in the marketplace from the bills, and whether Gore would cause the President to sign or to veto the legislation.

The handful of Senators and Congressmen who opposed the prospect of huge media mergers or the Bell political tide (in the name of opening the local markets and saving the long distance companies from extinction) could not have injected in the bills many pro-competitive positions, except for two facts. First, the White House veto gave Senator Hollings and the Senate Democrats negotiating power. Second, Bernie Ebbers, CEO of entrepreneurial WorldCom (later to buy MCI), had his headquarters in Jackson, Mississippi. Republican House majority leader Trent Lott of Mississippi had few big companies in his home state and was bent on serving the interests of all of them. Lott became an unlikely but reasonably reliable proponent of a Bell–long distance compromise.

A small, almost unreported story amidst the clashing of the giants was the proposed amendment to empower the FCC to fund classroom connections. If Jay Rockefeller of West Virginia had not led the Democrats to support the classroom connection initiative, the Democratic alliance might have dedicated all its energies to the economic issues in the legislation. Senator Rockefeller had become interested in the subject in order to promote distance learning in West Virginia. He understood the very practical fact that the many remote small towns of his state needed to import certain teaching over communications links, because they could not afford adequately diverse and well-trained faculty for their small and distinctly not rich student bodies. The Bell monopolies charged very high prices for communicating live video over short distances. Rockefeller was willing to give the FCC the power to order the phone companies to charge specially low prices for, in effect, carrying education to remote areas.

We needed Rockefeller to expand his agenda to provisioning the communication of education anywhere, and he was willing. He saw that if networks could revolutionize education through distance learning, they also had the potential to provide on-line libraries to schools that had few, if any, recently published books, to permit teachers to collaborate, to give parents a chance to phone or e-mail teachers. These uses of communication were making businesses efficient and responsive to employees and customers. Similar changes could happen in education.

Senator Rockefeller decided to champion the goal of the President and the Vice President to connect every classroom to the information highway. The necessary step was to amend the bill so that the FCC had the power not just to lower prices to schools, but to pay for building networks inside schools. This change was a matter of words. But its significance was to give the FCC the authority to command the spending of not just millions per year, but billions a year. My staff did not want to emphasize this cost, but those on the Hill who were concerned—both friends and enemies of the amendment—understood that in the midst of the din and clamor of the monumental lobbying battles among the communications giants of America, we were also debating at relatively whisper-like levels, with virtually no media attention, one of the most important education bills of the century. The funding that might come from the proposed authority granted to the FCC would be, in time, greater than the G.I. Bill, which gave a college education to more than 15 million Americans.

We needed a Republican co-champion on the Senate Commerce Committee to join Rockefeller. Unless one party has 60 votes—enough to close off debate—a bipartisan team is necessary for almost any legislative accomplishment in the Senate. Newly elected Olympia Snowe of Maine entered the debate. Senator Snowe's support was crucial because none of the other Republicans on the Commerce Committee was willing to support our effort to amend the telecommunications bill to authorize a rule-making that would connect classrooms to the Internet.

Senator Snowe, like Senator Rockefeller, believed in the need for distance learning. The classrooms of Maine are for the most part scattered and poorly equipped. Our technology proposal would bring the infinity of the Internet to every child in Maine. In her view, a purpose of federal government was to help poor states. She saw that the Republican draft of the bill had deleted the provision of the 1994 Democratic bill extending universal service guarantees to educational institutions. When we heard that she proposed to amend Pressler's draft bill to address this issue, we knew we potentially had the crucial Republican ally. Rockefeller persuaded her to co-sponsor the critical amendment, and the Senators' staffs began hurriedly drafting the language necessary to fund not only distance learning but also networking classrooms.

The Senate Commerce Committee was composed of ten Republicans and nine Democrats. Its debates were not televised. The committee's writing of the telecommunications bill was conducted in arcane language, witnessed and understood only by staffers and lobbyists. (I was not permitted to participate; I sat in my office hanging on phone calls from Judy Harris, Karen Kornbluh, and our other staffers who tracked the hundreds of provisions under discussion.) Every result in the bill turned on fine linguistic parsings.

Connecting classrooms raised questions of policy as well as semantics. Whether the bill should refer to "schools" or "classrooms" depended on whether one preferred computer labs in schools, or computers in every classroom. Should the bill guarantee access or cheap rates on existing networks? If the bill mandated only that the FCC provide communications to all schools at cheaper rates, we would have failed to accomplish much of anything. Most schools already had low-price phone service to the principal's office. But suppose the new law told the FCC to guarantee communications access in every classroom? Did that imply the construction of networks? On the other hand, explicit language ordering the construction of networks might suggest the installation of data networks designed for the Internet. The same bill eventually was amended (unconstitutionally, as it turned out) to protect against obscenity on the Internet. The Snowe and

Rockefeller staffers wanted to avoid such Internet controversies by relying on more general language like "access." Later, at the FCC, we would try to use such language as a basis for a rule that spent the billions of dollars necessary to network two million classrooms. That is, of course, if I could get the votes at the Commission; and if the appellate courts subsequently upheld our interpretation of the law.

Republican Senator McCain of Arizona led the opposition to the amendment that Senators Snowe and Rockefeller, President Clinton, Vice President Gore, and the education lobbyists wanted. McCain wanted school districts to buy their own communications facilities. The federal government should not help; the communications industries should not pay. We had explained to his staff that urban schools in particular were too poor to pay for internal networks, especially in their decrepit buildings, which are so difficult to renovate, whether for plumbing, electricity, or fiber cables. Typically school bond measures for these purposes are defeated in urban areas because most voters there (indeed, the majority in the country) do not have children at home. Altruism does not routinely win elections, even in our big-hearted nation. Only in suburban areas, where a greater percentage of voters are raising children, do school bonds routinely pass. For this reason, only a national mandate to network schools would do the job for urban areas, where many poor children live. John McCain and his staff rejected these arguments. They vowed to oppose us.

But Senator Snowe had become a firm ally of Senator Rockefeller. Karen Kornbluh, Al Gore's staff, and the staffers to Senators Snowe and Rockefeller scribbled versions of our preferred language. Senator Bob Kerrey's staff, led by Carol Ann Bischoff, joined at crucial moments. Phrases on paper flew out of printers, were passed by hand around rooms. As the hours passed, words circulated more slowly. Finally the carousel stopped, and a provision guaranteeing low-cost service was put to vote. All Democrats supported the language, but unless a Republican voted with them the amendment would not be added to the bill. Senator Snowe crossed the party line, leaving the other Republicans in opposition, and cast the deciding vote in favor. Meanwhile, Senator Hollings obtained many of the pro-competitive provisions he and the White House had sought. The Senate Commerce Committee then, on March 23, passed the entire bill.

The amendment's language did not make clear that installing the connections in classrooms was critical. And it did not specify that every classroom should be connected. At the suggestion of Karen Kornbluh and others at the FCC, staff members for Senators Rockefeller and Snowe, along with Carol Ann Bischoff, negotiated with Republican staffers to insert in the accompanying committee report the word "classroom" everywhere, as well as the phrases "make available" and "shall have access to." In the months and years to come, these additions helped our side at the FCC and in the appellate court.

I was amazed that such an important issue went unnoticed by virtually everyone outside the small group working in the committee deliberations, and that it passed only because life in Maine and West Virginia had taught good lessons to fine elected officials. But that vote was a good day.

For my maiden appearance before the National Association of Broadcasters in Las Vegas in April 1995, a bank heavily into commercial lending to television stations hosted a breakfast "in my honor." More than 100,000 people had come to Vegas for the convention, but only a hundred, about one-tenth of one percent, stumbled into a large dark room for cold eggs and the thin gruel of my remarks. The cursory introduction, in which the audience was reminded of my absence the year before, chilled the room further.

Throwing my carefully worked rhetoric into the gloom, I described a "New Paradigm" of broadcast regulation. Instead of vague exchanges between government and broadcasters about serving an undefined public interest, I advocated the adoption of "clear, concrete standards"—such as three hours of children's television. On the other hand, instead of unnecessary regulation of the business side of broadcasting, I would eliminate rules such as the one that precluded networks from distributing their feeds during the entirety of prime time. I would deregulate the business side of broadcasting and write clear rules that made concrete its duty to serve the public interest. My approach also called for rethinking the so-called high-definition television scheme. Instead of mandating the technology and ignoring the public interest benefits of digital broadcast, the FCC should let industry solve all the technical issues in the absence of regulation, but should require digital broadcasters to commit time to children's education and political debate.

The only FCC chairman cited in *Bartlett's Familiar Quotations* is Newton Minow. He became chairman in his early 30s, fresh from running President Kennedy's Illinois campaign. When he gave his first speech as chairman to the National Association of Broadcasters, it was one of the most powerful lobbies in Washington, as it is today. To support Minow, President Kennedy drove him to the NAB's clamorous convention, held a few blocks from the White House. JFK took along for the ride the first man in space, Alan Shepard, as a message of respect to the broadcasters, who were expected to support the race to the moon with uncritical and extensive coverage.

To the shock of the NAB, Minow told broadcasters that he loathed much of their product. Television, he said, was a "vast wasteland." Minow's criticism was akin to the secretary of defense saying he hated flying in a Boeing; to the secretary of commerce telling General Motors their cars stunk up the road. No one in broadcasting ever forgot the "vast wasteland."

My team tried to twist the great one-liner; I told the NAB "not to waste the vast land" of digital television. My sound bite had no teeth. Digital television was not part of anyone's imagination and could not be apostrophized, whereas anyone needed merely to turn on a television set to appreciate the accuracy of Minow's zinger, even without apprehending its faint evocation of T. S. Eliot. (Oh, those Kennedyesque allusions to the classics.)

Even if I had said something memorable, few were there to hear it. The small audience comprised mainly lobbyists, who could bill their time for attending. Nor could I obtain much press coverage. One major newspaper's beat reporter skipped the NAB because he had been to a convention of paging companies in Las Vegas a few days earlier and he did not like the town enough to stay over. The industry and the media had hung on Newton Minow's words; he was conscience, judge, teacher, commander-in-chief. But the chairman of the FCC was apparently of far less significance in 1995 than in 1961.

Unlike Minow, who dismissed the quality of television content, my intent was to inspire the industry by articulating a new paradigm for the relationship between the public and the broadcasting industry: no commercial regulation, definite "public interest" rules. But broadcasters did not like either part of the two-part agenda. The various players in the industry tolerated the government regulation of their business relationships because it was familiar. Affiliates rather liked FCC regulations because the agency's rules shifted value from the networks to individual stations. Affiliates had great influence on Congressmen, and as a result Congress, on both sides of the aisle, opposed deregulating the broadcasting business.

Affiliates and networks also disliked concrete public interest obligations because the true rule in the industry was to send shows over the air to make money, not to educate or inform. The NAB lobbyists asserted that free broadcast television tied the nation into a well-informed, experience-sharing community. But there was a difference between what the industry thought of itself as doing for the country and what most people outside the business thought it was doing to the country, and for itself. Many broadcasters did not understand the ire of families at the lack of good quality kids' shows, in part because advertisers, and not viewers, were the true customers of broadcasting. Advertisers wanted popular shows that drew big and identifiable audiences. A group of young children watching a half-hour educational show was a wasted half-hour for advertisers. The industry opposition to "public interest" rules was, in part, about the money.

Returning from Vegas, I concluded that my NAB speech, indeed, my broadcast agenda, had been too abstract. My job was not to describe to business audiences a "paradigm" of regulation. Business either liked the rules as they existed or wanted no rules. No suggestion of better rules was likely to be embraced. I should have told the broadcasters directly, on behalf of the American people, who I was supposed to serve, what I thought the industry owed the country, and not what the country was willing to do for them.

I thought I might as well be more direct at the Commission, because compromise in any event was not encouraged by the anti-public-interest climate engendered by the Republican takeover of Congress. Commissioner Barrett told *Broadcasting & Cable*, "While I believe that broadcasters can do better, I have been and continue to be unwilling to support the notion that we, by virtue of our position as regulators, are entitled to infringe on the rights of broadcasters." Government granted these "rights" under a license and had the lawful right to revoke the license if the broadcaster did not serve the public. But the NAB had successfully turned the law upside down in the minds of most of the FCC staff, the other commissioners, the trade press, and the Congress. Commissioner Quello added, "The idea of making every station in every market carry certain programming doesn't make sense." He called the kidvid proposal a "First Amendment time bomb" that would "self-destruct" in the Supreme Court. Commissioner Chong's new kidvid stance was equally hostile. Everyone concluded that I had no way to muster a majority for my children's television proposal. The question was what costs I incurred from advocating the kidvid rule.

On April 19, 1995, the federal building in Oklahoma City was blown into rubble. More than 150 people died. Everyone knew the bombers could have selected any government building. Indeed, for madmen the FCC was not an unlikely target. Three years earlier a psychotic had shot and killed one of the Commission's employees as she was walking toward the front door of a federal building. Even before Oklahoma City, I received scores of threatening letters every week, alleging that government uses the media to propagate evil.

Two nights after the Oklahoma City bombing, Betsy and I were hosting a dinner at our house for the German minister of communications, Wolfgang Boetsch. In the middle of the meal, I received a phone call from the Federal Bureau of Investigation.

"Your agency received a phone call warning that your house may be bombed. The report was forwarded to us. We have assessed the matter and concluded that we should alert you."

"What do I do?" I asked. I closed my mind to the vision of the warning ricocheting in the security bureaucracy for untold hours while the possible bomb was perhaps ticking in my boxwood.

"You might want the local police to search the environs."

I apologized to our guests, who left with dispatch. I called the local police, as advised.

"We've had a lot of these calls relating to government officials since Oklahoma City," the local authority said. "We can send a dog to check."

"Fine," I said.

"But our regular is in the hospital. He was hit by a car. We're using the backup."

Another security matter that it was best not to think about. I hung up.

The substitute canine sniffed the azaleas, the hemlock, the window wells, and the thick boxwoods across the front portico of our house. The dog found a golf ball and a dead bird, but no explosives.

A wave of bomb threats hit the FCC. Repeatedly, I evacuated the building. Everyone stood on the street corner, chatting, waiting to see if the building blew up. We were either in a farce or a tragedy; time would tell. More threats, increasingly ominous in tone. The FBI told me I should decide how to respond. I closed the FCC for two days. Then I decided that we could not permit telephone calls to shut down part of the government. For many weeks thereafter my assistant, Ruth Dancey, continued to receive anonymous calls promising various terrible acts. We were lucky; nothing happened.

While I was teaching at the junior high school I had spoken about at Georgia Tech, I had a girlfriend. She had red hair and freckles. She smoked a corncob pipe for laughs. She read Jane Austen. She told me that she and her twin sister were the girls on the Campbell's Soup can. She was an optimist, raised with her twin to do good with self-confidence and exuberance. A decade later, after she became a psychologist, a patient murdered her.

I had a friend from college. On the day after his son was born, three men jumped him when he walked out the back door of his office building. They beat him to death in the parking lot.

For many years Americans seemed to accept violence as part of the nature of our wild country. At last we woke from this delusion. The murders of my friends were not remotely acceptable. No murders are. No one should ever put killing in a context, or make excuses for violence. Violence is evil. So are its precursors—hatred and anger.

Most knew that in the background of the Oklahoma City bombing was a strain of overly harsh national discourse. Most turned against unbalanced animosity toward government. Most knew, without specific discussion, that democratic government was our way of acting together to create moral communities, and that a violent attack on government, whether by bombs or by more subtle means, was directed at all of us.

In May, the head of Sinn Fein, the political wing of the Irish Republican Army, Gerry Adams, sat calmly on the sofa in my office and talked of peace. He said coolly that he was in the United States looking for new ways to end the struggle in Northern Ireland.

I told him a story from my recent trip to Ireland. In the drawing room of American Ambassador Jean Kennedy Smith's house, I had preached the transforming power of the communications revolution. From the back of the room someone had called out, "Can you pour Guinness by e-mail?"

"No," I responded.

The voice declared, "Then there will always be an Ireland!"

As I finished my anecdote, Adams showed a very thin smile through his beard. I suspected he was recalling that the American ambassador's house had previously been the headquarters for the British colonialist rulers of Ireland. A green and prickly island, I thought. I switched the subject.

I said, "What if we were to connect all the classrooms in a Protestant and a Catholic school in Belfast to the information highway? The children could talk to each other through computers. They could find ways to end the violence, or talk about their favorite rock groups. It all could be put on the Internet. A lot of computers are made in Ireland."

Adams smiled faintly. He was bent on being agreeable. He needed go-betweens who would arrange for him to meet with the President. Such intermediaries, of whom he hoped I would be one, take a risk with their own reputation in seeking time on a presidential or vice presidential calendar. Adams, as an alleged participant in terrorist activities, was an especially dicey introduction to make. He had much reason to suffer indulgently my conversation about the Internet in Ireland.

In the information age, publicity precipitates debate. Media attention precedes thought. Celebrity empowers. Much change can occur because of the scrutiny of the public eye. The Internet builds on this lesson by creating new possibilities for expression and new ways to reach an audience. Whereas the history of Northern Ireland is tragically self-contained, the Internet admits no containment. Its genius is its infinitude. It interconnects all peoples, cultures, and eras. With a good tale to tell, an Internet narrator can reach anyone anywhere. The Internet can break the self-referencing cycles that mire any community of violence in justifications for unacceptable acts.

Later that week, reverting from the future of Ireland to the future of Al Gore's communications policies, I went to the White House to talk to the Vice President about the telecommunications bills in Congress.

"How is your leg?" I asked. Al had torn his Achilles tendon playing with some of his former congressional buddies on the House basketball court.

"It's coming along." The cast and crutches made his ceremonial appearances (a half-dozen or so every day) seem stiff and awkward—a metaphor for the widespread misperception of his personality.

We reviewed the principal differences between the House bill and the reasonably satisfactory bill the Senate Commerce Committee had passed. The Speaker and his lieutenants, Jack Fields and others, were writing a bill that encouraged rapid consolidation of the radio and television industries, entry of the local telephone companies into the long distance business before the local companies' own monopolized markets were competitive, the repeal of cable rate regulation while denying satellites the right to transmit broadcast television channels. Gingrich did not intend to give the Commission power to open local telephone markets. The Speaker also would not support the White House proposal in the legislation to link all classrooms to the information highway.

"Perhaps the Republicans do not take my veto threat seriously," said Al.

Gingrich's advocacy of deregulated monopolies was not the subject of any soaring, televised rhetoric (like the windy House impeachment hearings more than three years later). But the difference between Gore and Gingrich, between Democrats and Republicans, would matter to hundreds of businesses, millions of employees, and every consumer in the country. Scarcely a voter knew what was at stake. Indeed, we ourselves did not know that two-thirds of the country's economic growth in the remaining years of the decade depended in significant part on whether Gore could use the veto threat to force Gingrich to compromise.

An aide entered and handed Al a note. In the White House you cannot help but catch your breath at this intervention: it could be a routine reminder that the meeting time is over before you've gotten to your point; or it could be an international crisis disrupting not just scheduling, but the country's way of life. At the center of the world's news, the note could be about anything at all.

Al folded the paper, placed it on the table, and said in the calmest of tones, "Someone has been shot trying to climb over the fence into the White House."

Bombings and bomb threats, wars and shootings: National government was an admixture of life-and-death events, serious policy debate with enormous consequences, and a never-ending struggle to win the favorable attention of a distracted, elusive public. Al leveraged himself up on his cast and limped to the door to show me out.

"We'll win this legislative fight," he said. I did not know where he would find the political strength to sustain a veto against a Gingrich-authored communications bill, in light of the lucrative benefits the House Republicans were crafting for incumbent industries. Consumers had no voice with the Republican Congress. And potential new entrants in the telecommunications space had no lobby because they would come into existence only if the new law were written the way the Administration wanted. Still, the Senate Commerce Committee's bill was not bad, and I trusted Al's constancy.

On June 8, the full Senate began to debate the telecommunications bill. Senator McCain tried to amend the bill to strike the Snowe-Rockefeller provision. A majority of Senate Republicans joined him, but Senator Snowe led enough of them to the Democratic side to defeat McCain; he garnered 31 Republicans against connecting classrooms, but the amendment stayed in the bill. McCain then voted against the bill, but on June 15 it passed, 81–18, on its way to conference committee for reconciliation with any House bill that might pass.

McCain's attitude reminded me of the occasion when I asked Ronald Reagan's secretary of education, Bill Bennett, to support the effort to put the Internet in every classroom.

"I'm against it," Bennett said.

"Why?"

"Because I want to close the public schools. This sort of program could encourage people to keep them open."

On the House side, where Gingrich's right-wing ideology was in full swing, the Bennett view would eventually prevail. The House telecommunications bill would contain no commitment to connect classrooms.

At the Commission, we were acutely aware in our policy making that the wealth of the New Economy was accruing to the top third of the country ranked by income, while the lower two-thirds were not much wealthier than they had been 25 years earlier. If our policies could increase investment, job growth, and therefore economic expansion, then there still would remain the need for a President—such as Al Gore—to begin to meet unrequited claims of the middle class and the poor for health care, specialized education, technological training, and real hope for fulfillment of their individual destinies. Certainly, some benefits of technology should be put at the fingers of all children right away. We were, after all, in government for the purpose of doing something as opposed to nothing to create equitable opportunity. So we wanted to put the Internet in every classroom as soon as possible.

In June 1995, I went to the J. O. Wilson School, a public school in Washington, D.C., for an event with Newt Gingrich. The Speaker and I were going to celebrate the wireless industry's gift of a wireless network to the school. If Gingrich had his way, the J. O. Wilson School's network would be an isolated instance of corporate charity. The school's electronic library would be the setting for yet another misleading political event—an event where the children would be props and the pictures would not translate into positive legislation for any school.

We gathered in a hall crowded with kids, teachers, and reporters. The Speaker arrived. Not very tall. Softly he shook my hand. He told me we had to talk. He had a plan for me. I supposed he would tell me that the elimination of my agency would liberate the information economy and finally realize personal freedom, at least for the rich and powerful. I imagined the contours of a candid exchange of views with Speaker Gingrich. I would explain to him my conception of the Internet and education. I would win his sympathy through talk of a revolution in communications markets.

Information age technology overthrows existing education systems, I would tell him. First, instead of merely certifying students as meeting the standards of the educational institution, an Internet education system would focus on maximizing the capabilities of each student. Many children, for example, have some learning disability or some idiosyncrasy in learning style; yet almost none are tested to find out how they learn best. Sophisticated tests on the Net, cheap and available to all because of the scale of the network, could discover each child's distinctive ways of learning. Education could become a specialized benefit, not a commodity product.

Second, an Internet education would take place in fluid and non-geographic communities. Students would form communities of learners anywhere, anytime. And teachers would collaborate with each other at any distance. A good idea hatched in a classroom in Washington State could be at the fingertips of the teachers in Washington, D.C.

Third, by electronic mail, parents and teachers would work together to help children learn. Working parents who could not attend every PTA meeting would still be able to consult with their child's teachers. On the Net and with e-mail, new parent-teacher communities could change the management of schools.

Fourth, today teachers and students are lucky if their school libraries have a few books printed in this decade. The Internet could distribute the resources of education, and make a rich person's educational opportunities as ubiquitous as telephony or electricity.

This was the argument I wanted to make to the Speaker, but no chance presented itself. At the J. O. Wilson School, Newt and I posed with kids, looked at computers, and spoke not a word of the total difference in our views on how to create equality of opportunity for 55 million kids from kindergarten to 12th grade. I was mere background for the Speaker's attempt to identify himself with education, even as he schemed to eradicate any national role in that essential dimension of the American Dream. After the photographs, the Speaker thanked everyone and rushed to his car, neglecting to talk to me.

Meanwhile, the spokesperson for a Gingrich Republican front organization called the Progress and Freedom Foundation called for "a [broad] effort to replace the outmoded regulatory structures of industrial age government. The current system cannot be reformed," the spokesperson said, "it must be replaced, and the FCC is a great place to start." Put more simply, even though the Senate bill had given the FCC new powers, this group—amply funded by the telephone company monopolies opposing pro-new-entrant regulations—wanted the FCC eliminated.

While abiding my confirmation process in 1993, I had accompanied my wife to her professional society's annual meeting, the American Psychological Association convention in Toronto. In a batch of seminars, experts reported on the effects of the media on children.

The average American child is in front of a television 55 hours a week. As channels have multiplied, broadcasters and cable have developed greater ability to target programs to audiences. This sophistication has generated many new genres of programming for audiences that include children. Some studies of such programming's effects on children concluded that television viewing correlated with falling grades and increasing truancy and delinquency. Dozens of studies showed that violence on television desensitizes child viewers, making them more willing to tolerate and even to inflict violence. Television is even linked to an increase in childhood obesity.

I summarized these findings to my staff one morning in June 1995 as the President jousted with Congress over the budget.

"How about this title for a speech," I suggested. "'Television Makes You Fat.'"

"You'll be laughed out of town if you say television makes kids fat," Judy Harris said.

"I was sort of kidding," I said. They looked unconvinced. "But don't you agree that we have to take on television? No one was ever a well-known FCC chairman without scolding television."

"I hate you being known as a scold," said Blair.

"Not that you aren't one," Judy assured. "But I think we should be somewhat concerned about the prospect of taking on the broadcasters when our side is under such political pressure."

"Al and Tipper will be holding a Families Conference in Nashville again this July," I said. "The topic is media. We have to make our contribution. We'll press harder for children's television rules, but we have to explain the whole picture. We need to articulate a philosophy of the government's role with respect to media."

Karen Kornbluh joined in, "We should examine the media from the vantage point of children."

Everyone looked at Karen.

"That's great," I said. "I'm looking forward to your draft of the speech."

"Who'll help?" she asked. Murmuring vague assurances, everyone else quickly departed.

I was convinced, however, that by launching a critique of broadcasting I would be applying Blair's insight that we would gain political power whenever we could steal the Republicans' thunder. The pernicious impact of the media on family life was a traditional Republican theme. Moreover, if the Commission was going to show true intellectual integrity, we had to give meaning to the public interest standard. It was a duty on broadcasters that liberal academics and conservative ideologues disparaged, but it was the law—and it mattered to American families.

Several weeks later I landed at the airport in Knoxville, Tennessee, on my way to the Alex Haley Farm, the house of the late author of *Roots,* the book that gave rise to the television serial that had taught more about American slavery to more people than all the books ever written on the subject. Now the place was used by the Children's Defense Fund for an annual summer get-together to plan African-American advocacy in Washington.

At the Haley farm, I said I hoped the group would join me in militating for a networked society that reached all children. Children's educational television and connected classrooms mattered especially to poor children, I said, because they promoted universal equal opportunity. These goals were the new ends of the civil rights movement in the 21st century.

My hosts, led by Marian Wright Edelman of the Children's Defense Fund, said that they dreaded the new Congress's direct attacks on funding for welfare, its attempts to end the school lunch program, its hostility toward the poor. They were fighting desperately to hold on to their historic gains. They had no capacity to go on new crusades. (My successor, the diplomatic and perseverant Bill Kennard, the first African-American to become FCC chairman, much more successfully made the connection between our communications agenda and civil rights.)

I went from Knoxville to the Gores' annual conference on families, held in Nashville. The topic for discussion that year was Families and the Media. President Clinton attended: big, southern, friendly, but restrained, making an effort to play second fiddle to his Vice President. The President announced that he would veto the telecommunications law unless it contained a mandate to have the FCC order a new technology—the V-chip—built into every television so that parents would be able to block out violent shows.

Then the President and Vice President each said they would support the children's television initiative. I had become part of the Administration's political agenda—perhaps the first time in history that FCC issues were in the center ring of the political circus. Al singled me out in the crowd. I stood up. The auditorium applauded. The event made the national news. It was intoxicating; it was much more important to be there in Nashville than at, say, an NAB convention.

Two weeks later, in July, the slowly coalescing Gang of Three— Quello, Barrett, and Chong—agreed to issue a further notice of proposed rulemaking relating to children's television rules, while announcing that they would never vote for a rule that required shows for children. The notice asked for comments. Lobbyists would write still more briefs. But according to the Gang of Three, no vote on a new rule itself would occur; or if it did, no rule would be passed.

I told the press that I had made progress. I explained that the broadcasters faced a challenge to explain in writing why they would not support a simple rule requiring every television station to show at least three hours of educational programming per week. The reporters barely suppressed their laughter at my attempt at positive spin. The Clinton-Gore support in Nashville had only galvanized the Gang of Three, supported by the congressional Republicans, into firmer opposition of the children's television initiative.

One day at the Fox News studio on Wisconsin Avenue in northwest Washington, after I finished that day's kidvid pitch, I passed Dan Quayle in the Green Room. I was selling children's television; he, his new book. I introduced myself, and he said amiably, "That's a good job, the FCC. Are you doing it the regulatory way or the deregulatory way?"

"I think deregulatory," I said. I intended to give the former Vice President a polite answer, but his question gave me pause. I wanted to eliminate rules granting commercial advantages for incumbents, while making clear those rules that imposed on businesses reasonable obligations to society. Quayle had summed up the issue crisply. I had not answered squarely. On a net basis, I calculated, I was deregulatory. But I needed to articulate my message more clearly, and to find an appropriate stage.

To speak at the National Press Club, you invite yourself. When Blair told them I intended to launch a critique of the impact of the media on children, they happily agreed to provide a forum. For the FCC chairman to rap television was a blast from the past. Moreover, the print media relishes reporting negatively about television for at least two reasons: everyone reads such articles, and just as old money mocks parvenus, print gets off on knocking the electronic media.

Dan Quayle's question gave guidance for my July 27 speech. As stated in Karen Kornbluh's draft, I was "deregulatory" on economic issues and "regulatory" in demanding social benefits. But I needed to clarify that the proposed new rules stating "clear and enforceable public interest requirements" were justifiable interventions in the marketplace.

I said that such rules would protect freedom to speak without fear of government pressure, while enforcing the legal condition on the broadcasters' license to use spectrum. Vague standards for the "public interest" condition could permit government officials to exercise lawless discretion. Specificity in rules meant accountability, and that meant less possibility of abuse or unfairness by government. Without specific rules, how could any broadcaster know what it was expected to do?

Relying on the brilliant legal thinking of FCC general counsel Bill Kennard, his deputy Chris Wright, and my adviser Julius Genachowski, I expressly rejected Mark Fowler's view that the public interest standard was only a word game. He had said, "The public's interest, then, defines the public interest." But under our new doctrine we argued that broadcasters had a duty to promote the well-being of society, which is an interest we all have as citizens in a well-ordered public life. Moreover, established evidence had documented the troubling behavioral effects of repeated exposure to media. I analogized broadcast media to the open spaces of public parks and to billboards near schools—both places where the Supreme Court had said government could regulate to protect children. I said parents needed "something to choose" and the "power to choose." That meant we would write rules requiring children's television and the V-chip.

I was much blunter than at the NAB convention, and in consequence the broadcasters (as well as First Amendment–absolutist liberals) disliked my speech as much as they had disliked Minow's 1961 speech. In reaction, Commissioner Chong effectively repudiated the Children's Television Act of 1990 by remarking, "Maybe children's television is a noncommercial function. Public broadcasting can do it, they want to do it, and they do it well." (I was always surprised that some believed the FCC could ignore laws that imposed duties on all broadcasters, not just non-commercial stations.) I responded that commercial broadcasters owed the country for their free licenses and special breaks. We announced that the Commission welcomed debate on this topic, and solicited e-mails at kidstelevision@fcc.gov. We regularly publicized the number of e-mails we received supporting our kid-vid initiative. We wanted to demonstrate the power of the information democracy.

Our lawyers concluded that the Children's Television Act had given the Commission the power to write a new rule requiring specific, concrete public interest obligations. I still did not have the votes at the Commission to pass such a rule. But my efforts plainly supported the President's political goal, as crafted by Dick Morris, of enumerating specific differences between his views and those of the Republican Congress. The Republican Congress did not welcome this coincidence of purpose. They decried my independence from their prerogatives. Many members lambasted me in public and private. The trade press delighted in quoting criticism, the less balanced the better. But my message firmly occupied the middle ground of reasonableness. The challenge was to get my message heard.

Then Karen Kornbluh called from Capitol Hill with predictable but bad news. The House Republicans had refused to insert into their telecommunications bill Ed Markey's proposed language requiring the FCC to connect every classroom to the Internet. For all his talk about a new information age in which the next generation could flower, Speaker Gingrich did not want the federal government to guarantee that every child be taught with, and about, the new technologies. His talk was truly cheap.

On August 4, the House passed its communications bill. They had deregulated cable, let the local Bells into the long distance market under certain modest conditions, taken a few steps to open the local telephone market to competition, increased the possible concentration of ownership in both the radio and the television industries, and ordered the digital television license giveaway. Much of the bill was unacceptable to the White House. Ironically, the bill required many new rulemakings at the Commission. Even though the House bill was written to favor the telephone company incumbents in the regulations that implemented the law, the Commission was not going to be phased out soon. The issues of competition and monopoly were too complex for Congress to articulate with specificity in a statute. They needed the FCC to do the detailed work, even with Gore's friend as chairman. (Later, the House Republicans would resort to vituperative rhetoric—coupled with assaults on the FCC's budget and threats of investigatory hearings—as their means of having their way on specific rulemaking.)

We held the Bell companies and the Speaker responsible for killing our classroom connection proposal on the House side. But if our side could insert the Snowe-Rockefeller classroom connection language into the legislation negotiated by the Senate-House conference committee charged with reconciling the two chambers' bills, then in the resulting FCC rulemakings I could try to bring Gore's dream to reality. In the conference committee negotiations, everything depended on Snowe's support, Democratic advocacy, and the White House veto threat. How we would muster a majority at the Commission for our desired results on any of the dozens of prospective rulemakings—that was a problem to be addressed later.

Meanwhile, waiting on the legislative process, I continued my kidvid campaign. In August I told a group of Chicago broadcasters (with Newton Minow in the audience), "The country will be watching broadcast television's new season this fall, but it will also be watching the broadcasters." We successfully placed this one-liner in some of the trades. Blair sought at least two or three quotable phrases per speech; he said that in the age of out-of-context remarks, the rest of my speeches were filler.

Minow came up to me after the speech and smiled broadly. "You and I bookend television in America," he said generously.

In the Chicago speech I also said that convergence and deregulation meant that broadcasters should buy their new digital spectrum licenses at auction. Nobel Prize–winner Ronald Coase, the Chicago School economist, had raised the spectrum auction idea decades earlier. Every Treasury Department had sought spectrum auctions to raise revenue. Even Bob

Dole, prodded by Bill Safire, had spoken on the Senate floor against the digital television spectrum giveaway. (He wanted to repeat with digital television spectrum the success of our PCS cellular auctions, which no Republicans mentioned that they had not voted for.) In one of the most grievous manipulations of politics by the electronic media in history (naturally unreported by that media), the broadcast lobby retaliated with the threat of using their government-gifted airwaves to advertise against any politician who dared agree with Dole.

A self-serving maxim of broadcasting is that television station owners do not allow their political opinions to affect programming content. I never met a television journalist who agreed with that assertion. One reporter told me, for example, that his management had killed his story on the digital television giveaway. Another explained that few reporters would risk their careers by doing stories management disliked. Reporters would censor their own reporting based on their assumption of management's preferences. They could determine these preferences by reading *Broadcasting & Cable* magazine. No internal memos needed to be sent. But never before the anti-Dole campaign had broadcasters used their own advertising time to lobby for their own interests.

Both outrageous and false, their ads said that spectrum auctions would kill free television. The statement was absurd. The FCC needed only to pass a rule ordering that the spectrum be used exclusively for free broadcasts. We told reporters that the NAB attack on Senator Dole was an offense to democracy and to the 1934 Communications Act's imposition of a public interest duty on broadcasters. The print media happily writes negatively on television content, but criticizing the lobbying tactics of media businesses strikes closer to home. A few liberal commentators wrote about the broadcasters' tactic, but most criticized me for chilling the exercise of free speech by seeking to require kidvid shows. We responded, through speeches by general counsel Bill Kennard and myself, that by imposing an obligation to teach, we would not be telling anyone substantively what to say. Television should teach, we said, but it could teach anything it wanted—creationism or evolution, Milton Friedman or John Kenneth Galbraith.

Julius Genachowski persuaded Cass Sunstein, a constitutional law scholar at the University of Chicago, to articulate arguments from the Constitution to support us. Barry Diller, providing industry support, wrote an editorial in the *New York Times* calling for a specific public interest standard. Peggy Charren persuaded Senators who were sponsoring the V-chip that they should also stand for creating good shows as well as giving parents the power to block bad ones from the home.

The Gang of Three told the trade press that I was on a frolic: wrong on the law and incapable of getting a majority for a new rule in any event. The career staff, and some on my personal staff, fretted that open contentiousness among commissioners frustrated the resolution of dozens of virtually invisible matters that the Commission had to decide every week. But I believed that I had to seek public debate if I wanted public opinion to empower me to run the agency.

We wrote our new legal theories into speeches to law schools—Pittsburgh, Brooklyn, Boston College, Berkeley, UCLA, USC, George Washington, Howard. That made the Gang of Three even more angry. In their view, I was using the general counsel's resources for my policy goals, outgunning their tiny staffs and undercutting their authority. Because the 1934 Communications Act said I was the CEO of the agency, I felt I was well within my rights.

I expanded the range of issues for my public advocacy and involved a broader group within the agency. The International Bureau prepared speeches I gave in Geneva and Berlin advocating open markets in all countries. A new office for small business and minority issues generated proposals for including all minorities in the communications revolution. With excellent historical research by the agency, I recalled to women's groups the accomplishments of the first female FCC commissioner, Frieda Hennock, who in the Truman Administration had invented, in effect, public broadcasting in America.

My primary target audience was the American public. We were trying to cure the Commission of the disease of invisibility. Our adversaries were not only the Republican Congress, but the sleep of public opinion. We knew that the Congress would take the broadcasters' side against us as long as the public did not react negatively. But voters are sympathetic with criticism of television. They do not trust the media. Our goal was to tap into that feeling. That might deter Congress from taking my head off. Public debate was a defense against private destruction.

Responding to my new public advocacy, the Republican Congress threatened to reduce the size of the FCC's budget. There was no joy to be had in arguing against any downsizing of government. I began the most aggressive effort to reduce the scope of the FCC's activities in agency history. My target was the FCC field offices. After study, I concluded that the principal and misbegotten purpose of the field offices was to do work for industries or other governmental agencies that should do the work on their own. A television station thought its signal did not reach as far as it should; the local field office would do measurements. A ship needed to have its radios checked; the local field office would help. The police wanted help tracking a bad guy; the field office would provide extra staff. And more than two dozen people in the field offices spent their time primarily giving lectures about such matters as how to obtain a short-wave radio license. The Commission field offices were helpful to the television stations and police departments. But no one could explain why the beneficiaries should not pay for this help.

Blair and I proposed to close virtually all the field offices. The career bureaucrat who ran the group refused my direct order to recommend a major cutback. I issued the order to the next in command, who also refused. Finally, the third in command agreed to make the recommendation to the full Commission. Then the bureau chief relented. Finally, the Gang of Three refused to vote on the reduction. The trade press reported (to its own confusion) that the chairman, as a New Democrat, wanted to shrink the agency, and the pro-Congress commissioners were resisting the downsizing. The Gang of Three reversed their opposition. We had won another battle.

Eight Politics Matters

October 1995 – January 1996

Standing on the bare ground—my head bathed by the blithe air, and uplifted into

infinite space—all mean egotism vanishes. I become a transparent eyeball; I am

nothing; I see all.

Ralph Waldo Emerson, Nature

n Washington, a room with a view describes a room where others can get a good gander at you and your colleagues. In the best of such rooms, the Hay-Adams Hotel dining room, everyone examines the eating groups in order to decode the lobbying alliances of the day. But when Ann Lewis—pink-cheeked, gray-haired doyenne of the White House spinners—and I met to align our messages, we selected a coffee shop in the anonymous dead zone between the White House and Georgetown.

As a matter of law, the White House could not tell the FCC chairman or the commissioners how to vote. But naturally I, and any agency head, preferred the White House to approve of my agenda. Few are successful in any endeavor without learning the value of partnership. Moreover, the power of the White House to drive or block any agenda was, especially in the midst of the Gingrich Revolution, my primary source of support.

Assuming an alert curiosity on my part, lobbyists eagerly brought news of Administration reactions to any and all of my proposals. Nearly always the source was anonymous, although the lobbyists usually implied that the President was angry or unhappy with opposition to their views. But why should the FCC's chairman not be able to consult directly with the White House? The law prohibited not discussions, only unwritten direct advocacy on a particular issue. Furthermore, the chairman was supposed to discuss matters with Congressmen and their staffers under penalty of condemnation for failure to "work with" the Hill. From time to time, then, I met with Lewis in order to learn about politics and to decide how to choose my fights. At an October meeting I told her my themes.

"Kids' TV," I said. "That's the main thing we're doing that most people already seem to care about. Getting the classrooms connected to the Internet. Isn't that the most important thing we're doing that people eventually will care about? I can't believe that opening telephone markets to competition is a voter issue."

"Cable rates," she said. "Consumers look for something concrete."

When Ann Lewis was analyzing voters, she seemed to visualize the specific people, each of the 30 million plus we would need to win the 1996 presidential election. Everyone said that was impossible. Clinton was a one-termer. Possibly he thought so himself. (Perhaps the Monica affair started out of hopelessness. Stranger behaviors have come from much less than wrecking the country's oldest political party. No one understands the private misery of a President—so at odds with the public trappings of pomp and prestige—so based on the inevitability of taking everything personally.)

"The Republicans will insist on repealing cable regulation," I said.

Lewis shrugged. "Our message focuses on families; theirs, ideology," she said. "Voters have moved beyond the Republicans' ability to reach them with scare words like 'liberal' or 'tax.' People want government to produce deliverables. Family-friendly television is on message. I'll poll the classroom connections. No one understands the Internet. We do not know how to ask that question with precision. But I'll try."

"We could just call it technology in the classroom," I suggested. "Or in education."

"The Vice President has persuaded people to feel positively about technology," she said. "This is a big change. Technology causes unpredictable change, and people don't like that. Change threatens jobs, produces anxiety. The elites believe in the benefits of innovation, but voters do not. Al has turned those attitudes around. He has increased America's confidence in the future."

Government comprises many discretionary decisions by many people. Executive-branch leadership provides general guidance, interspersed only occasionally with specific direction, and can succeed only by achieving general alignment with popular opinion. (Corporate leadership is no different, except that in business the relevant constituencies are consumers and the financial community.) There are only two paths to success, and hence to obtaining the authority to make the myriad decisions unnoticed by most people. First, move to agree with public opinion. Second, move public opinion to agree with where one stands. Each is difficult because opinion is volatile, and decisions have effects. The Republicans' problem, as Ann Lewis saw it, was that they were aligned—and were eagerly making decisions that fixed in history that alignment—with where opinion had been, but not where it would be.

Apparently, the Republican leaders were confident that they could overcome the unpopularity of their agenda by spinning the media, trusting the public's indifference to politics, and using their wealth against Democrats to create a three- or four-to-one margin in spending on attack ads. Lewis predicted that the House would pass a terrible budget, and that voters would be very unhappy with the cuts in health care. The Republican assaults on various popular programs had helped our side enormously. Al, for example, had done well in his Big Bird speech. (Gore and Public Broadcasting System president and former FCC commissioner Ervin Duggan had lambasted the House for threatening to eliminate PBS.)

Leaving lunch, I concluded that pressing the kidvid rule was good politics as well as good policy. If my advocacy galvanized the alliance of the broadcasters and the Republican Congress, they would together swing away from public opinion. Voters did not like government telling television networks what to show, but they did not mind rules requiring decent things: specifically, shows for kids.

Congressman Ed Markey and Peggy Charren had success in rallying Democrats on the Hill to support kidvid. Education groups organized an e-mail campaign directed at Congress and the Gang of Three. When Ann Landers printed my letter calling for a minimum requirement of educational television, Quello blasted me for "unprecedented" attempts to go outside for support for the kidvid rule. "Outside" meant outside the noose of lobbyists that was tight around the FCC's neck. The strands were the Republican Congress, the broadcast lobby, and the trade press. One trade press reporter told Blair and me that a group of 75 people—lobbyists, trade press, and lawmakers—were "all who mattered" to the FCC. But all 75 were mobilized against us. My hopes for success and my ability to contribute to the President's comeback required that I ignore the 75; I had to make millions of Americans, and not dozens of insiders, matter to the FCC.

Fortunately, Ann Landers is more powerful than any Washington lobbyist. None of them can reach tens of millions of voters. In the new public information democracy, the greatest political power comes from activating networks that exceed traditional expectations. Most politicians respond to a few hundred people; a thousand phone calls signify a grassroots movement. In the information age, tens and hundreds of thousands of voters can build Web communities of informed advocacy. Today's much-derided public opinion polls foreshadow politicians' responsiveness to networked communities—at least, so one must hope, in light of the need for a vaccine against the power of money over Congress.

Technology in classrooms polled very well. The White House passed the results to sympathetic Senators and Congressmen. But we were far from sure that the conference committee could fashion the compromises necessary to pass a telecommunications bill the President would sign. Congress was splitting along party lines on most issues. The industries were also backing off on compromises they had struck. The Bells liked the House legislation too much; their premature self-congratulation alarmed the long distance companies. MCI decided it had lost the legislative wars; it began to lobby the White House for a veto, which would kill the bill. But AT&T was undecided. The company's Washington hands did not like the bills, but CEO Bob Allen was willing to roll the dice. The conference committee negotiations still might lead to a law.

As the telecom giants scratched their strategic heads, stomped around the Washington ring, banged their high-revenue bellies, the new Internet economy—emphasizing growth over profits and attack over defense—began to take shape without them. In July 1995, Netscape went public. The stock soared—the first of the Internet "bubble" stocks. Founder Marc Andreesen, a huge barefoot Currier & Ives lithograph of a farm boy, pushed not a plow but a browser—the means by which anyone could type a phrase or two into a personal computer and then launch their eyes across invisible roads of loops, switches, and lines to some other computer's presentation of pictures, text, voice. The browser was a ticket to ride a telescope into infinity.

Thanks to a far-sighted, or accidentally smart, FCC decision in the previous decade, the cost of that browsing was zero. In 1984 the Commission had declared that communication of bits zipping through networks (called "data") was not the same as voice conversation (although on long-haul routes both data and voice are digitized) and that it deserved separate legal treatment (although it shared the voice network). The Commission allowed the local phone companies to charge the long distance companies about three dollars an hour for the use of the local loop while connecting a long distance voice call. These are the so-called access charges that contributed billions to the phone companies' bottom line—allegedly as much of 40 percent of their profits. But for data, the FCC did not allow the telephone companies to charge anything extra for use of their lines. Hence, when Internet usage, and therefore data transmission, proliferated, telephone companies correctly calculated that they had lost (or failed to make) hundreds of millions of dollars because they were not allowed to treat the transmissions as voice calls. Even more galling, on average an Internet call used the telephone lines ten times longer than a voice communication; the Bells were outraged that Net users got a long, free ride on their networks. In the absence of the FCC's decision, the Internet would have been so expensive to use that Andreesen's Netscape would not have been a hiccup, much less one of the first bubble stocks of the Internet.

Another benefit of the Internet, at least for me, was that it proved the merit of the collapse of the Bell Atlantic–TCI merger, as well as those of other telephone-cable mergers in the wake of the FCC's cable rate decision in 1994. Those proposed mergers were premised on the belief that the cable and telephony companies should build proprietary networks that delivered video through switches, on channels resembling the circuits of voice telephone calls. The Internet model accommodated any number of different pipes (or "solutions") to every home, because Internet transmissions could use any or all interlinked networks. Indeed, cross-network transmission was the original purpose of the Internet software protocols; that explains the "inter" and the "net" of the neologism. By contrast, the 1994 telephone-cable mergers would have created a powerful force behind out-of-date technology, in favor of a closed system and against the trends of the Internet. It is even possible that the merged entities would have had the economic incentive and political muscle to stifle the growth of the Internet. The unintended effects of cable regulation, it seemed, had been lucky for the country.

One day in October, Intel's Andy Grove telephoned.

"I'm just off my bike," he said.

Was it Silicon Valley jargon? Perhaps a bike was a testing cycle, or a state of being?

"I'm on sabbatical," he explained.

"Where are you calling from?" I asked. People always ask that when they're buying time. Except for the Vice President and other old friends, no one ever telephoned to give me good news. I was trying to think how I might have alienated the Valley folk.

"I'm here at our place on Lake Tahoe. I was riding on my bicycle, when I realized we're in a war. It's a [expletive] war between the packet-switched networks and the circuit-switched networks. You can't let them [meaning the circuit-switched, voice-optimized network builders, also called the Bell companies] win."

When Grove called me, engineers had not yet fully figured out how my grandmother and I could talk to each other through packet-switched technology. The packets had a tendency to get lost. Grandma might say "hel," but the "lo" would be misdirected to Schenectady, where it would slip unaccountably into, say, a telemarketer's pitch, as in: "Low low prices!" Meanwhile, the "hel" standing alone might not capture Grandma's meaning. Eventually, the TCP/IP protocol would find and reroute the missing syllable, but Grandma and I would have had a disturbing conversation. In brief, the Internet was not sufficiently reliable for voice communication and wouldn't be for some time.

But, as Grove envisioned, it will be. Indeed, the Internet's future is multimedia. Through packet-switched communication, voices and pictures and numbers and words would be exchanged at extraordinarily low cost over fantastic distances. In the future when Internet technology is perfected and my grandmother would phone me, I would say to her, "Look at your great-grandson Adam, he's already over 6 feet tall." Looking at my film-quality full-motion home video on her computer-phone, she would respond, "Why not get him on the line?" I would give him a ring in his college dorm, and on his hand-held picture phone he would bring his handsome face into our three-way video conference.

Andy's apocalyptic vision of a war between data and voice was based on the surmise that the phone companies would not promote progress toward this packetized multimedia future. Americans spend $200 billion a year on circuit-switched services and less than $10 billion a year on packet-switched communications. The voice-oriented phone companies were defenders with great risks of losing market share. Next-generation data networking companies were attackers with little to lose and vast wealth to gain. Intel, as well as the rest of the computer hardware world, wanted packet-switching to prevail because the enormous data flow of the new networks would require new, complex, and profitable chips to organize the information for consumer and business use. Intel, in short, was a pro-bandwidth company. However, packet-switching must use a critical portion of the existing network—the multibillion-dollar system of copper lines, or loops, that run between any grandmother's telephone on her bedside table to the telephone pole on her street, and on to the first switching station in her neighborhood, from where the circuit is opened to any grandson in any town. From first switch to last switch, an Internet communication may use long-haul fiber and cheaply bypass the complicated telephone company networks. But at its genesis and at its conclusion, it rides a local loop. Someday wireless, cable, and fiber optic connections will provide alternatives to the loop. But for now, more than 98 percent of residential Web traffic originates and terminates on copper.

Andy Grove understood that the local phone companies would be irresistibly tempted to seek to charge large fees to consumers to use those loops. After all, the Bells needed the money, or at least wanted it. Moreover, the Bells would want to raise packet-switched communication costs to levels that did not radically undercut the pricing of circuit-switched calls. When Ann Lewis said that the country was growing more comfortable with technology, she did not mean that incumbent businesses were happy with new competitive threats.

If Grove was right about the "war," there were reasons not to throw the power of government behind the voice-oriented incumbents. Hundreds of billions of dollars of new investment would build the data networks of the world—that meant enormous job creation. The data networks would be cheaper and more efficient—that meant consumers everywhere could buy more communications services. The data networks would accomplish more tasks more quickly—that meant they would increase corporate productivity. The result would be the increase of economic growth, the decline of unemployment, and the reduction of inflation: the triple economic wonder of our times.

At least once a week in my 48 months of public service I was told by someone that the purpose of the Commission was to create a "level playing field." No one meant it. The proponents of this view wanted someone else to be buried under their "level" field. And I never believed our job was "leveling." Should a jury declare a defendant neither guilty nor innocent, but only express a neutral view? Should a competitively advantageous technology be suppressed either by monopoly or regulation? We were decision makers. Everyone knew it. Everyone, in Congress and in industry, wanted decisions to go their way, but, in any event, all wanted decisions made. Then the affected parties would alter form and function to accommodate the decision. And results would unfold. We could perpetuate and extend policies favoring the existing voice-based monopoly networks. Or we could open markets to new, growth-oriented, risk-inclined entrepreneurs building data networks. If Congress passed the new telecommunications law, we would find that we had to choose.

In November 1995, the conference committee negotiations on the House and Senate telecommunications bills were in full swing. My staff and I played a supporting role, advising all sides on any issue they raised. Senator Fritz Hollings and Congressman Ed Markey were outnumbered on the committee by the pro-Bell conferees, but as the Administration's allies, their hand was strengthened by Gore's veto threat.

Senators Rockefeller and Snowe, who were not on the conference committee, beseeched Hollings and Markey to insist on classroom connections in the negotiation. No business interest supported the classroom connections. It was a mouse that the elephantine businesses might step on as they pursued their long list of goals. Worse, the local telephone and long distance companies knew that from them would come the money to connect the classrooms. They thought of it as a tax: each preferred the other to pay, hence their common wish was that neither would pay. Naturally they were allied with the House Republicans against the provision, although they were anxious not to confront the sponsoring Senators—especially not inexhaustible Jay Rockefeller, who did not hesitate to tell CEOs how strongly he felt about his provision.

The consumer groups wanted to make sure the local telephone companies did not pay because they believed the charges would be passed on to consumers as an addition to the local telephone bill. Although I tried to induce guilt about children in the chief representative of the consumers' lobby in America, I understood that citizens as consumers were his interest; citizens as parents was the focus of other advocacy groups. The deletion of the Snowe-Rockefeller provision was all right with him.

The education lobbies wanted any or all of the companies to pay. They were primarily concerned about getting *some* money, as opposed to none. The idea of directing auction revenue to connecting classrooms had been killed by the bipartisan imperative of directing all new revenues to balancing the budget. No way to connect classrooms existed except the

Snowe-Rockefeller provision. The computer hardware and software industries did little to lobby seriously for the initiative. I had never found a way to broach the subject to Bill Gates, and the Silicon Valley companies did not see the classrooms provision as central to their businesses.

In the wrestling match of lobbyists and conferees, a compromise would be a reduction in the amount of money required. The Snowe-Rockefeller language stated no number, letting the FCC discharge the controversial duties of fixing the amount in our rulemaking, deciding who paid, and coping with the consumer reaction. But the range of spending could be sharply reduced by a change in the definition of the program's goals. If Congress ordered only discounted rates, and not a guarantee of access for every classroom, the program would be transformed from ambitious to insignificant.

"If they take out 'classrooms,' we lose," Karen explained. "If they delete the word 'access,' we're doomed. Installing lines to give access to classrooms costs billions. Discounted rates for schools, merely a few million."

The great fact for our side was that the co-sponsor, Senator Snowe, was a well-respected Republican and a spokesperson within her party for family issues. Even if the Republican House members dismissed her wishes, still the Republican Senator who had sponsored the bill, Larry Pressler, might still be reluctant to disregard his colleague's view.

The Vice President had listed classrooms as part of his non-negotiable agenda. But Karen and I knew that the White House might not veto the whole legislation over the classroom connections provision. There was too much in the legislation that might improve the economy to risk losing all over one issue.

Another risk was that the bill—groaning under the pressure of the lobbyists, heavy with favors extended to numerous businesses—threatened to collapse into the void of legislative inaction. Time was passing and the end of the session approached. MCI increased its criticism of the bill. If AT&T also decided to oppose the process, it could probably succeed in killing the bill.

Meanwhile, the trade press continued to report that I had committed myself to a quixotic, ill-advised campaign for children's television at the expense of harmony among the commissioners. I felt that virtually everything done behind closed doors at the Commission could go wrong. And everything we could force to be discussed publicly had a very good chance of turning out right. My conclusion: force public debate on all disagreements.

The Gang of Three responded by arguing through apothegms. On various issues, they repeatedly used three statements: (1) "This is too regulatory." That meant that any policy designed to serve more than a simple goal of gratifying a particular special interest was opposed. (2) "This is micromanagement." That meant the proposed rule would have an impact on a particular special interest. (3) "I'm for a level playing field." That meant they would vote against rules designed to share a monopoly's advantages with rivals. These statements did not admit discussion; that was their purpose.

Despite the contentiousness on the eighth floor, I occasionally made an effort to be a clubbable chairman. To this end, one day that fall, I visited Jim Quello's office. As usual, he was friendly enough; at least he was willing to have me sit down. Of the other two in the Gang of Three, one would rarely meet and the other would never meet with me alone.

Jim said, "I'm thinking about serving another term. I've got the experience; I've been around enough that I've voted against everyone twice, but I have a lot of friends in this town. Thinking about another term."

My heart sank. Would the FCC never move into a new era?

We recruited in academe for a candidate to fill Quello's post. Professors made careers out of criticizing the FCC. But no one wanted the job.

I met with a respected Democrat who was close to the President. "Jim's term expires in 1996," I said. "The President can't renominate him. He doesn't support anything the President favors: not auctions, not competition, not children's television, not anything."

She responded, "That might be right. But if you strike at the king, you must kill him."

The king. In Washington a kingdom lies in the power to vote. Or to hold up votes. If the House-Senate conference committee reached no agreement, the FCC would lack a mandate for action from Congress. Nor would I have the votes at the Commission to pursue my agenda. I could continue the public relations campaign for kidvid—I asked Oprah's business partner for an appearance on her show (no); I met with athletes' agent David Falk to get help from professional basketball players (no)—but I ran the risk of becoming a crank. I could negotiate individual deals with cable and telecom companies to put the Internet in every classroom without a new law, and opening monopolies to competition would be at least remotely possible if I could obtain support from the Gang of Three. But without a new law they inevitably would block these efforts. They could deny my main chance for success. They could drive me literally or spiritually from office.

The press reported that I had a problem "learning to count to three." They meant that my agenda was in irons, floating in the Sargasso Sea of Washington futility. In Washington, if you push for something and fail, you are much worse off than if you had never tried at all. Right or wrong is not as important as who's up or down, in the view of media who (according to their secular code) report on the popularity of moral stances but not the moral issues themselves.

Katharine Graham's house in Georgetown is across the street from the formal public gardens known as Dumbarton Oaks. An elegant but short circular gravel driveway leads to a stately but short staircase, appealing but not intimidating from the curb. A grand house is one that cannot be seen from the road; one where the adjacent gardens are private, reserved for tête-à-tête strolls of the great and powerful.

Mrs. Graham is the capital's royalty, the Queen of the Fourth Estate. But she does not have a grand house. You could call it a home, which is how you know that in Washington, unlike any other great American city, it is not about the money. Although they may possess wealth, the royalty of the government and the media do not distinguish themselves by amassing private fortunes. They do seek to direct vast spending of public monies, and they are exquisitely sensitive to the wishes of private wealth. So perhaps Washington is in a metaphysical way indeed all about the money. But in habits and appearance Washington, as the blues singer Huddie "Leadbelly" Ledbetter put it, is "a bourgeois town."

An immoderate zeal to make or unmake reputations—the currency of the capital—has been endemic to the *Washington Post* at least since Watergate. (Nothing scars like success.) Since the 1970s, in the quiet style of American revolutions, the *Post* has used words to grind public consciousness to the cutting edge of a guillotine. The "click, click" of its printing press echoes like the *tricotage* of Madame DeFarge. To encounter a top-notch *Post* reporter is to brush against the possibility of image death.

The paper's hostile attitude toward authority—even to the possibility of doing good in public service—could fairly be regarded as particularly justified by the actions of the Federal Communications Commission.

In 1974, President Nixon asked his staff whether someone could take away the *Post*'s television station by protesting the FCC's otherwise routine renewal of their licenses. On his infamous tapes, Nixon said, "The main thing is the *Post* is going to have damnable, damnable problems out of this one. They have a television station . . . and they're going to have to get it renewed."

After Nixon's request, as with Henry II's plea to have someone rid him of the "meddlesome" Thomas à Becket, untraceable bad acts occurred. Specifically, known Nixon allies in Florida filed protests at the FCC against the *Post*'s valuable television licenses in Florida. The Commission to its shame purported to treat seriously the preposterous claims and refrained from ruling against them until long after Nixon had resigned. An immediate corollary of the protests was that Wall Street financiers grew skittish over the initial public offering of *Post* stock that Mrs. Graham had planned. With the support of Democrat Warren Buffett, her investor and friend, Mrs. Graham weathered the skepticism, floated the stock, and took down the President.

Under the circumstances, even more than 20 years after the FCC's conniving with the Nixon White House, I was delighted when she invited me to her home. The December 1995 occasion was a party for Bill Gates's first book, boldly titled *The Road Ahead.*

In the drawing room, Gates looked wide-eyed behind his glasses, small in the crowd, and completely comfortable as he expressed in a short speech his profound confidence in the information highway. He had just completed one of the biggest self-promotions in history. His own image personified Windows 95. That had become the hottest and fastest selling software in the history of the industry; total sales in 1995 alone were $2 billion. His personal fortune had risen by many, many times since I had met him first in Pamela Harriman's dining room in Paris in March 1994, many times even since lunch with him in Redmond.

In his talk, Gates did not speak of a "network of distributed intelligence." He had long since discovered the Internet, and was reinventing Microsoft to adapt to it. If the consumer could buy a computer that retrieved application programs from the Internet, the risk for Gates was that hot-selling Microsoft applications compatible with his profit-manufacturing Windows operating systems might not have such a special claim on the customer's eyes, fingertips, and wallet. And if incompatible applications became popular, Windows' market power would diminish.

While he spoke, I thumbed through his book. Eureka! I found my name in the chapter on education. After his speech, I handed Gates the book for his signature. "Have you done that giveaway yet?" he asked, referring to our discussion in Redmond earlier that year.

"It looks like Congress will make us give the television licenses away if they pass either the Senate or House version of the telecom bill," I said.

He wrinkled his nose, shrugged his shoulders, and wrote in the book. In the noisy swirl of the party I could not explain that the telecommunications law's fate turned not only on the conference committee's negotiations but also on the larger fight between Speaker Gingrich and President Clinton. If the President vetoed the big budget bills, it was possible that neither side would agree on lesser bills like communications reform.

When he finished writing, I thanked him, took my book and drifted away. He had endearingly inscribed: "The years ahead hold a lot of promise. Your job will not get simpler but it will be even more important than ever. Bill."

This opinion was not shared, for example, by the Republican Congress. Like the post–Civil War Congress, it believed in its power to run all the government over the head of the President. It believed it had a right to command the actions of regulatory agencies. But the principal battle over the competing points of view of the White House and the Congress was, by late 1995, the budget.

On November 13, 1995, by refusing to appropriate the necessary funds, the Republican Congress had shut down the government for six days. Eight hundred thousand government workers were furloughed. It was high farce and critical symbolic politics. As the President explained, the extremist Republicans had denied myriad public benefits to the American people. Polls registered a huge lift for Democrats. Compounding the Republicans' political mistake—and inserting an element of bathos that no fiction writer would dare—Speaker Gingrich complained that he had been snubbed on the President's plane to the funeral of Israeli Prime Minister Yitzhak Rabin, who had been assassinated on November 4. At a November 15 breakfast with reporters, Gingrich had said that the perceived slight was "part of why you ended up with us sending down a tougher interim spending bill."

The great world of budget battle was reflected in my small one. In December, at the annual test of character known as the Chairman's Dinner where all my world was represented, I had the crowd laughing with me, and at the Congress: "I was trying to figure out how to be funny. David Letterman gave me his files of Stupid Chairman tricks. But I'd already done them all. Steven Bochco said just postpone the speech 'til after 10 P.M. and then take your pants off. Then for inspiration I started thinking about the Commission. What's funny about the Commission? Furloughs. Not funny. Furloughing auction staff because of a budget crisis, which prevents auction staff from raising money to balance the budget? Funny. Not ha-ha funny, but weird funny."

If the Republicans were going to make themselves a laughingstock for the country, I certainly wanted to join in the fun.

Meanwhile, Senator Fritz Hollings and Congressman Ed Markey held the Senate-House conference committee hostage, insisting that Al Gore would indeed cause the White House to veto any telecommunications bill that they did not like. They insisted on a compromise that gave the FCC real power to open local telephone company monopolies, and that let the FCC connect every classroom to communications networks. The last of these issues kept being pushed to the edge of the table by the volume of debate on the other, heavily lobbied topics. But in part for fear of further characterization as being mean-spirited in light of the budget battle, the other conferees did not dare to strike the Snowe-Rockefeller provision. That would have given the President still another basis to explain to the country how relentlessly the Republicans opposed the use of government to promote the public good.

In the second week of December the conference committee's deliberations approached a climax, even as the Administration and the Congress came to loggerheads in the negotiations over the budget. The Gingrich Congress said it would again, for a second time, let the government close if Clinton did not accept their cuts in programs in the budget. The President stood firm. The Congress closed the executive branch on December 15. But at the same time, the Gingrich-allied conferees caved in to Senator Hollings and Congressman Markey, and the conference committee passed a bill that the Democrats and the White House could accept. The Snowe-Rockefeller provision was included.

How did it happen that this frail hope of radical economic reform and significant social benefit achieved consensus, while larger issues were irreconcilable? One explanation is that the Bell companies, unlike in 1994, did not ask their allies to kill the law, and their habitual opponent AT&T

also supported the law. The big long distance company had the most to fear from the reform, and its own Washington operatives believed that the FCC might well interpret the law to give the Bells vast powers to attack AT&T's long distance market while protecting their own local monopolies. But the top management of AT&T was somehow convinced that even though I lacked a majority at the FCC, the company could count on the Commission to promote competition in opening local markets. There was little basis for this decision and its degree of uncertainty in execution was vast. Perhaps AT&T was beguiled by its own vision of using its famous brand to attack the local market while successfully defending its long distance market share. As it turned out, the company had no competitive strategy, and its top executives lost their jobs for this reason, but that was unforeseen in late 1995.

An equally important reason for the conference committee compromise was that all other relevant industries—cable, broadcast television, radio, wireless—won various benefits from the law. They all wanted it, and the conference committee did not want to deny them. But perhaps it was also the case that the Gingrich faction was consumed or distracted by the budget battle.

On December 20, Al Gore announced that the conference committee's work was acceptable to the White House. The President would not veto the bill. Al was proud of the reform law that would be delivered to the country, that would jump-start the information economy, that would connect every classroom to the Net.

Congress, however, had not yet voted on the conference committee draft, and the shutdown crisis had aggravated tempers. The Republicans erupted in a fury at the notion that Gore was taking credit for the result of the conference committee work. Jack Fields, Bob Dole, and others said it was far from clear that they would let the Republican Congress vote for the conference compromise. They wanted still more consolidation of the broadcast industry than the bill permitted. The government was still closed.

Sitting in the silence of the shut-down agency, Blair and I did not know how the American public would react to the budget fight, and we underestimated the impact on the President's popularity. Our solitude was interrupted by the sound of wheezing from the waiting room outside the chairman's office. An Asian country's delegation had arrived to hear how American government would handle the communications revolution. In the absence of working elevators, they had puffed their way up the eight flights of stairs of the FCC. Blair and I welcomed the Asians into my poorly lit office (no one to replace the dead bulbs).

I explained, "The legislative branch has shut down the executive branch."

"Ho ho," chuckled a representative of the newly democratizing country, "in our nation it works the opposite way."

Some in our country asserted, as George Gilder had said to me in late 1993, that in a networked world citizens would form self-organized communities that dispensed with inefficient techniques for cooperation like representative government. A closed government, they thought, was a step in the right direction.

Industry, however, understood that when the government closed, the rule of law was at risk. Without clarity from the FCC about the rules, businesses were less able and willing to make investment contracts, attract foreign capital, enter into export or import agreements. Then everyone made less money.

Citizens understood that a closed government could not create the public goods that, in our country of stupendous private wealth, are the means of assuring some semblance of equal opportunity. The paradigmatic picture of the shutdown was the family turned away from the closed museums on the Mall in Washington, D.C. After a long trip from Ohio or Iowa, these citizens and voters discovered that the Gingrich-led Congress had interfered with the family Christmas vacation. And this was the same uncompassionate Congress that would not provide *Sesame Street* on television, or hot lunches in public schools.

Gingrich's righteous right-wing rhetoric was associated with nonsensical callousness. Seen through the eyes of the children wondering why they were standing on the capital city's cold streets with no way to get into the National Air and Space Museum, the Republican policies were in trouble.

Politics in the American democracy consists of standing up for principle and sitting down to compromise. The Gingrich Revolutionaries forgot this teaching, perhaps because Bill Clinton so maddened them. They came into office punching at Bill Clinton, asserting in all ways their moral and intellectual superiority. But they could not land a punch on the ever-sliding President.

After a year, the Gingrich Congress tired of swinging at air, and elected to march steadily at the White House. As it swung its roundhouse rights, it leaned too far forward and lost control. Clinton stepped in and began landing rapid combinations to the body: you're wrong on social security, out of step on education, mean-spirited in your attacks on public broadcasting. Clinton cared about the country. Congress cared only about itself. So the judges, the people, scored the bout. Poll numbers gave the result. Gingrich lost the war for public opinion. Humiliated, in January he appropriated the money to reopen the government.

During the December shutdowns, working out of their homes, my team members had hammered out the terms of our approval of Westinghouse's acquisition of CBS. Copying the White House's selective approach to controversy, I decided that I would not allow the Commission to vote on the item unless Westinghouse agreed to show three hours of educational television per week. I assumed correctly that Westinghouse's sensible CEO Michael Jordan valued approval of his merger far more than his fidelity to the NAB's uncompromising opposition to my kidvid rule.

Barry Diller explained his view of our strategy to the journalists. He told the trade press that public interest performance had begun to ebb among broadcasters but that "frightened broadcasters, if frightened properly, tend to do the good thing."

Another part of our calculation was that the Gang of Three commissioners would explode at my assertion of the chairman's authority to control the agenda for voting. Lacking a majority vote, I had obtained the promise I wanted from CBS. The Gang of Three indeed rebelled and attempted to undo the deal, erasing "children" from the text of the item. Blair and I then blundered in not publicizing the controversy vigorously. We did not explain to the press the Gang of Three's editorial tactics.

In the new vacuum, Quello's staff was particularly adept at mischaracterizing the fight. In their telling, I had conceded the legitimacy of Westinghouse's purchase of CBS but was holding up the approval of the deal for procedurally improper reasons. For failure to have trumpeted Jordan's concessions and for not having obliged Westinghouse's lobbyists to force the Gang of Three to go along, I was labeled as holding up the deal for vindictive reasons.

As always, however, the Republicans helped by going too far. One of their House subcommittee chairs—a faithful Gingrich lieutenant—called to tell me he was planning a public hearing to investigate the accusation that I had "extorted" Westinghouse to show kids' programs.

I asked, "Doesn't extortion involve something illegal? An illegal means or an illegal end?" I had refreshed my memory with a peek at Black's Law Dictionary.

He said, "You could be in a lot of trouble."

By then, our Westinghouse decision, even as ruthlessly edited by the Gang of Three, had been issued. Jordan, a man of his word, had not withdrawn his promise to show more educational television. Even more important, the President had triumphed in the shutdown wars. Feeling carried by the tide running in my favor, I succumbed to the urge for bravado.

"Congressman," I said, "make my day."

There was silence. I continued, "Put the hearings on TV and you'll make us both famous. I'll be for kids and you'll be against me."

Soon after, one of his staffers sent word that the Congressman had decided to let the matter drop.

Congress sheepishly returned to work in January 1996, and both houses voted on January 5 to reopen the government. As the guns of the budget battle were silenced, congressional Republicans complained about the "regulatory" nature of the conference committee telecommunications bill before them. But the Republicans had to demonstrate their usefulness in some way. For a legislature, that proof lay in legislating. (The next, even more frustrated Republican Congress would reject that approach as it sought to justify itself in a misbegotten impeachment.) Moreover, the industries involved in the legislation were ready to move their own fights to the FCC rulemaking process.

The President stood firm on the broadcast consolidation issues. In particular, he would not sign the bill into law if the Republicans inserted an amendment allowing newspapers and television stations to merge in a single city. He told people that he could not have been elected governor if the media in Little Rock had spoken with only one voice. The Republicans backed down on all their attempts to alter the conference committee compromise, except that Bob Dole was not yet satisfied.

Senator Dole sought revenge for the broadcast lobby's attack on his advocacy of digital television license auctions. He had been reluctant even to vote for the telecommunications bill because it ordered the giveaway of the spectrum to the broadcasters. To win his support for the bill, I negotiated with his staff the terms of a letter that he sent to the Commission demanding that it hold off granting the broadcasters their digital television licenses until spring 1997. That way, if he was elected president in 1996, he could reverse the Telecommunications Act's giveaway. With my agreement to this letter, Dole allowed the Senate to vote on the conference committee bill.

Senator McCain railed against the broad powers granted to the FCC in the bill. He garnered a couple dozen Republican votes against it, but on February 1, the Senate and House passed the conference committee version of the telecommunications bill. President Clinton agreed to sign the bill into law.

Congress had not been mindful of Senator McCain's repeated warnings against transferring power to me. Now, in the wake of the government shutdown, the Telecommunications Act of 1996 made me, at least for a limited time, just as Gates's prophetic inscription had stated, one of the most powerful persons in the communications revolution.

PART 3 **Remember Who You Are**

Nine **Chance of a Lifetime**

February 1996 – May 1996

So I . . . make my way over to Tibet, and I get on as a looper at a course over in

the Himalayas . . . and who do you think they give me? The Dalai Lama,

himself. . . . So we finish eighteen and he's gonna stiff me. And I say, 'Hey, Lama,

hey, how about a little something, you know, for the effort, you know.' And he

says, 'Oh, uh, there won't be any money, but when you die, on your deathbed,

you will receive total consciousness.' So I got that goin' for me, which is nice.

Bill Murray in Caddyshack

The leaders of government and the titans of the communications industries gathered in the Library of Congress reading room for the signing of the telecommunications law on February 8, 1996. The location, selected by the Vice President's domestic policy adviser Greg Simon, was intended to recall Al Gore's long-ago promise to create an information highway on which the schoolgirl of Carthage, Tennessee, could go to the Library of Congress.

The President brightly (and, as it turned out, correctly) announced that the new law would lead to fantastic economic growth, but that its best feature was the authority to connect all classrooms to the Internet. Under the pressure of the moment, even Republicans like Tom Bliley, chairman of the House Commerce Committee, agreed that the Snowe-Rockefeller provision was perhaps the most important feature of the new law. The Vice President, on this day of his success, beamed at the passage of a critically important law that largely failed to effect the twin prongs of Speaker Gingrich's agenda: it regulated anew (instead of deregulated) the telephone company monopolies and it extended (instead of contracted) the guarantee of public benefits from the communications sector. The communications executives made a point of congratulating Gore; they knew that he would have controlling influence at least on the way I, if not the full Commission, interpreted the law. Al accepted the ritual of respect with grace, and happily arranged the signing pens on the railing in front of the President. Bill Clinton, glowing like a sunrise, appeared to transcend the crowd.

The White House handlers had placed the President and Vice President on a dais above the congressional leaders. Gingrich appeared diminished by the setting, and by the burden of watching the President celebrate. He muttered conspiratorially with assorted cheerless Republicans. Polls in the wake of the shutdown showed his popularity plummeting.

Gingrich did not look up at the President during the event: getting caught in that posture could have been an embarrassing photograph. Outside their private offices, experienced political figures always act as if they are on stage. The attitude (chin up, eyes searching for the lens, lips peeled back in an amalgam of confident smile and shark's bite) is infectious. Whenever I was near the President, for example, I found myself grinning to beat the band, as if I were competing for a bit part in a terribly uplifting movie.

Bob Allen of AT&T looked pained. Perhaps the Washington ritual, replete with hypocrisy and code, appalled him. Or perhaps he suffered recurring bouts of worry about his company's fate in the rulemaking battles that the ceremony would kick off. My own staff's early readings of the law's hundreds of cross-referencing and ambiguous paragraphs suggested that Allen's company faced serious risks. The Bells' networks covered huge geographic areas, and no one had enough money to build from scratch similarly sized systems. Congress had rightly decided not to force the Bells to sell off pieces of their networks; indeed, the law did not bar the Bells from merging. Neither the economy nor consumers would benefit from dissipating the essential efficiency of these systems: namely, that the cost of carrying a single additional call approached zero. This efficiency was, however, what the economists called a "network effect." If the marginal cost of an incremental phone call was nearly zero, and the incumbent could charge nearly zero to retain a customer, no new entrant could hope to compete against the incumbent. One solution that could be discerned in the law was to let new entrants share and connect to the existing network at prices that reflected the efficiencies of the Bells' existing networks. Such a rule, however, would madden the Bells even as it gave the long distance companies and start-up companies a fighting chance to enter the local market. By contrast, as some read the conference committee's handiwork, the Bells could plausibly argue that the FCC should let them invade Allen's long distance market by the end of 1996. In that event, AT&T should fear losing one to two percent of its 75 percent residential market share per month, with no effective way to compensate by taking share at the same rate in the local telephone market.

Although his fate was in the FCC's hands, Allen did not approach me. Instead he stood rigidly in the swirl of politicians, like a man trapped in a bee swarm. Not far away, Ray Smith of Bell Atlantic, who had masterminded the Bell company strategy, was beaming.

The Bells had prevailed in the law on issues such as denying their adversaries in the Department of Justice a large role in implementing the statute. But they also believed they had won a much more debatable proposition—namely, that the law empowered the state regulatory commissions and not the FCC to decide how to open local markets to competition. Historically, the Bells were most influential with the states, second most persuasive with Congress, and third and least successful in their lobbying at the FCC. But at all three levels their threat to raise local telephone prices, their huge numbers of unionized employees, and their century-long experience in mastering the regulatory and political arts gave them great power. They expected that Congress would persuade the FCC to allow the states to set the rules for competition in the local market and that the state rules would be favorable for the Bells. In other words, they thought I would give up the chance to be the master builder of the information sector's competition rules.

To this day, I cannot imagine that the Bells thought I would abandon voluntarily the chance of a lifetime. Perhaps they assumed, as so many lobbyists did on other issues, that I could not win three votes for my point of view. Or perhaps Ray Smith and the other Bell CEOs were sure that Congress would browbeat the FCC into writing the rules their way in 1996. Perhaps they counted also on the backup plan of electing their ally Bob Dole as President in November. In that event, by at least 1997, the Bells would have an FCC that would help them vanquish the long distance companies, integrate their local monopolies with long distance facilities, and consolidate in their own ranks.

I sat on the far edge of the crowd, having been ousted from the center by a guard responsible for seating Congressmen. Left to my thoughts on this day of accomplishment for the legislators, I mused about the day 27 years earlier when I had passed hopeful notes in the same Library of Congress to thin, blonde, knobby-kneed, bright-eyed, literary Jori Woods. She was on her way back to Stanford, and I to Yale for senior year. The 3,000 miles made a difference for us; perhaps she would not have turned (so quickly!) to someone close at hand had I been able to send her e-mail over the Internet. But now that library was at last bringing me good luck.

The passage of the new law placed me on a far more public stage. But I felt that Congress—in the constitutional sense—had asked me to exercise the full power of all ideas I could summon. And I believed that I and my team had learned, through many failures, how to succeed. Later, I realized that we knew almost nothing of the complexity and importance of the tasks in front of the FCC.

Like, I suppose, any son, I calibrated myself against my father. A brilliant lawyer, he believed he should have been an architect; he imagined he could have had a happier life in construction than in litigating about construction projects. My father's stories taught me to fear the possibility of remorse.

To battle against the risk of regret, my FCC team worked harder than any of us had ever done before. Meeting in several overlapping groups of about a dozen people each (organized according to the lanes of the information highway) we dedicated almost three weeks to studying the possible readings of each word in the 150-page statute. The conference committee compromises had produced a mountain of ambiguity that was generally tilted toward the local phone companies' advantage. But under principles of statutory interpretation, we had broad authority to exercise our discretion in writing the implementing regulations. Indeed, like the modern engineers trying to straighten the Leaning Tower of Pisa, we could aspire to provide the new entrants to the local telephone markets a fairer chance to compete than they might find in any explicit provision of the law. In addition, the law gave almost no guidance about how to treat the Internet, access charges, data networks, the principle of affordable telephone service that was called universal service, and many other critical issues. (Three years later, Justice Antonin Scalia agreed, on behalf of the Supreme Court, that the law was profoundly ambiguous.)

In effect, our rules would decide when, whether, and how new entrants could compete against the Bells in the local telephone market, Bells could enter the long distance market, companies could merge, rural telephone companies could provide service in high-cost areas, classrooms and rural health care clinics could be connected to the information highway, televisions would have V-chips, commercial television could show public interest programming, and dozens of other questions.

The more my team studied the law, the more we realized our decisions could determine the winners and losers of the new economy. We did not want to confer advantage on particular companies; that seemed inequitable. But inevitably a decision that promoted entry into the local market would benefit a company that followed such a strategy.

We decided that our fundamental goal was to encourage any business to attack monopoly incumbents. Incumbents like the Bells or AT&T, we reasoned, could become attackers in other markets. After all, why should the FCC not try to stimulate the Bells to invade each other's territories? They appeared to abhor such uncollegial behavior, but it would benefit consumers and the economy. (In 1999, my successor Bill Kennard extracted from Southwestern Bell a promise to enter other Bells' territories as a condition to approval of its acquisition of Ameritech.)

Some months earlier, during our continuing search for political allies, Blair had taken me to visit his friend Governor Jim Hunt of North Carolina (white frame house, iced tea in the study). Leaning forward, his eyes squinting with seriousness, the Governor said, "I have a piece of advice. Be bold." He held out his right hand, with thumb and forefinger pinching tightly this nugget of guidance.

Recalling this piece of pithiness, I said to my team, "I want to be bold."

Governor Hunt was a wild success with voters by never commencing bold initiatives; President Clinton was reconfiguring his presidency after this model. Counterpunch, not first move, was the recommended political strategy. But the law required that the FCC make decisions: we had to offer proposed interpretations of the new competitive reform model. And these had to win the approval of the Gang of Three. If they rejected my proposed rules, I would lose all power, reputation, and credibility. I hoped they underestimated their strategic importance.

I was convinced, however, that we had assembled from new recruits and promotions within the agency a team that would correctly determine the desirable reading of the new law. Their interpretations would create competition, investment, entrepreneurship, benefits to the economy and to every citizen. But I did not know if Blair and I could invent the political strategy that would permit the Commission to do the right thing. The starting point was to convince everyone in the agency, in the press, in the financial and lobbying community, that we knew very well what to do.

"I want to be bold," I declared again.

Bold rhetoric from the top means hard work for everyone else. To master the material in the law in a hurry, we held a dozen large meetings in my office per week. The teamwork exposed as many people as possible to one another's thoughts. I tried to convince everyone that Congress expected them to make the final decisions, and that I would not let politics have any effect on them. I hoped it was true.

In the second month of our deliberations, March, my team agreed on our core principles of interpretation: promote investment, encourage entrepreneurial ventures, stimulate the growth of the Internet, do not transfer value from one incumbent to another, do not directly raise local telephone prices, create a uniform national set of rules, and guarantee immediate and tangible public benefits—especially the Internet in every classroom. Behind all our decisions were the motives of stimulating economic growth and innovation. The law, as we learned to interpret it, would encourage new companies to create thousands of new jobs. The new entrants would make the existing companies offer more and better services, like second lines and high-speed connections to the Internet and many so-called vertical services, like call waiting and phone mail. As consumers bought new services, the economy would grow, and the belief that any company's success came from another's failure (the static model of historic telecommunications debate) would be put to rest.

To create the conditions for competition everywhere in the country, we would write rules that forced the state commissions to follow national rules for connecting to the existing phone network. I tried to bring the state commissioners on my side by bringing them into our deliberations—we even traded staff with them. But despite the cries of the Bells and the Republicans for "federalism" (meaning the abandonment of a national policy the law was supposed to bring about), I was not going to create voluntarily a Balkanized regulatory system. We would dictate for the country a range of prices that the local phone companies could charge to their new competitors for leasing the use of the existing companies' networks. The states would set specific prices within the range. I considered that a compromise with utility commissions.

Our rules would encourage the development of new companies

called CLECs (competitive local exchange carriers). Many of the CLECs, as it turned out, were builders of new data networks. These new networks are generating access to the Internet from homes and businesses. Within four years all small- and medium-size businesses will use the Net; and within not much longer three-fourths of all homes will have Internet access. Already more data, measured by volume, travels across America than voice traffic. This data surge in turn attracted investment in new long-haul data companies like Level 3, Williams, Global Crossing, and Qwest. (The purchase by Qwest of US West, a triumph of data over voice, was another unforeseen but significant effect of our choices.)

After competition developed, we intended to end state regulation of local telephone prices charged to consumers. We would put the state regulators out of the communications business. Perhaps that was one of the reasons they did not welcome our assertion of preemptive federal jurisdiction.

A constant concern was my lack of a reliable majority. To avoid losing the support of either Congress or the Gang of Three, I could try with the Republican leadership or my colleagues to write our rules by consensus. I rejected this option as both impractical and unlikely to lead to a truly pro-competitive result. I was left then with the necessity of rallying public opinion behind our approach. Blair and I saw that we needed favorable press, and we needed to keep the armies of lobbyists pacified or confused.

Almost everyone at the agency thought it was unbearable that Congress had commanded the FCC to conduct specific rulemakings in statutorily set time periods. The most burdensome were the obligations to write the interconnection rules by August, and to obtain a recommended rule on universal service (including connecting classrooms) from a joint board of five state officials and three FCC commissioners (Commissioners Ness, Chong, and me) by November. That, in turn, was intended to lead to a final universal service order by May 1997. The impossible deadlines, in fact, were a stroke of luck. They permitted my team to rush the items past the other commissioners to votes, insisting on our interpretations of the law, and brooking no delays. If we could do our work well, quickly, and with approval in the press, we had a chance to push through on our terms the more than 100 decisions that the law required. Thus, our slogan: to meet or beat all deadlines.

To put even more pressure on the other commissioners, I announced that I expected to obtain a unanimous vote on all items. If the Gang of Three could not agree with my team's recommendations, I hoped to invoke memories of the Republican shutdown of government. I wanted the Gang of Three to fear that the public would blame them, as it had the Congress, for failure to produce results.

The day after the law was signed, we had FCC career staff announce a detailed schedule for the many dozens of rulemakings and other decisions. Never had the Commission announced in advance when it would decide a series of matters. Traditionally, that was the greatest of eighth-floor mysteries. The lobbying community praised me for helping them to organize their work. But the deadlines denied the lobbyists and the Gang of Three the use of delaying tactics to build opposition to our recommended decisions.

If the lobbyists had time, they could assemble coalitions against any particular reading of the law. They could generate letters from Congress, articles in the newspapers, telephone calls from prominent people, ad campaigns on television that would alarm even otherwise supportive Congressmen. They could cause suggestions of reappointment to reach Jim Quello (whose term expired in 1996) and Andrew Barrett (who was already serving past the expiration of his term, hoping for an extension), could woo Rachelle Chong with hints of career advancement (over me!).

Even without regard to such obvious emoluments, the other commissioners did not wish to be unpopular. There was no joy in that role. It was better to be smiled at than frowned upon, invited to movie openings and trade association dinners than ignored. Hence at any moment the incumbents' lobbyists could drop unbearable weight to break an individual commissioner or bring heat that, like a furnace, could put steel into the collective will of the Gang of Three.

Speed would kill us if our policies were mistaken or did not win public approval. To maximize the advantage of knowing what we wanted to do before others knew what they wanted, we began to articulate our principles in public and to explain our detailed tentative conclusions in private. Anyone could get a private meeting with me or my staff to be informed on a topic, but the complexity of the issues was so great that hardly any lobbyist could apprehend the totality. That was another advantage for us— provided that we ourselves were not overwhelmed by the degree of difficulty. Let it all hang out, we said to ourselves, and we will have our way by dint of the overpowering nature of our logic and the pressure of the pace. Our teams held dozens of public forums, gave speeches, did interviews. We had the power of ideas, and we used it.

By publicly explaining our goals to everyone (state regulators, congressional staff, reporters, the financial community), we won confidence in our decision making and deterred incipient opposition. Committing to unanimous votes created the impression of a moderate, compromising attitude on my part. In mere months we planned to undo 60 years of rules and reshape the structure, rights, and responsibilities of the cable, satellite, television, and wireless industries. But, as we all told everyone, our plan was to do so with modest steps phased in over time, perfectly predictable, in no way unsettling to the markets.

Commissioner Barrett was a good ally on minority issues and a very able lawyer, but I was concerned that the Republican Congress would promise to persuade the President to reappoint him in return for his allegiance to Commissioners Quello and Chong. (There was no question that the Senate Republicans had at least a veto over the Republican FCC seats). Instead, one prominent Republican Congressman asked Barrett to stay, but he could not deliver the Republican Senate leadership's support. Perhaps Barrett had been too moderate for the Gingrich Congress. In any event, with his term expired, no reappointment in the offing, and the private sector beckoning, Barrett stepped down.

At most, then, I faced a Gang of Two; the pair could not insist on anything and could only block rulemakings. While that tactic had served them in 1995, in 1996 we hoped they would be afraid to disregard the congressional deadlines.

Even as we planned rules mandating that the telephone companies share their networks (as if a championship football team had to lend its stars to the challengers), Blair and I were able to make common cause with the most vociferous critic of intrusive market-opening government rulemaking. Senator John McCain supported our critique of the congressionally mandated gift of airwave spectrum to the broadcasters. The Senator said publicly, "I am completely dismayed about the giveaway aspect of this legislation. One thing I want to make perfectly clear to the American public is that Congress, at the behest of special interest groups, has turned its back on $30 billion of potential revenue which could have been used to fund vital and important programs."

This speech, emanating from hours of discussion between his staff and mine, gave new momentum to our efforts to dismantle the FCC's high-definition television plans. Microsoft, as directed by Bill Gates after our Redmond meeting, supported my argument that the market, and not the

FCC, should decide how to exploit the second channels. In the new law, Congress had predictably ordered us to give the broadcasters the blank channels on the analog television dial—for example, channels 6 and 8 in my hometown, where no over-the-air signal existed—for digital broadcast. But Bob Dole's letter postponing the handout had given us a year for public debate. In that year Microsoft would argue for technological transmission standards that would permit integration between their software and digital broadcast. Even if Gates had thought the spectrum was not wide enough for true broadband delivery over the air, nevertheless the Internet and data compression techniques together promised to make the digital television spectrum a usable over-the-air conduit not just to television receivers but to PCs and hand-held devices. And during the Dole-won year of delay on the giveaway, I could continue to bang on the broadcasters to give back to the country kidvid and free time for political debate, if they were to be given the spectrum for free.

A key to success in public life is to have a great advance man. One of the best was Bryan Gruley of the *Wall Street Journal.* We were at the Artists' Rights Dinner in the ballroom of the Century Plaza Hotel in Los Angeles in February 1996. Many actors and directors were coming to honor one of their own for a lifetime of achievement. Gruley had come with me to do an in-depth interview about the telecommunication law's shift of power into my hands.

We walked into the party like we were walking onto a studio lot. The first star we saw that night was Tom Selleck. He had not successfully made the transition to film after *Magnum, P.I.* Perhaps as a career move, recently he had become a political activist. But he was a Republican. For this reason—and because he had not made it in the movies—the liberal organizers gave him a bad table.

Gruley hurried me past Selleck and into the well of the ballroom. Beefy but light on his feet, Gruley plowed through clutches of unknown long-haired males and undiscovered short-haired females. He steered directly toward the central scrum. A fawning circle stroked the hands, shoulders, and arms, and snapped flashbulbs at the head, of a famous director. I could not see over the grinding shoulders to spot the honoree.

I had been invited, naturally, to be lobbied. The movie artists wanted the FCC to order that all television sets have dimensions in not the traditional three by four ratio but nine by sixteen, which was a much more horizontal shape, like the CinemaScope in a movie theater. The artists sought this government intervention as to the shape of television sets so that the screens would not cut off the action on the edges of their films. The premise of their politics was that the purpose of the FCC was to gratify cinematographers and directors.

Hollywood dislikes government (First Amendment fanfare on the soundtrack) when politicians ask for something that undercuts revenues, like free television time for public debate of political issues, or a promise not to use cigarettes to convey coolness in story lines. When the issue is commercial (directors versus networks; studios against networks), then no one scruples about asking government to regulate to their advantage. That is called pro-business regulation.

The artists' problem with the television screen format did not stem from constitutional concerns about freedom of expression; it was a commercial concern. The studios wanted to sell their product to the television networks for the maximum price. Therefore the studios did not impose on the networks any meaningful constraints on cropping or editing. They even relinquished control over running time (networks wanted the right to speed up videos to maximize ad time). The artists wanted government to intervene on their behalf because each had given away artistic control of their film content as part of the studio's purchase of the product. In short, the artists wanted the government to stop them from selling out—it was classic Hollywood to treat the FCC like a psychiatrist or personal trainer whose job was to curtail the client's bad tendencies.

With the studios and television networks against the artists, the Commission would never even bother to vote on the preposterous proposal that it redesign by rule all television sets to ensure that the complete image from the original movie remained intact. Knowing how hopeless and wrong-headed was the cause espoused by my hosts, I nevertheless enjoyed the star-gazing. Unlike a Washington fete, however, virtually no one recognized me.

"You're the chairman of the FCC," said Bryan as he pushed me forward. "They should learn who you are."

"They think Washington is the state up north where DreamWorks money comes from," I said.

"The FCC controls TV. Directly or indirectly, Hollywood lives off TV. They need to know you're in charge of something that matters to them."

"You're absolutely right, Bryan. Put that in the *Journal* and give them copies."

"Onward," he said, and he thrust me through the crowd just as the featured cinematic auteur was shuffling toward his seat. Surrounding the head table was a group larger in number than the available unassigned seats. Bryan explained to several males in suits that I was important. He persuaded only the raffish Washington lobbyist for the film studios, Jack Valenti, to force an additional chair for me into the charmed circle of the honoree's table.

From my new seat, I could feel the warmth of the glow shining from the star sitting at the next table over. Anxious not to be caught staring at Sharon Stone as if she were, say, an eye doctor's chart, I scanned the rest of her table. James Woods was at her side. He's very witty, they say, and an MIT graduate. Couldn't I be sitting there? James and I could discuss the engineering of the Internet. And Ms. Stone might be interested in the burdens placed on the FCC by the new Telecommunications Act.

When it comes to seating at banquets, the grass is always greener where one is not. With a sigh, I turned to the earringed person on my right. His long black hair streamed down to the shoulders of his velvet-collared black tuxedo jacket. Shrouded in anonymity, I genially asked, "So what brings you here?"

"Her," he said and jerked a thumb toward the winsome girl by his other side. She was unknown to me. She might have been thought to be a child, but in the dry heat and bright light of L.A., the maturation process occurs more rapidly than in the East.

"She?" I asked.

Pitying my ignorance, he said, "She's Marty's daughter."

Marty? A famous television show starring Ernest Borgnine as a Brooklyn butcher? Perhaps not the reference. I looked around the table. Joe Pesci, next to the daughter of "Marty," was wrinkling everything from the musculature of his neck to the scalp above his hairline so as to make maximally vivid his appreciation of the remarks made by the figure on his other side with the fantastically bushy eyebrows: the honored guest of the evening, Martin Scorsese.

I turned to the youth: "You are seeing Marty's daughter?"

"We got engaged today," he said. He turned toward his fiancée. On cue, she turned. They kissed. Not a peck but a cinematic chew. He turned back to me: "I'm on the photography crew on Marty's movie."

As with the English aristocracy of yore, Hollywood romance may have a commercial quality without incurring anyone's disapproval.

"What's the movie?" I asked. "And congratulations."

He shrugged, "It's about the Dalai Lama. Kind of a political story."

"I'm kind of in politics myself," I volunteered. "Communications." I roused no interest.

At the adjacent table on the other side, away from Sharon Stone and James Woods and the surrounding talent, were George Lucas, Steven Spielberg, and Jeffrey Katzenberg. As waiters plucked the remains of the meal from before me, I dashed across the short but great divide between me and that triad of celebrity. I reminded Lucas who I was. He slowly responded to my reintroduction of myself.

"We're going to connect all the classrooms. Just as we discussed at your ranch. It's in the law. We got it in the law. But now we need you to help persuade the commissioners to vote the right way."

Lucas nodded slowly, benignly.

"Let me know if I can help," he said.

"I sure will," I promised, truly.

Hoping that after I left he would explain who I was (if he knew) to Steven and Jeffrey, I returned to a moment of anxiety about whether the coffee was truly decaffeinated, and then abided the actors' beseeching speeches in praise of their potential employer, the great director Scorsese. James Woods won the Kneeling Oscar for Most Obsequious. Then the circulating began en masse. As I set off aimlessly, Gruley happily reappeared.

I thanked my Virgil: "That was a great dinner table."

"Did you get any good quotes?" he asked.

"My job was quotes?"

"For the story. I need a lead."

He looked around, then pointed out Sharon Lawrence, the television wife of Sipowicz on *NYPD Blue*. She was a honey blonde with a breathless purse of lips and eyes as big as floodlights. She glided between tables and chairs in our general direction. Bryan positioned us across her path and called out, "When are you having Sipowicz's baby?"

She giggled. The television pregnancy was plainly an affair of a pillow under the skirt. She was slender as a hope.

"This is Reed Hundt," said Bryan, jerking his thumb at me. "Reed's the chairman of the FCC."

Sharon briefly looked me over. I do not look best in a tux, I think; my

neck is too thin. A thin neck framed by the black and white of a tux sug-
gests a bookish and perhaps bloodless nature. Not fun. Not living large. As
Sharon's gaze raked me, I lowered my chin in the manner instructed by my
Yale Drama School coach.

"Whoa," she said in a soft southern accent. "I know you. My father's
a broadcaster in North Carolina. You're the guy in charge of all this legislation, digitalization, telecommunications thing that's going to change the
world?"

"That's my job," I replied, grinning like a puppet on a stick at the
serendipity that she had grown up in one of our regulated businesses.

"Wow," she said. "That's big." She gently exhaled her sweet breath
around the word "big."

"It's even bigger than she thinks," wrote Gruley in the lead of his
front-page story in the *Journal* on the importance of me. A huge article. A
double entendre of the special Hollywood mixture of crass and grand.
What a swell party it was.

In March I met with the Vice President in his office to discuss our
agenda for the election year. He showed me to the armchair next to him. I
knew I was long past the era of dog food. He no longer had to defend me
against the lobbying pressure of the cable industry. The negativity of the trade
press was beneath his attention, and in the general publications (those read
every day by everyone in political life) I was avoiding violent criticism. Most
important, by transferring power to me the new telecommunications law, by
extension, had empowered him. All to the good, and with good timing, I
thought, for in November he faced the electoral challenge that would determine, among many other things, whether my public service would have a
purpose.

"The new telecommunications law is an amazing accomplishment,"
I began. "I marvel that it was passed. You should feel very good about it."

"You've got quite a responsibility," he said, diffidently.

"More than 80 separate rulemakings," I said. He nodded.

"We won't be upsetting the markets with our interpretation of the
new law," I explained. "The law requires radical reform but it permits us
to do that reform in stages. I don't want to cause immediate upheaval in
any industry."

I knew hundreds of lobbyists would besiege him. He nodded. I was
asking him to discount everything alarming that he would be told about

the implications of our actions. I wanted him to understand that I knew it was an election year. If Bob Dole won in November, the FCC rulemakings, as well as a thousand other actions of this Administration, would be undone. So we might just as well take the constraints of the politics into account. It would be unwise to rattle the business community by shifting value radically and suddenly from one industry to another. If AT&T expected us to write rules that doubled its market capitalization and halved the Bells, we would disappoint them. If the Bells feared that my pro-competition rhetoric translated to a devastating hit to their bottom line, they should relax. I provided no such specifics—did not want to embroil Al in such details—but knew he would understand the general point. My message was no different from what I was already telling the financial community. I wanted to calm investors who might think the new telecommunications law meant the return of the mad bomber of the cable industry.

The social goals of the law were a different matter. There we did not shy from controversy.

"Connecting classrooms is still going to be a huge political fight," I warned.

Indeed, Republican Tom Bliley, chairman of the House Commerce Committee, who had praised the Snowe-Rockefeller program at the Library of Congress, proved to be a vigorous and cunning adversary of the classroom initiative. He had already warned that the FCC's attempts to "read into" the Telecommunications Act would be likely to "stir up a hornet's nest on Capitol Hill, which would not bode well for the agency's future."

"Just tell me what you need," Al said. "For the schoolgirl in Carthage," he added, smiling.

"I will need the White House staff to be cool," I said.

"I'll take care of it," Al said.

I stepped confidently out of the tiny, tidy mansion into March's breezy blowing suspicion of spring. The light green tulip fuses pierced the perfect mulch of the borders, promising exquisite flower beds within the month. I could be confident that if we did the right thing in the right way, the Vice President would make sure that the White House would support and defend us. It is a fine thing, I thought, to have the favor of your king—or your vice-king.

On the other side of the country, in Los Angeles, the winds are blue. When they blow hard, the skies are scrubbed of whites and gray and a brilliant promising cerulean dazzles the cortex. On such a fine day in L.A., joy explodes in the heart. So the Los Angeles County Unified School District superintendent told me on a March Saturday, as we pulled telephone lines in an elementary school in Mar Vista, a low-income community.

"I have never been so optimistic about change," the superintendent said. "In the 30 years I've been in teaching this is the first time big businesses have volunteered to help schools. Not just next door to their plants or headquarters, but all over the district."

This was Net Day 1996, the idea of Eric Schmidt and John Gage of Sun Microsystems. It was a day of metaphor. They were connecting Silicon Valley and classrooms by bringing business volunteers to pull telephone lines into some of the country's worst-performing public schools.

To dramatize the statewide California event, the President and Vice President would pull wire in one city, Commerce Secretary Ron Brown in another, Education Secretary Dick Riley in a third, and I in Los Angeles. In hundreds of schools all told, volunteers would demonstrate the power of the Net to bring people together.

The superintendent held a coil of telephone line. It looks and feels like plastic rope. I stood on a ladder, reaching down for the end extended to me. I fed the line into a hole in the ceiling, where invisible hands dragged it deeper into the inner structure of the old school. Descending the ladder I joined the superintendent in the conference room to await the appearance of the President and the Vice President, via video feed, from a school in Sacramento.

Some think that volunteerism could substitute for adequate national funding to build and operate networks: this is a favorite Republican fantasy. No one disparages charitable impulse, but numerous studies demonstrate that private altruism rarely extends its benefits far outside a set comprising the donors themselves. For the most part, the haves give to other haves—the have-nots depend on government. A politician who insists that charity, especially corporate charity, is a cure for poor public education, lack of health care, or any other inequity in opportunity is just pulling the proverbial lamb's wool over a cruel conscience or, as the case may be, subconscious.

A teacher named Rhonda Toon, a teacher in Barnesville, Georgia, put it plainly in a letter to me: "I hurt when I see the Net Days with technology going out to a school here and a school there. I know we have to start somewhere, but for this technology to reach schools everywhere it has to be affordable. . . . Please, please help us." Toon became a grassroots organizer of support for our rulemaking at the FCC to implement the Snowe-Rockefeller amendment.

The video feed from Sacramento failed. Nevertheless, the national news carried photos of the President and Vice President in shirtsleeves pulling line in a school. Mission accomplished. Getting the votes for the FCC rulemaking was left to be done. Net Day had usefully underscored the importance of our rulemaking.

The new telecommunications law gave the FCC the power to create funding for something. But it provided no guidance as to the size of the funding, where the money should come from, and what it could be used for. We intended to fulfill the President's promise that all classrooms would be connected to the Net by the next century—not a bad fact to remind people of in the presidential election of 2000, I thought. Only about 10 percent of two million classrooms had some communications link, so the scope of our mission was daunting. I told every audience that the FCC should and would raise the money to meet this goal. The more often a prediction is asserted, the better its chance of coming true. But I did not have a reliable majority on this issue for either the joint state and federal board vote, which had to recommend a rule in November 1996, or the FCC vote on the rule itself and other universal service issues in May 1997.

April in Maine is not spring, especially in Bangor, but Karen Kornbluh and I took our chance on the northern weather to win the ally necessary to pass a rule in the joint board and the FCC that would put the Internet in every classroom. It was the same person who had co-authored with Senator Rockefeller the successful amendment in the Senate Commerce Committee. She had been a hero in the legislative fight, but Senators rarely have the time to run campaigns on administrative rulemakings. That was what I needed from Senator Olympia Snowe.

At the door of a Bangor junior high school, Karen and I stood with the school principal, a handful of teachers, and a dozen kids under the shifting layers of clouds that gave deep dimension to the cold sky, and greeted the Senator. Although what I most wanted to do in government depended on this visit, I was disheveled, on edge. Karen and I had gone to the wrong gate at Logan Airport in Boston. Making this discovery in horrible discussion with the indifferent ticket taker, we had run out of the terminal, across the parking lot, and through another terminal—past a rack of huge tangy pretzels, through the pack of squinting limo drivers, each holding a steaming paper cup in one hand and a pastry in the other, beyond the shiftless lobsters waiting in murky water for the first and last flights of their lives. I ran hard and sweated from neck to ankle, but the right plane had left without us. The next jet got us late to Bangor. I feared the ill omen.

The Senator—big smile, firm handshake—was, fortunately, a little later than we were. She had tarried at another meeting with constituents. Grateful for the demands of democracy, I followed her into the school.

The kids welcomed their Senator with low-key Yankee hospitality, but when they showed her the Internet it was as if they were sharing a precious secret. The principal explained that most classes could not explore the Net, because the school was incurring enormous communications bills from the telephone company for the new lines installed to connect the computers. The school district was not rich enough to provide the connections to every classroom without financial help from Washington. The teachers and students were concerned that they would be excluded from the opportunities of the future if technology did not connect them to the outside world.

Afterward, the Senator spoke at a news conference. "The Snowe-Rockefeller Amendment," she said, "grew out of a firm belief that the people of rural America should not be left behind by the telecommunications revolution. This provision will be critical to our state's health care providers, schools, and libraries because it will ensure that they have affordable access to the tremendous information technology of the future."

When the telegraph was invented, Nathaniel Hawthorne wrote that at last Maine and Texas could talk to one another. Henry David Thoreau sniffed that they had nothing to say to each other. But the truly insurmountable barrier between people of different regions proved to be that during the 19th century the telegraph cost a dollar a word to use. Now, 150 years later, the children of Maine and Texas could cheaply talk to one another, pass e-mails in the cyberspace version of notes, and go to the Library of Congress, if the FCC would pass the right rule to connect their classrooms to the Net.

After the school event, Karen explained to the Senator's staff that we lacked a reliable majority in both the joint federal-state board of commissioners and the FCC. She gently broke the news that either the board or the Commission might interpret Snowe-Rockefeller in ways that stripped it of meaning, by limiting either the use or the amount of its funding. Karen said that we wanted Senators Snowe and Rockefeller to lead a fight for ample funding of the construction of broadband networks into every classroom. Senators sometimes called me to express their views on a matter. Al D'Amato, for example, once recited to me a litany of curses and asked whether I would let him repeat them on the radio; this was his way of defending Howard Stern. On occasion, Senators assembled groups of senatorial signatories to letters advocating certain statutory interpretations. But no one could recall a Senator personally leading a lobbying campaign directed at encouraging state and federal commissioners to adopt a particular rulemaking. That is what Senator Snowe agreed to do. Yet even with Snowe and Rockefeller leading a bipartisan campaign, I was not confident we could obtain more than token funding for classroom connections. Certainly the FCC's history of skimpy efforts to create public goods, such as children's television, justified concern.

The upcoming election was also a gate through which the classrooms initiative had to pass. The Republican state and federal commissioners on the joint board were, after all, loyal to their party. If the voters put Dole and the congressional Republicans in charge, then the Republicans would believe the election winners should decide how to apply the telecommunications law. Based on the Gingrich Congress's opposition to a strong FCC and Snowe-Rockefeller, a Republican Commission's rulemaking on opening markets and connecting classrooms probably would be scaled down to near invisibility. Given this possibility, the joint state-federal board would wait to vote on its recommended rule until after the November elections, in order to see who won. In effect, the country was voting in November on whether to promote competition against the Bells and to connect classrooms to the Net.

From Bangor, I went to the city of renewable expectations, Las Vegas, for the National Association of Broadcasters' annual convention in April. My consolation for the predictable unpopularity of my speech (kidvid, digital television auctions) was arrival on Air Force Two with the Vice President. The NAB routinely neglected the usual convention amenities (greeting by a high-ranking association official at the gate, limo, hotel registration completed in advance, big room, fruit basket), but traveling in Al Gore's ten-car motorcade to the hotel would obviate the slights.

On the plane, Al revised the draft of his speech line by line, word by word. He dictated changes to punch up the language advocating serious commitments by broadcasters to serve the public interest. On landing, we raced (the motorcade always moves quickly) to the convention. He did a bang-up job, extracting hearty applause from a reluctant audience.

The day after Al's speech, to a much smaller audience in a dark room marked by a sign that misspelled my name, I told the broadcasters that even though Congress had ordered the FCC to give away the digital television licenses free, I intended to attach strings to the giveaway. I said the new law meant me to do so by its reiteration of the broadcasters' historic duty to use all licenses to "serve the public interest." The audience was as silent as a dark channel.

Next on the convention tour that year was cable, in April, in Los Angeles. Again, I went with the Vice President. In L.A. everyone wants to be someone different tomorrow from who they are today. Lawyers want to be screenwriters, writers want to be actors, actors want to be real people, and all real people just want to put reality behind them—that's why they move to L.A. to begin with. (Another such personality-altering destination is, of course, Washington.) Visiting Los Angeles, Al Gore and his lieutenant at the FCC sought a characteristically Californian fresh start with the cable industry. The new law had let cable out of the Washington regulatory doghouse, and the industry, sprinkled in light of its entrepreneurial history with an unusually large group of Democrats in its high ranks (unlike most established industries), was delighted that the Vice President was there to brag on its prospects.

Our intent was to communicate our great support for cable's investment in renovating its systems. The 1996 law had repealed rate regulation, effective in two years. That topic was behind us. Now cable had to take on the telephone industry. The method in 1996, as opposed to the days of the Bell Atlantic–TCI merger, was to turn the cable pipe into broadband Internet access. Al explained with energy and technical insight the broadband pathways that cable could build to every home in America. He received a standing ovation. The next day they gave me the same enthusiastic response when I explained how intransigent the broadcasters were on children's television and how eagerly the cable industry had supported our effort to connect every classroom. I predicted that the cable industry would vigorously build high-speed Internet connections everywhere in the country—its existing fiber and coaxial cable, after all, already passed 95 percent of all homes.

A few days later, I flew to San Francisco to give a speech to Children Now, a conference of children's advocates. Geraldine Laybourne was the other keynote speaker. She had invented in Nickelodeon a new sensibility toward children. I begged the conference attendees to help us persuade the broadcasters to go along with a rule requiring educational television. The next day, Laybourne told everyone she was going to invent a new kind of children's programming, to prove the impossible was inevitable. But she had no vote at the Commission, and without a rule requiring kidvid, the most creative programmers would not get carriage on television.

On a warm, tulipy May day on Capitol Hill, I had lunch with the tall, handsome member of Congress who I felt would surely support our new democracy initiative. I explained that in return for the huge giveaway of the digital television licenses, we should insist that the broadcasters give up a billion dollars of free air time for political candidates to run ads. The recipient candidates would have to promise not to buy time. But they would then be free from the burden of constant fundraising. I said many candidates, particularly Democrats outgunned by the Republican largesse from business interests, would take this deal.

"One thing that will never happen in my lifetime is free TV time for politicians," said my friend.

"What?" I should not have spoken so sharply; people in public office should be treated with respect, except when talking about them behind their backs.

"None of the members wants free time. Virtually everyone has a safe district. Why would they want their opponents to get the boost of free TV time? Then they might not get so easily re-elected."

"This is depressing," I said.

He explained that most members are afraid of local broadcasters. At first glance, the fear seems groundless. Local television does not run editorials for or against candidates the way local newspapers do. Television networks do not go after a President the way the major newspapers do. No sharp-edged editorial writer sits anchor on the nightly news. The broadcasters do not give huge piles of money to campaigns, like tobacco or health care companies do when they want to stop legislation. But the typical member of Congress is afraid the television station will not put him on the local news. They can make him a non-person. Then he would be no better off than the unknown challenger.

If the member had free advertising time he would be sure to be well known, of course. But then the challenger also would be well known. That,

gressional friend explained, is the opposite of any incumbent's goal.
purpose of television in commerce is to make sure that whatever was
bought yesterday will be bought tomorrow: soap, salsa, software, sneakers.
I was learning that the purpose of television in politics is to make sure that
most seats in Congress do not change hands.

According to the modern politics of money, incumbents benefit from
television's insatiable need for advertising purchases, because access to
money increases the probability of re-election. The traditional saving grace
was famously voiced by California State Treasurer Jesse Unruh, a practi-
tioner of the art of politics in the 1960s: "If you can't drink their booze,
dance with their women, take their money, and still vote against them,
what's the point of getting elected?" But in the 1990s the point of honor—
voting against big donors—was often absent.

Today too many members of Congress vote the way the money wants
instead of the way the people would want. This cannot be easily proved,
but many in politics are convinced this is the truth. Some believe that their
own consciences and the purposes of their contributors are in perfect alignment. Many Republicans, however, know that much of the agenda of their
contributors is not supported by the majority of the country. Without the
money their party raises in vastly greater amounts than Democrats, they
would not be in power. Perhaps they feel this system of financing politics
is meritorious, because they and their contributors know better how to run
the country than the people who would be selected in a less money-directed
process. The representatives of money usually hold this view, in most countries and in most eras.

The lanky, photogenic Congressman stood up and pulled a chicken
salad sandwich from a box brought by an aide. "Lunch," he said. I took a
bag of chips.

"I'm not saying things don't change," he said. "But TV has not
changed politics for the better."

I munched on the greasy, salty Cape Cod potato slices, thinking that
it takes a businessperson of poetic genius to know that the taste of potato
chips evokes Cape Cod. The Congressman continued, "Nowadays it takes
maybe $10 per vote to pay for the TV time you need. And TV time is get-
ting more expensive than ever, if you're trying to reach a mass audience."

"That's because cable channels have attracted many people to narrowly targeted programs. Only very expensive shows like sporting events
can draw big audiences on broadcast TV anymore," I said, showing off a

little learning. "The more expensive the show that attracts a big audience, the more expensive the advertising to that kind of audience."

"So you see why you're wasting your time trying to persuade Congress to order free time. The expense of running a campaign in the TV age benefits incumbents. Besides, voters don't care about money in politics. They care about money in their pocketbooks. That's what you need to worry about."

He was referring to the recent *Washington Post* headline that read, "Phone firms seek higher local rates: average bill would rise $10 a month to subsidize service." The story was about the local phone companies' threat to increase the cost of regular phone service in order to pay for connecting classrooms to the Internet and to offset loss of market share to new entrants. He was telling me that my two primary policy goals at the FCC—connecting classrooms and competition—could hurt the prospects of Democrats to win back the House, or even to hold their current vote count.

Disinclined to take my friend's practical and well-meant advice as the last word, I went to Senator John McCain, co-author of the McCain-Feingold campaign reform bill. I hoped he would believe that requiring the broadcast industry to give back free time for political debate was modest compensation for the digital television spectrum windfall.

I felt that Senator McCain would be indifferent to the fact that we were in opposing parties. Most Americans care little about party label. Inside the Beltway things are different. Yet I believed I could trust John McCain, and that he would be my ally in fighting for free political advertising time on broadcast stations.

I explained that as a matter of law the Commission could interpret the general public interest test of the Telecommunications Act to require each broadcast station to provide free time to candidates for public debate. Earlier in the year, presidential candidates Steve Forbes and Bob Dole had bought so much time for advertising in Iowa that local car dealers could not purchase their routine spots advertising weekend deals. I explained that a candidate accepting free time would have to agree not to buy additional time. In this way we could curtail both campaign fundraising and egregious spending on ads.

McCain told me that he would support my free-time initiative. He seemed, like Olympia Snowe, to be willing to take on the most powerful special interests even in his own party to do the right thing for the country. Moreover, a rulemaking at the FCC on free time would increase pressure on Congress at least to vote on McCain-Feingold. In a fair vote, with public attention to the issue, campaign reform legislation would pass over the opposition of the Republican leadership.

The President cared about campaign reform. His staff did not believe voters cared, and did not want him to spend time on an issue unappealing to voters. Nevertheless, he agreed to announce his support for an FCC rule ordering broadcasters to grant a billion dollars' worth of free time to candidates. The Vice President had long supported free time. The billion dollars was less than three percent of the industry's advertising revenue, but enough to liberate campaigns from the money chase.

A few independent groups of broadcasters like A. H. Belo Corporation in Dallas publicly agreed with us. Barry Diller, as always, was willing to stand up against the NAB. He told me that the campaign system was evil and that he would join us in trying to fix it. I called Rupert Murdoch, and he said that the United States was the only country that did not provide ample opportunity for political debate on broadcast television. He also would publicly support our free-time initiative.

The President, John McCain, Barry Diller, and I held a press conference announcing the President's support for the FCC's proposed rule ordering broadcasters to donate free time. At a subsequent FCC hearing, Murdoch and Bill Bradley joined the alliance.

After the FCC hearing, McCain asked me, "Do you know who was the toughest adversary I ever faced?" His eyes were gleaming as he lifted his eyebrows and cocked his jaw at me. I was sure he was about to say the North Vietnamese. Not for the last time, he surprised me. "The toughest adversary I ever faced was the networks," he said. "They're the toughest."

We then won still another ally. Paul Taylor, a *Washington Post* reporter and friend from college, had returned from the lengthy and harrowing assignment of covering Nelson Mandela's peaceful revolution in South Africa. The history of a people is shaped by the three great modern forces— technology, economics, and politics—but the history of a life is how by luck, skill, and pluck you negotiate these currents. Taylor had been shot and seriously wounded, but he recovered, and chronicled brilliantly the reversal of centuries of history. Now he had decided to be a revolutionary in his own way in his home country. He quit the *Post* and obtained a grant from the admirable Pew Foundation to work on fixing campaigns in the television age. With wonderful Walter Cronkite, he was assembling a coalition called Free TV for Straight Talk.

Taylor thought no candidate should be able to use the free time unless willing to go on television in person, as opposed to using the time for
attack ads. Taylor understood that no technologies are value-neutral; all
technologies advance some human behaviors and deter others. For example, political advertising on television discourages consensus building and
reduces voter turnout. After the typical campaign air war of attack advertising, the uncommitted do not want to vote for any candidate. Taylor
wanted to make elections positive experiences in democracy. Candidates,
and not their advertisements, should address voters on television. My mission was to win the free time for such straightforward campaigning.

Relying on the support of the White House and John McCain, I
pressed the issue in public and in private meetings with broadcasters, who
were obliged to visit in order to lobby for the rulemaking that effected the
giveaway of the digital television spectrum. Although the law did not permit the FCC to auction the digital licenses or give them to anyone but the
broadcasters, I implied that I would not permit the handover until I got
what I wanted on transmission standards (I preferred to reject the transmission specifications made by the television manufacturer–broadcast alliance, on the ground that they were compatible with TVs, but not PCs)
and the public interest (kidvid and free time).

Republican Congressman Jack Fields questioned my motives on kidvid, classroom connections, and free time. He told the trade press, "Chairman Hundt takes a great deal of direction from the White House and most
of that is in the direction of social engineering. The White House wants to
use the FCC for policies it cannot pass through Congress." But with the
support of McCain, I was sure we could force the Republican Congress to
reform even the campaign finance system that benefited them so greatly.

Ten Help!

June 1996 – October 1996

Liberty and monopoly cannot live together.

Henry Demarest Lloyd, Wealth against Commonwealth

The aggregation of large fortunes is not at all a thing to be regretted. On the contrary, it is a necessary condition of many forms of social advance.

William Graham Sumner, What Social Classes Owe Each Other

Sandwiched among the meetings with staff and business leaders were weekly trips on my public campaign for children's television, free time, and connecting classrooms. In San Francisco and Atlanta, Los Angeles and Chicago, and all the other major cities of the country's different regions, my staff found an audience for a speech, orchestrated meetings with information sector business executives, sent me to newspaper editorial boards in search of positive editorials. Good articles we blitz-faxed to the relevant Congressmen and Senators for the specific city. By covering the country, we were able to cover the Congress. On most trips I phoned reports from the road to the Washington trade press. I had to feed the beast. They would write every day, and if I did not give them material, someone else's (critical) commentary would fill their pages. I was convincing them that I had a winning message. Eventually, we persuaded the trades to follow my travels the way the major press follows the big cheeses of an Administration. Publicity precedes persuasion. The other commissioners and congressional staffs read these stories as if they were box scores from a rival team's road trip.

I had two themes: private competition to drive investment in the communications revolution, and public benefits to come from the revolu-

176

tion. On competition, I had two sub-themes: clear, enforceable rules opening monopolized markets to entrepreneurs, and the elimination of regulation where competition existed. We focused on a trio of public benefits: kidvid, free time, and connecting classrooms. These were public goods and social investments that most Americans felt needed doing and that the allocative efficiencies of capitalism would not widely distribute. We did not dwell on consumer protection. In a competitive market it is the competition that protects consumers.

Our message struck some as government activism. Others decried new entitlements. But we believed we had synthesized good economics and fairness. Ultimately results—real investment and real benefits—would affirm or discredit our agenda.

As our teams worked round the clock on the rules implementing the new telecommunications law, we became increasingly aware that under the new law the FCC inevitably would tilt the potential to create value toward or away from the incumbent industries that the FCC had traditionally nurtured—the telephone, cable, broadcast, satellite, and cellular oligopolies. We might write the rules to encourage only a trickle of entrepreneurship, minimally eroding the market capitalization of the incumbent firms. Or we might craft the rules so as to cause a flood of new investment and innovation that would wash away the advantages of the incumbents—and erode their market capitalization. It was an unavoidable choice. No truly neutral option existed. The new telecommunications law could have been interpreted in any way: for or against existing monopolies, for or against innovation and investment.

One southern Senator asked me, "How'd you like that Telecom Act?"

"I've studied it a lot," I said.

"Then you know we put everything in there. Then we put its opposite in." And he laughed, slapped me on the shoulder, and walked away, still chuckling.

Even determining how to write the rules in accordance with our own intent was unimaginably difficult. Nothing in the law or the record provided all the details necessary for such exact rulemaking. Our team had to understand every piece of the world's most complex engineering system: the United States telephone network. (Our economists created a statistical model of the economics of telephony, and posted it on the Internet as an aid to rational discourse.) Other teams were obliged to rewrite the rules governing the wireless, cable, and satellite industries. And in still another room, Blair and Julius led the team that rewrote the rules for digital television.

During our deliberations, the captains of the communications industries paid their visits: Bernie Ebbers, the bearded rebel from Mississippi who was building the phone company he ambitiously called WorldCom, wanted cheap access to the local loop for Internet communications. The Bell CEOs pushed us to let them enter quickly the long distance market from which they had been barred by the now defunct Justice Department order that had broken up AT&T in 1984. The heads of AT&T and MCI, outgunned in Congress, asked us to write rules that gave them a chance to enter the local markets before the Bells came after their long distance business.

Unlike the cable regulation experience, I aspired to tell each businessperson what we were thinking, and I asked for their reactions. I convened a private sector group (one representative from each of long distance, local telephony, cable, and wireless) to meet with the heads of the Commission bureaus and other key staff. We asked the group to agree on the rules they wanted to see from us. The company representatives debated in good form, but concluded that we should raise local telephone rates to all consumers. If the consumers paid more, then new entrants and incumbents could make more money.

We rejected this unpalatable proposal. Consumers should pay more for communications if they wanted to buy new products and services that competition and innovation would generate. That is indeed what happened. But at the time we had no idea that the Internet would be the cornucopia of these new consumer goods—from on-line stock trading to high-speed streaming video.

Blair and I had preached that the FCC staff should never give us political advice. I said I only wanted to know the right thing to do. Now they were giving me what I asked for, testing whether I could translate my rhetoric into reality.

The staff wanted me to adopt rules encouraging cheap, efficient entry into the local telephone markets. Specifically, they wanted the interconnection order to give new entrants the right to share and connect to any piece of the existing network at very low prices—essentially the prices that the existing telephone companies charged themselves for using their own networks. This approach would permit the most efficient firms to prevail in competition (fairness for economists), and, by the way, would kick off an investment boom. They acknowledged also a risk that promotion of new entry would cause the stock market to sell off the Bell stocks, bring the Dow crashing down, shake consumer confidence, and even threaten the President's re-election (not concerns for economists).

To protect against the downside, I tried to persuade Wall Street analysts that we would act prudently—so, they should not short Bell stocks. Our approach would require incumbents to share the use of their networks at, in effect, fair wholesale prices to their new rivals. The effects on retail prices would develop slowly over time, as the new entrants built their own networks to connect to the existing networks. The new construction would exploit new, cheaper technologies, and gradually retail prices would drop. But the short-term effect on the telephone companies' revenues, unlike in the case of the cable rules, would be minimal.

We had decided to reject the long distance companies' petition to reduce radically the access charges imposed by local telephone companies for long distance traffic. Nor would we order local telephone companies to provide service at very low wholesale prices to their rivals. These measures would have hurt the existing telephone companies immediately. By contrast, over the long term, our interconnection rules would enable new competitive phone companies to build a network of competing but connecting networks. Competition would force the Bell companies' networks to become part of this new, constantly evolving, technologically innovative system. Most of this plan we did not explain because no one asked. Indeed, in a hearing, one Republican Congressman told me that the market reaction to our rules was irrelevant. He would not have held this view if analysts had sold off Bell stocks because of our policies. But Bell stocks rose during our deliberations.

To the editorial boards of *Barron's*, the *Wall Street Journal*, the *New York Times*, *Fortune*, *Forbes*, I argued that our rules would spur economic growth, create competition, and lead to deregulation. I was concerned about rapid consolidation of the radio industry and mergers among the Bells. But I firmly believed sheer bigness was not bad, as long as our rules let new entrants challenge incumbents through innovative business plans and new technologies. We even persuaded the *Journal* to editorialize in support of our auction philosophy (auction everything, from digital television licenses to satellite slots to phone numbers!)—although the paper would later turn its op-ed page over to the Bell company attacks on us. For the right wing, pro-entrepreneurial government action is much worse than no government at all.

The majority of Congress, and certainly of the House and Senate Commerce Committees, strongly favored the Bell companies' interpretations of the law. To pressure us into reading the law against new entrants and entrepreneurs, the House held hearings in which the members lectured us on how they wanted us to interpret the law. Some members read their statements directly from papers written by lobbyists. Many echoed the Bell company refrain that our pro-competition policies would force the Bells to raise local residential rates. Unless we let the local telephone companies charge high prices to entrepreneurs who wanted to share or connect to their facilities, they said, the companies would raise local rates.

All the members knew that local rates were regulated by state commissioners, but they wanted us to discourage new entry in order to maintain the monopolists' revenues. The local regulators could continue to keep residential rates low and business-line prices high. This historic deal (where businesses paid more for communications services than they would in a competitive market) discouraged investment in the new technologies, such as data networks, that the businesses wanted to buy. The irony was that the Bells and their congressional allies in effect wanted the FCC to apply Cable Act–style rate regulation, while I preferred a deregulatory, pro-business-customer attitude toward the law. I was convinced that we would produce more benefits for consumers by giving them a choice of suppliers than by regulating retail prices.

The unforeseen effects of the Internet created far more options than communications has ever before provided. Not only can consumers choose among wireless companies or Internet access providers. Now they have new choices for everything under the sun: all the books in the world (Amazon.com), any kind of used car (autobytel.com), millions of flea market items (eBay). We adopted policies that opened the local market to different vendors of telephone service, and discovered to our happy surprise that the most aggressive users of the new rules were a class of company almost invisible in the legislative debate: Internet service providers and builders of data networks. These firms built the physical links of the Web and enabled the e-commerce that is revolutionizing sales and marketing. This was luck that perhaps we deserved from the pro-competitive approach that we firmly espoused.

A few congressional allies supported our aggressive pro-competition view of the law. Most valiant was Ed Markey, who used every hearing of the House Telecommunications Subcommittee to urge that the FCC should aggressively open all closed markets. Without him, the subcommittee might have more vigorously worked against our choices, and galvanized the Gang of Two against my staff's recommendations. On the Senate side, Fritz Hollings was our best champion on the competition issues.

Notwithstanding the economic importance of reshaping communications markets, the public was much more interested in our continuing focus on television issues—children's television, free time, and the digital license giveaway. The purpose of commercial television is to make shows popular with a broad audience, to collect an audience for the purpose of advertising to it. Advertisers pay more for access to a big audience. Our educational television proposal required stations to broadcast three hours a week of shows that might catch the imagination of children, might teach them, or at least would try to do so. By definition the audiences for these shows would be much smaller than those for adult programs. (Or, as Blair used to say, shorter, given that they are kids.) Therefore, advertising support would be far less.

I argued that a show of creative genius, if given a chance by our rules, could destroy the assumptions of broadcasting. *Sesame Street* was the quintessential example. By appealing to the power of inspiration, I hoped to win the support of the creative community, which was traditionally leery of any government rulemaking that affected content, and hence was usually an ally on the left to the right-leaning NAB's opposition to public interest regulation.

The NAB lobbyists, however, still believed that because I could not "count to three," my kidvid and free-time efforts were futile. Even after Andrew Barrett retired from the Commission, the broadcasting lobbyists were smugly sure that I could pass no rule to require kidvid, much less free time or digital television auctions. But our kidvid campaign was directed at public opinion, not at Commissioners Quello and Chong. I believed we were helping the President and Vice President win re-election, and we were persuading Congressmen to help themselves at the ballot box by urging the NAB to compromise. In any event, following our tactic of strategic intransigence in 1996, I generally refused to compromise any issue with my fellow commissioners. When we addressed, for example, even insignificant spectrum licensing issues, I insisted on auctions against the inclinations of

Commissioner Chong and occasionally Quello. Where we made exceptions to this style, we shielded our conciliatory steps with strong rhetoric. Every result we claimed as total victory—precisely the opposite of the FCC tradition celebrating consensus and compromise.

As the FCC progressed in the announced sequence of more than a hundred different acts of adjudication and rulemaking, I publicly praised the other commissioners for speedy implementation of the new law. But if a commissioner caviled at some part of a proposed rule, my office complained to the interested parties and to the press that the congressional intent to move quickly was imperiled by the commissioner's indecisiveness. In private our team might not be able to reason successfully with my fellow commissioners, but in public debate we would prevail on any issue because we had more horsepower to think through and argue about the issues. Moreover, we believed our positions were right, and were willing to submit to the judgment of popular opinion.

Our continuous advocacy of the broadcast issues also sapped the resources of Commissioners Chong and Quello. Moreover, although neither had an abiding incentive to agree with me on the Telecommunications Act rulemakings, the complexity of the FCC's tasks overwhelmed them. My teams amounted to more than a hundred people; the commissioners had only three on their personal staffs.

In response to our pressure, the other commissioners told anyone who would listen that I was arrogant, imperious, stubborn, self-righteous, deceitful. They tried numerous forms of embarrassment, ranging from leaking confidential documents to (my favorite) drawing a caricature of me on a wall.

The truth is that everyone wants to be liked, even a chairman. I told the press I had taken John Dingell's advice and grown thick skin. It was not true, but our strategy required this response. Paradoxically, when the other commissioners read about my indifference to them in the press, they became more convinced that they were obliged to give in to me.

The Commission never would have mastered the economics, law, and philosophy necessary for our work but for the brilliant team Blair and I had assembled—Berkeley economist Joe Farrell, general counsel Bill Kennard, deputy general counsel Chris Wright, bureau chiefs and deputy chiefs Gina Keeney, Richard Metzger, Larry Atlas, Don Gips, Meredith Jones, Michelle Farquhar, office heads and deputies Bob Pepper, Elliot Maxwell, and my own personal staff—Julius Genachowski, Ruth Milkman, Mary Beth Richards, Tom Boasberg, Greg Rosston, Jackie Chorney, John Nakahata. Senator Joe Lieberman, my mentor and friend, told me that I had the finest team in public service since the New Deal, although, he added, he was not really old enough to know for sure.

But our most difficult political challenge remained the rule putting every classroom on the information highway. The first step was persuading the joint board of state and FCC commissioners to recommend the rule in November 1996. The second would be a vote on the rule by the full FCC in May 1997.

Part of the challenge was to explain why communications technology belonged in classrooms. Unconnected computers had been in many classrooms for years. They had accomplished little, cost a lot to maintain, and did not capture or inspire imagination. Computers in closets were evidence to support the argument of Republicans that teachers, not tools, were the problem in education, that public schools wasted money on technology (and everything else) and that privatizing public education through vouchers was the only solution to declining performance.

To respond, I had to explain the Internet. To explain things they do not really understand, lawyers resort to analogy. I said the Internet looks like a plate of spaghetti, behaves like trains in a switch yard, and spreads like kudzu vine. I said it changes everything. In the words of Jimi Hendrix, a six becomes nine and I don't mind.

Having gotten attention with this opening, I then would note the way the Net had changed the Commission. I had unplugged the Commission's 25-year-old mainframe Honeywell in 1995. Our decisions and speeches were on the World Wide Web. By e-mail, anyone could praise or complain directly. Because of the Web, no lawyers and no lobbyists would stand between us and the people. If all that could happen in government, imagine the reforms in education that the Internet could cause.

The right wing's most insidious argument was that the Internet gave children access to pornography. Trying to ban pornography on the Net was like trying to keep handwriting off bathroom walls. But the right wing's greatest challenge in trying to paint Democrats as pro-pornography was that the Administration and the Commission in still another rulemaking would assure the installation of the V-chip in TVs and PCs, so that parents could filter violent and pornographic imagery from the material available to their children. Fighting bad technology with good technology proved again the usefulness of an active government.

A friendly Republican Congressman told me that Congress would never appropriate the funds to put the Net in every classroom, so in his view, our rule should order the communications industry to pay for the networks. The money would come from the industry, but would go back to it through competitively awarded contracts supplemented by local and state matching funds. The plan was unprecedented, elegant, and very large. Based on a McKinsey and Company consulting study by the brilliant Peter Bisson, the total cost would exceed $10 billion over five years—the largest national effort for K–12 education in the country's history.

Most Republicans in Congress, however, held to the line that the federal government had no concern with local education. They wanted the joint board and the Commission to give scant effect at most to the Snowe-Rockefeller provision in the telecommunications law. In the face of congressional opposition, to win the votes at the joint board in November and the FCC in May 1997, I needed not just arguments but a skilled lobbyist as well.

A friend directed me to Ira Fishman, a member of the President's Whitewater defense team. Ira explained that he had promised his wife he would return to his law practice and spend time with his children. I asked for a year. I told him he would be famous. He said he did not want to be famous, but he gave me the year anyway. He refused a title, took a tiny windowless office deep inside the maze of the building, befriended the other commissioners' staffers, and refused in all respects to take my tactical advice.

Our lawyers understood that the hastily written language of the Snowe-Rockefeller provision, and the accompanying congressional report, was ambiguous—at least in the view of lawyers, for whom anything is of debatable meaning. Various companies, led by the Bells, were quietly working against the Clinton-Gore goal of linking all classrooms. Their lawyers and lobbyists told the state and FCC commissioners that Congress had not commanded them to create a fund for connecting all classrooms. Indeed, they argued, the FCC was not truly obliged to provide the money at any particular time. Nor could it provide for building networks in classrooms.

To persuade the state and federal commissioners otherwise, I wanted public controversy. I wanted editorial boards and community leaders to verbally bludgeon the joint board. I proposed that we woo them privately and pound them publicly. Ira did not agree. He intended to encourage gentle but insistent inside-the-Beltway lobbying of the joint board and the commissioners by education groups, Education Secretary Riley, and friendly Congressmen, and especially Senators Rockefeller and Snowe.

The teachers' associations and other education groups had never before played a role in the Federal Communications Commission's processes. Ira, Karen, and Rockefeller's staff sparked the creation of a lobbying group—EdLink—dedicated to our cause. Led by Anne Bryant, the group commanded the appearance of power: millions of members of the PTAs and two million teachers in the teachers' unions were nominally part of EdLink. This new lobbying group was intent on creating a multibillion-dollar national spending program through the traditional Washington way of persuading lawmakers and regulation writers.

At my request, Bill Gates visited me at the Commission to discuss technology in classrooms. His handlers whisked him in quietly, seeking near anonymity for the richest man in the world. I thought it was wonderful that he visited. In fairness, the folks in the office were more excited when Quincy Jones came to seek extra broadcasting licenses. For that matter, Oral Roberts's visit sparked as much interest when he came to plead for a grant of a national religious television network to battle the devil loose in our country. Clint Eastwood, who rendered everyone the most starstruck, also visited, but only to ask me for a radio station license in Carmel. He suggested that I come out to Pebble Beach to inquire into the matter. "Bring your sticks and we'll play a round," Dirty Harry said. I did not grant any of these licenses, but the pleasure of being charmed by celebrities made me long, momentarily, for the pre-auction era when the FCC chairman could gratify the great with giveaways of public property. Gates, on the other hand, I had asked over to hit up for money.

Gates was undoubtedly the most powerful and famous private sector person ever to meet with an FCC chairman. His personal fortune was approximately equal to the total net worth of the lower-income half of all America: 125 million Americans in the aggregate were less wealthy than Bill Gates alone. With continued growth in our economy, Gates will be a trillionaire in his lifetime, as will at least two of his past and present colleagues. (Instead of suing him, the Department of Justice should have negotiated the terms of his will.)

Not only Gates's wealth, but also our country's, is more likely to grow if we improve average education levels. Somehow education creates wealth: an unvarying correlation in economic statistics is that more educated workers are paid more than less educated workers. Every year our information economy generates several thousand new job classifications, but many require more education than the average level found in today's workforce. Technology in every classroom from kindergarten through 12th grade is one of the prerequisites of preparation for success in the 21st-century economy.

My goal was to convince Gates to use his immense eleemosynary capability to stimulate widespread increases in education levels, and to help me win the votes for the right Snowe-Rockefeller rule. Gates asked me how I was going to pay for connecting classrooms to the Internet. I explained that, if I could get the votes from the state commissioners and the FCC, our rule would collect the money from communications companies.

"It's the only way to get the connections paid for," I said to Gates. "Otherwise, while rich school districts and private schools will buy the networks and computers, the public schools generally will lag behind. The result inevitably would be an increasing gap between the rich and the non-rich in our country. But there's a problem," I continued. "Snowe-Rockefeller will pay the cost of connections, but schools don't know what to do with the connections. The money could be wasted."

Gates began to rock gently, a sign that he was interested.

"You could create a foundation that will teach the teachers," I said. "Call it the Guide on the Side Foundation. You could have teams that work with schools to decide what software they need, what teaching programs they should install, how to link parents and teachers, how to download sophisticated tests. You could change the face of education."

I said that a high-speed data network should tie all classroom PCs together. We did not want schools to spend money on out-of-date solutions. But the national government could not teach all 100,000 elementary and secondary schools how to use technology for two reasons. One, the Republican Congress routinely opposed national programs to bolster education. They said education should be a local function, even though on the local level conservative Republicans typically voted to limit spending on public schools. Two, in the absence of a long-term agreement on how to fund Social Security, Medicaid, and Medicare, neither the Administration nor Congress would propose significant spending on any new initiatives.

He nodded. The Internet changes everything. He had seen that. He had reinvented his company from selling self-contained worlds to purveying tickets to the Net. He took it as a given that the Net would change schools. He had already written that in his book!

Gates said that he agreed with my goals. He had created a foundation to focus on education. But he received innumerable requests for money. He did not have time to sort them out. Most he simply rejected. He would probably join Warren Buffett in leaving money after his death for population control efforts. But I had made a very intriguing suggestion, he said. He promised to think hard about the idea of the technological advisory foundation.

As Gates talked, his voice rose in pitch like an engine getting revved up. He looked into space as if listening to his own words. He was thinking out loud, about time and technology. By contrast, when some public figures talk they are on mental cruise control, quoting themselves without attribution. The small jokes and polished phrases are off the shelf of the gift shop of gab that the speaker owns.

John D. Rockefeller considered himself a steward of God-given wealth. But in his time government spending was much smaller, and private charity relatively more important. Now, many think the government has taken the responsibility for most large social problems. The fortunes of the new cyber-rich are so great, however, that we could be entering a new era of smaller government and greater world-changing private philanthropy. Some among the new rich disclaim such responsibility. The prospect of inheritance taxes forces them to create charitable trusts—like it or not—but often, after they are in the grave, they leave to the anonymous officers of these eponymous non-profits the problem of determining how to spend the wealth. They rarely put the creative sparks that created their fortunes to the tinder of noncommercial activities.

But Bill Gates—self-taught, self-defined, forward looking—will be able to make a mark on the country in his lifetime not just from commercial success but by creating public benefits on the scale of his wealth creation. I thought Gates's gift of technological advice, if he made it, would be the strongest possible endorsement for technology in education. It would also help me get the votes for the program. With his support, we would force the state commissioners to pass the right recommendation and make the FCC commissioners vote it into a new rule.

Looking for public officials who would help jawbone the state commissioners, I went to Omaha, on the edge of the Great Plains, to speak to the Western Governors Association. I said the classroom initiative could mean hundreds of millions of dollars for the school districts in their states. They needed only to urge the utility commissioners in their states to inform the members of the joint federal-state board, and FCC Commissioners Chong and Quello, that they should vote to connect every classroom to the Internet. Most of the governors and state regulators were Republicans. They could be very persuasive with the Republican members of the joint board and with the FCC commissioners. But the governors shrugged their collective shoulders. As Republicans, they appeared uninterested in a national program that inured to the credit of Clinton-Gore.

Indeed, one Republican governor from the West later called me to explain that he used convicts in state prisons to pull telephone lines into classrooms. No federal funding was necessary. I did not have the heart to tell him that the construction of a modern data and voice network required skill and training. I was tempted to ask if the parents or the unions had expressed any concerns about the types of crimes committed by this curious scab labor that would be working in the schools. But I decided to let the moment pass.

While in Omaha, I visited Warren Buffett. Bill Gates and he took long train trips together, a sure sign of friendship. I wanted Buffett to talk to Gates about the foundation that would advise schools on how to install a communications revolution in their classrooms.

Buffett chuckled and smiled when he welcomed me, as if technology amused him. Unpretentious paneling, wall-to-wall shag rug, old chairs—Buffett's office was the downstairs den my father built in our house in the 1950s.

"What brings you out?" he asked.

I explained I was pitching the western governors to support the connecting of classrooms to the Internet.

"That Internet is fantastic," Buffett said. "Use it all the time. Play bridge with my sister on it. She's in California. Foursome all over the country."

The richest man of his generation was riding the information highway to a bridge party in cyberspace. Communications produced a wonderfully benign revolution.

Buffett continued, "Of course, I never invest in technology. Know nothing about it." I thought that he had done quite well enough in any event. Then I explained what I had asked Gates to do. I asked Buffett if he would help me persuade his young friend. Since I was there, I also asked if he would support my rulemaking on free time for political debate. I knew he had joined a group of prominent business leaders who were lobbying for campaign finance reform. Buffett explained that his group would follow John McCain's lead.

"Next time you come out," said Buffett cheerily, "let me know in advance and we'll have a steak."

A steak invite from Warren Buffett, a foundation pitched to Bill Gates. I was playing the outside game at a high level. But I had failed to make a winning bid with Buffett. He would throw himself behind the free-time cause if John McCain led the business group in my direction.

Meanwhile, Ira Fishman stayed inside the Beltway and worked with the teachers' unions and the staffers of Senators Snowe and Rockefeller. When I returned, Ira took me to see another group of Senators, led by Jim Jeffords, Republican of Vermont, who were advocates of national efforts to reform education. Following Senator Jeffords, they joined the Snowe-Rockefeller lobbying effort. The problem, as I saw it, was that outside Washington the interest in policy issues was thin, on the level of a hobby, less passionately pursued than, say, bridge on the Internet. Or it was eccentric, as with the view that the incarcerated population of a state could substitute for the Communications Workers of America. Washington was playing a key role in shaping the information age, but that news did not reach outside Washington.

In July, as the Republicans gathered in San Diego for their national presidential nominating convention, Commissioner Quello unintentionally weakened the NAB position on kidvid by exposing it to ridicule. He explained in a speech that Blockbuster Video carried so many educational videotapes that our rule requiring broadcasters to show kidvid was unnecessary. Within hours, our staff had told reporters that Quello's view amounted to "Let them eat videotape."

Bigger issues than children's television were on the agenda in San Diego, but everything in politics relates to everything else. Politically astute Republicans liked Elizabeth Dole's walk through the convention hall, but they did not get joy from the kidvid issue. It made them look stingy and uncaring. Meanwhile, congressional Democrats enjoyed the issue's concrete definition. Our side wanted one half hour per day of decent kids' shows from each television station. The Republicans wanted none. Polls showed our position had overwhelming popular support. Moreover, the difference between the parties on this issue also reinforced the impression left by the winter government shutdown that Republicans were mean spirited.

Congressman Ed Markey gathered signatures from a majority of the House of Representatives supporting a three-hour minimum requirement. Some Republican Congressmen in swing districts signed Markey's letter. The letter was the first time that a majority of the House of Representatives supported a specific, quantified requirement of the broadcasters' public interest obligation. Congress had validated the new constitutional theory of broadcast regulation that our team had articulated the previous year.

As the Democratic National Convention approached in August, the NAB and its Republican political allies worried that they were giving too delectable an issue to the White House. The NAB had no wish to see a Democratic President re-elected or, worse, a Democratic House returned to power. The children's television debate was becoming a national issue, and it was at least one of a range of reasons why an undecided voter would go Democratic. The broadcasters had not lost at the Commission, but they—thanks primarily to the White House and Ed Markey—had been defeated in the court of public opinion.

The broadcasters passed the word to Jim Quello. He was supposed to take a fall. After 20 years of combat against an effective children's television rule, he would have to reverse his vote. It was a bitter time, but he was loyal to his people. He told the Associated Press, "I'm saying for the first time, three hours a week is a reasonable amount."

Commissioner Chong required more time to cope with the NAB's change of mind. Indeed, she caused so much difficulty in the negotiation of the rule that an NAB lobbyist told Blair that the organization could count only on us to write a sound rule. As a moderating influence, we relied on Ralph Gabbard, president of the NAB Television Board and a Kentucky broadcaster who had long favored a compromise. Gabbard made public a letter drafted by him, Blair, and Julius that set out the terms of a reasonable children's television rule.

Children's advocate Peggy Charren called the agreement on the rule "a big victory for families and children in America." She said in the *Washington Post*, "It's nice to see that the democratic process works. You just need persistence and hope that you don't die during the process." She richly deserved the Medal of Freedom the President later gave her.

We orchestrated with Al's staff a summit on kids' television at the White House for Monday, July 30. We would get national television coverage for our triumph. At the White House, Bill Cosby, Barry Diller, and many other icons of television said actors should work kids' shows for scale, suggested an Emmy for educational programming, and praised the networks and the affiliates for agreeing to help educate kids. According to the mores of Washington, the victors praised the vanquished. Gloating does not win votes, and regulation was a disfavored word in the semantics of New Democrats. But the victory added to my team's power to persuade the other commissioners to go along with all the rulemakings required by the new law. Political success breeds more political success.

On the campus of Stanford University a few weeks later, the eucalyptus drooped in the blazing sun. In the classroom where I was to give my pitch, the dust in the air glittered like the welding points on a microchip. Tom Campbell, a Republican Congressman from California and a professor at Stanford, had invited me to speak with the angels of the New Economy—Lew Platt of Hewlett-Packard, Scott McNealy of Sun Microsystems, Jerry Yang of Yahoo! and others—to persuade them to lobby for the rule funding networks into every classroom in America.

I told the business leaders that their great powers could change humanity's future. They unfolded and folded their wings, and nodded in agreement. They knew that the personal computer was always a communications device. The more robust and extensive were the networks (more bandwidth and more lines to more places), then the more PCs and more software would be sold.

I said the new Telecommunications Act had given the FCC the hardest non-wartime job ever given to one administrative agency and that we needed their help. But the new law's most exciting feature, I said to the business leaders, was that Congress had given us the power to pay for connecting networks to every classroom, every library, and every health care clinic in the country. I praised the work they were doing in Silicon Valley to revolutionize education. The executives had created a foundation called Smart Valley, Inc., that was using technology to revamp public school education there.

I explained that unfortunately Smart Valley depended on local wealth and expertise that did not exist in most of the country. The Smart Valley businesses were not headquartered in Maine or West Virginia. That was why Senators Snowe and Rockefeller had attached their amendment to the telecommunications law; they wanted all schools to be in smart valleys.

Lew Platt, CEO of Hewlett-Packard, the original billionaire-creating success story of the Valley, explained that the Smart Valley initiative showed what corporations could do to benefit public schools. I said these corporations could make a still bigger contribution if they lobbied for the rule I wanted.

Scott McNealy, CEO of Sun Microsystems, said that there was no point in giving schools technology until they changed their curriculums. I replied that I could not change what school districts decide to teach. But I could build networks to every child and teacher in the country. If we built it, wouldn't curriculum change come?

McNealy pointed out that the Valley had provided the workers and corporate sponsorship for Net Day. Sun had led the volunteer initiative. More than 10 percent of the classrooms in California were connected to communications because of Net Day. I agreed that the Net Day event was tremendous. But even if Net Day volunteers were everywhere, schools needed money to complete and to operate the new data networks. The right FCC rule would fund modern Internet Protocol data networks and the continuing maintenance and use of such networks. The program would cost billions of dollars, according to the McKinsey and Company study.

Jerry Yang, a founder of Yahoo! had become a billionaire before he was 30. He embraced our idea: "We should do this. Our future customers will come from these classrooms. We want everyone on the Web." I had no argument with that view. But what followed?

Although the angels did not oppose my proposed rulemaking, they did not offer to help. Their corporations were generous to their local communities. But business does not traditionally lobby for good causes in legislatures or in administrative agencies. The CEOs correctly believe their shareholders expect management to focus only on political issues that directly relate to the corporation's performance. Leaving the Stanford campus, I felt that the promise of the meeting had evaporated in the hot dry California afternoon.

Ira Fishman stuck to his inside-the-Beltway advocacy with the education organizations and the Senate staff members. The education associations and the Senate staffers began discussions with the telephone companies about the funding mechanism. I asked Ira if I should abandon my cross-country campaign. He said that the purpose of my public advocacy was to neutralize our possible congressional opponents, who read local newspapers, and to convince the commissioners, who read all press. In information politics, such intangibles matter. So, I kept on going. I would stick with my message until absolutely no one would pay attention anymore, or until we won.

Shortly after returning from Stanford, in the beginning of August, it was time to unveil our most important economic decision under the new telecommunications law—the interconnection order. The initial reaction to the order was very positive. Merrill Lynch reported to investors that the interconnection order had "smoothed the way for local market competition." Morgan Stanley called it "evenhanded." CS First Boston said the ruling "hits the mark."

However, the incumbent telephone companies and their congressional friends were appalled, in particular by our imposition on the states of a method of calculating the price paid by the new firms to share the networks of the existing local telephone companies. The Commission had reversed, in their view, the Bell victories in the legislative battles that led to the law. Representative Jack Fields declared, "If the Interconnection Order is not a simple and honest mistake, and Chairman Hundt has willfully and intentionally disregarded the specific language of the Act and the intent of Congress, then he should step aside and he should resign. Or the President should appoint someone who can read." Representative Billy Tauzin, Republican from Louisiana (he had been a Democrat until the 1994 election results came in), claimed that our rules "ignored much of what the Congress did and went into a level of bureaucratic detail . . . that is not anything near what Congress had in mind."

What Tauzin meant, presumably, was that the FCC should have let the states write the rules—because then the country would have had 50 different sets of rules, advantaging the local phone companies and devastating the business prospects of the new entrants. To avoid debating the substance of our reasoning (which ultimately the Bells challenged in court for years), the telephone company lobbyists ridiculed the length of our rules. I explained to reporters that the new rules were only two-thirds the size of the Little League baseball rulebook—although I admitted that the baseball rules were more important.

Under our interconnection order, capital markets funded new entrepreneurial business plans. Skilled employees quit their jobs at AT&T, the Bells, and elsewhere to start competing companies. New businesses proliferated: within three years there were 6,000 Internet service providers, 250 new competing local telephone companies, a half dozen new long distance companies, dozens of new equipment vendors (the arms merchants to any commercial revolution).

Economists began to suspect that the communications revolution might be producing record productivity gains. Apparently, computers alone produced no efficiency or productivity gains. But network communications of massive data (spreadsheets, balance sheets, sheets of numbers, payroll lists, customer lists, lists of products) made computers, at last, into tools of efficiency. Networks simplified businesses, increased the number of people one person could manage, reduced layers of bureaucracy. Communications, not computers, apparently set off the big bang of productivity growth that was at the heart of the American economic boom.

At the end of August, I went with my eldest son, Adam, to the Democratic National Convention, that year held in the Chicago Bulls' arena. In the box for the Vice President's staff, everyone looked around, checking who was in, learning who was out. I recognized everyone: you can't be in an in-group unless you know everyone there.

The Democratic Party then and now describes many issues in terms of their impact on the next generation. Al Gore, in accepting the vice presidential renomination, listed the specifics of the Democratic commitment to children. He included our rule requiring three hours of educational television from every station per week; the FCC, perhaps for the first time in history, drew extended applause from a political party's nominating convention. Then he said the Administration would guarantee that every classroom in the United States would have access to the Internet. More applause. One of the staff members said to me, "Now these ideas belong to the White House."

The goal of public benefits from the communications revolution had become part of the campaign platform of the country's leaders. If the President and Vice President won re-election, I could claim the voters' mandate for connecting classrooms. If Clinton-Gore lost, our key initiatives would be scuttled in any event.

As Congress reassembled after Labor Day for its fitful pre-election session, I reported to Jay Rockefeller our progress on the vote of the joint board of state commissioners. I explained that we wanted the joint board to recommend that the FCC adopt a rule guaranteeing about $2 billion a year to the classroom connection program, to be matched with about $2 billion from state and local funds. And we proposed that schools could use the money both for building networks and buying communications services.

Leaning forward, peering through thick glasses, Rockefeller seemed to descend like a time traveler from the country's business and political history into the present. He was a legacy, but he was bent on creating his own country-shaping record of accomplishment.

I told him we needed a unanimous recommendation that the FCC pass a rule spending billions on building networks in classrooms.

"Why unanimous?" he asked.

"Because I don't have three votes at the FCC. A partisan split in the joint board would lead to a split vote at the Commission. Then at the most I'd have the other Clinton Democrat and myself; two to two and we'd lose."

"Olympia and I worked hard for that law," he said. "We'd both be unhappy if it weren't put into effect as we intended."

Two of the key state representatives on the joint board came from Missouri, one from South Dakota, one from Florida, one from Washington state. We assigned to each one several lobbyists from education groups in their states. In a series of public meetings, teachers' groups, PTAs, academics, and Senator Rockefeller testified in favor of connecting classrooms. After one of the meetings a joint board member, a conservative Republican, told me that he had been called to the phone on a Sunday night by his wife. She had said that "Rockefeller was on the phone."

He told her to stop kidding around, but when he took the receiver, "What do you know. You could have knocked me over with a feather. A Rockefeller calling me."

I asked him if a feather would knock him on my side of the vote.

"It's a possibility," he said. But he was still undecided.

Senator Snowe called the joint board members. Education group lobbyists shadowed them. Education Secretary Richard Riley charmed them.

I was informed that Microsoft believed education was too controversial politically. Bill Gates had thought hard about my suggestion. He would make major personal charitable commitments, but not now.

I was crestfallen at my failure to elicit useful business support, but Ira said my public advocacy had helped rally the education lobby, particularly the teachers' unions. These allies were critical to our chances. Moreover, he said, we had deterred Bell company opposition to the initiative. The Bells did not want a battle where, like the broadcasters on kidvid, I could label them publicly as anti-children. The Bells' agenda was to fight interconnection in court, persuade the FCC to let them into the long distance market, and constrain the FCC's reduction of the access charges they received from the long distance companies for originating and terminating long distance calls. Opposing a kids' initiative was not worth the distraction from their other efforts.

That fall, our crucial friend among broadcast affiliates, Ralph Gabbard, died suddenly while on a business trip. Overlooking the various deficiencies in my relations with broadcasters, he had sided with what he considered our wise decision of calling on broadcasters to do more programming for children. The broadcast lobby had put enormous pressure on him to recant, but he had stood firm. Ralph once told us that the secret to making good decisions was experience, and that experience came from making bad decisions. In this kindly way, he suggested that perhaps our early mistakes on broadcasting issues had taught us a few good lessons. After we showed we had learned them, he was a key ally for us.

A few weeks later, the state commissions and local Bell telephone companies obtained a court order blocking our interconnection rules decision. Our interconnection order culminated 20 years of debate in Congress and was based on review of about 20,000 pages of comments. We had written 48 pages of rules and 500 pages of reasoning. The Eighth Circuit Court of Appeals, however, sitting in Kansas City, Missouri, listened to our lawyer for 15 minutes of oral argument and then enjoined the national rules opening the local telephone company monopolies. Judicial activism reigned in Kansas City.

In their abrupt questioning during oral argument and curt discussion of our decision, the panel of Republican-appointed judges had revealed a bias toward the Republican–local-telephone-incumbent–states'-rights side of the debate and against the Democratic–new-entrant–federal side. According to the court, the states and not the federal government had the sole power to open local telephone markets to competition.

I considered it absurd to believe that Congress would pass an allegedly national law but give the power to write the rules and carry out the enforcement only to the states. To the trade press, I compared the trio of judges to Chinese emperors inside the Forbidden City second-guessing the way farmers planted rice in the provinces. I enjoyed my analogy, but our lawyers were doomed to read it in opposing briefs filed in the continuing litigation.

An irony of the injunction was that it frustrated our plans to ease regulations on the local telephone companies. As a quid pro quo for incurring local competition, we intended to permit the local Bell companies to enter the long distance market less than a year after our interconnection decision went into effect. I was in conversations with the CEO of Ameritech and the chairman of the Illinois Public Utility Commission that I hoped would result in Ameritech selling long distance service in Illinois by early 1997.

When the appellate court in Kansas City barred the Commission's rules from going into effect, it derailed that plan. As a result, while I was at the Commission, Bell companies did not take the necessary steps to open the local markets, and they did not obtain permission to enter the long distance market. In this way, the appellate court slowed the deregulation promised by the law, and frustrated the promotion of competition. Nevertheless, because the states took steps to emulate our rulemaking in their own reform processes, investment continued (even if more slowly) in new entrants in the local market. And while the incumbent long distance and local companies proceeded deliberately because of uncertainty about the new rules, investors poured billions into new companies building new long distance networks (Qwest, Level 3, Williams).

But we knew that if Bob Dole won the November election, his new FCC would reverse course and accept the appellate court's ruling as the correct reading of the law. The new companies' funding would dry up. Even if the new companies survived, their cost of capital would rise and they would cut back on their competition plans. Fortunately, polls showed Bill Clinton and Al Gore running ahead of the challengers.

In October 1996, Blair and I paid a visit in Los Angeles to Mike Ovitz, Disney's vice president, to try to find common ground on digital television and kids' television. Disney is a parallel country to the United States with an electoral process in which tickets are votes. Michael Eisner had been popularly elected for several terms, but like Franklin Roosevelt he was prone to switching vice presidents. Jeffrey Katzenberg had been bumped from the ticket. Mike Ovitz was the country's new vice president and heir apparent.

Blair and I arrived on time. That was bad. We had to be a little late: one of the rules of power in the Hollywood world. So we sat in the parking lot in our incongruous van until we could become late. The FCC had purchased our vehicle in an auction of items confiscated by local police. ("We always do auctions," Blair apologized to me, as we examined the adjacent Porsches, Ferraris, and Mercedes.)

After an appropriate time, about as long as the trailers before the feature, we made the trip through the cool corridors of ersatz sandstone into the Ovitz suite. Ovitz made us wait in a narrow hall outside his office, but left his door open so that we could hear him laughing on the telephone. We understood the lesson. Our time was not as valuable as his time, even when his was dedicated to no purpose.

When only minutes remained in the time period allocated for the visit, he welcomed us in: carefully managed clockery. Like Bill Gates when he visited my office, Ovitz met unaccompanied by staff members. In Gates's case, it was an un-self-conscious act by the firm's proprietor; in Ovitz's, the pretense of supreme power within the organization. Selling this message, Ovitz said, "Everyone said I was a fool to meet with you alone. They said you are dangerous."

I smiled. Blair, by my side, also smiled. Blair has two smiles: a sweet one and a mean one. Ovitz did not know that. He did not see the sweet one.

Ovitz said, "They told me if I agree with you, you'll use that against me and if I disagree, you'll use that against me."

"And if you don't do either, I'll say you were indecisive." I meant it as a joke. It could have been taken as a joke. But L.A. audiences are tough, and Ovitz was the mirror of all L.A. audiences. He did not laugh. Instead, he slithered around the office like a gecko on a tree trunk, perhaps necessary in an office that was a forest of unnatural shapes, exotic plants, edgy furniture. He ignored my puzzlement as to where to sit. He was in charge of the meeting, and would conduct it on his terms.

I stood awkwardly until after some time, Ovitz came to rest, in a contingent manner, on an object that was meant either as a table or a chair. He then pointed to an impossibly low couch resembling the back seat of my '87 Buick, but covered in what appeared to be the skin of a rare if not extinct species. Blair and I sat, as ordered, and predictably found our knees above our waists. A posture of weakness: we were fixed in place, facing difficult leverage problems should we wish to rise up.

"I was meeting with the Premier of China," Ovitz said, looking down at us and extending his hand as if to suggest that although China was many miles away, it was within his grasp. "Jiang Zemin. I told him he would have to stop misappropriating our content. Inexcusable piracy. But I invited him to Disneyland. He's accepted. I've told the White House. I think it will be a good trip."

At the time, the question of whether our President would go to China or their leader would come to the United States was in doubt as a result of China's record on freedom of expression and its unhappiness that the Taiwanese head of state had gone to his college reunion at Cornell University. Ovitz's foreign policy evidently transcended these disputes.

I told him that the American digital television policy was well on the way to becoming a catastrophe. I felt that I was describing to him a remote tragedy, like a ferry sinking in the South China Sea, in which he could not rationally be interested. Perhaps as a Mandarin of the American bureaucracy, I was simply speaking an alien language. I attempted to impart the story line of our broadcast agenda. The spectrum granted to the broadcasters would be ill-used if the government allowed the massive giveaway to proceed as planned, I warned Ovitz, because the broadcasters would not take the risks and spend the money necessary to take advantage of the digital medium. I predicted that the free, over-the-air medium called broadcast television would die for lack of profits unless the government stopped limiting ownership and began to allow Hollywood studios to buy networks, the networks to own the shows they broadcast, and the networks to buy more stations. At the same time, I argued, we needed to toughen the requirements on broadcasters to give us programs that serve the interest we have in a well-educated and well-informed public. For example, the broadcasters should grant free air time for political debate during elections.

Ovitz stared blankly at me as if I was an over-the-hill actor, no longer worth an agent's time. He looked at his watch. A piece of stage business. I got it, and excused Blair and myself. We labored upright and, in the gleam of Ovitz's false smile, found our way out.

Next we were invited to lunch on a studio lot with Richard Dreyfuss. He was mystified by our presence. He was not, however, curious. Hollywood was a sufficiently huge and complex country to satisfy his craving for knowledge. Washington was a place outside his range.

Steven Spielberg showed up. He had on a couple layers of jackets and a bush hat typical of the jungle of Hollywood. He was at that level of celebrity where he no longer needed, or could get, a good haircut or nice shoeshine. As guards and couriers scurried about, I had my picture taken with the celebrities.

Then the agents of the Hollywood artists swarmed around us. They had used the stars to attract us, the oldest trick in the movie book, and now they would extract their payment: I was their captive audience. As they had done on my night with Sharon Lawrence at the Artists' Rights Dinner, they asked that the FCC command that all television sets in the United States be shaped in the dimension of movie screens—wider, not taller.

I tried to indicate receptivity in the hope of being invited back to meet some more celebrities, but I knew that the FCC would never dictate the shape of 200 million television sets. Hollywood may dictate consumer taste, but politics is much more responsive to people and markets. If the creative artists wanted different screen dimensions, they would have to make shows that motivated consumers to buy larger screens, instead of trying to persuade the government to dictate to consumers what sets they must buy to watch movies on television.

I had not found anyone in Hollywood interested in making something useful out of digital television. If my side won the presidential election, we would have to resolve the digital television issues without help from the creative community.

Eleven **Elections Matter**

November 1996 – April 1997

Man has always craved recognition and fame. . . . But an individual's

achievement may be absorbed by a reality that is far more than personal.

Otto von Simson, The Gothic Cathedral

O n November 7, in the immediate wake of the bliss-fully boring re-election of Clinton-Gore, I sum-moned the joint board of state and federal com-missioners to vote on whether they would recommend that the FCC adopt a rule funding classroom connections. We decided to ask for enough funding to pay for networks in all schools in four years: we would take $2.25 billion in money from communications companies and match it with $2 billion from local school districts. The matches were weighted by wealth. School districts where federal money subsidized hot lunches for most children would pay 10 percent of the net-working cost, and 90 percent would come from the money we collected from communications companies. Wealthy school districts would be re-quired to pay up to 60 percent of the cost, and 40 percent would come from our fund. But every school had to raise some local money, to demonstrate a commitment. We would fund public, private, and parochial schools. We wanted all teachers and students on the Internet. This program was not about taking from the rich to give to the poor. It was about creating new cyberspace communities, so that the Internet could change learning as well as business.

Ira Fishman organized a last volley of phone calls from Jay Rocke-feller, Olympia Snowe, Dick Riley, and many lobbyists from the education community. I believed that the election meant the joint board should vote for the recommendation to connect classrooms. The President had set the goal of connecting all classrooms by 2001. He had repeated this call twice in State of the Union addresses and again at the Chicago nominating convention in August. Al had spoken about it across the country. Now that Clinton-Gore had won, everyone believed we had a mandate.

The board unanimously recommended that communications companies contribute about one percent of their total annual revenue. Matched with the local school districts' contribution, the total of $4 billion a year thrilled all of us. Moreover, the joint board specifically suggested that the monies should fund the construction of networks in classrooms. A normal Washington story is of a monumental effort to move a peanut an inch. Yet the joint board had recommended the largest single national education program for grades K–12 in our country's history.

On the grounds that a good offense was the best defense, I wanted to draw maximum attention to our triumph; some on the White House staff were afraid to announce the magnitude of the win for fear that it would attract congressional criticism. They had their way. Official White House reaction was muted, although Al was delighted.

Later in November, a Microsoft lieutenant came to the eighth floor for final negotiations with the NAB on a new technological standard for the transmission of the digital signal. Gates wanted broadcasters to use a particular protocol that would make the digital broadcast in a manner suitable for display on a computer screen. In addition, the Microsoft solution would be easily compatible with their software, which they wanted to inject into every new "digital" television receiver made to view these new signals. I had suggested that Microsoft should finance the building of the digital television broadcasting towers that each of the country's approximately 2,000 television stations had to construct. This would cost Microsoft at the most about a billion dollars. In return, broadcasters would accept Microsoft's preferred transmission standards. Microsoft negotiated hard, but offered nothing to broadcasters. The broadcasters preferred their own standards. None of the other commissioners was willing to override the NAB on the issue. Finally, we called a halt to the negotiations and compromised on no governmentally mandated standard at all. This result is what my team had favored all along. If Microsoft had not won what it wanted, without their help we could not have obtained our desired result.

In December, still powered by the wind of the election victory, I flew to Southeast Asia—the Philippines, Indonesia, and Singapore—to join

Trade Representative Charlene Barshefsky in urging the Pacific Rim countries to sign the World Trade Organization agreement on telecommunications. If they did not, we had decided, the United States would back out of the deal. At stake, in the view of Gore, Barshefsky, and me, was whether the communications revolution would be an American or a global phenomenon.

The basic points of the treaty were the same points set forth by Al Gore in Buenos Aires in March 1994 (when I had stood up the broadcasters' Las Vegas convention). Since Al's speech, Peter Cowhey of the FCC's International Bureau and I had been presenting the case for the treaty to each foreign delegation that visited us, and in trips to ministries of communications and trade around the world. We wanted every country to allow foreign investment in communications, to establish agencies like the FCC to create the rule of law for competitive entry into previously closed markets, and to issue interconnection rules like ours.

In 1995, Barshefsky and I had difficulty in explaining why other countries should create regulatory agencies, while our Congress proposed to eliminate the FCC. Nor could we advocate successfully that others promise by treaty to adopt pro-competition interconnection rules until the passage of the Telecommunications Act in February 1996. But until the November 1996 election, the other countries had been suspending judgment on the American-led negotiations. Now they interpreted the President's re-election as a mandate for his trade policies. As a result, we brought into the agreement most of recalcitrant Asia.

Late in January, the World Trade Organization negotiations came to a head. Our message was that the communications revolution had technological, economic, and political dimensions. If nations adopted the new politics of competition, then the new digital technologies could create wealth everywhere. Ambassador Barshefsky and I worked the phone in her office, while our staffs negotiated in Geneva with the other countries. The President and Vice President called certain key heads of state. Finally, we obtained the promises of 69 countries to adopt a pro-competitive policy that mirrored the American rulemakings, including the creation of an FCC-like entity in each country. The President approved the deal. We hit headlines around the world. Even as I began thinking about the end of my time in office, I was being cloned.

At the FCC we coupled with the WTO deal an aggressive policy to drive down international long distance telephone prices. Almost half of all national calling starts in, passes through, or ends in the United States. alls originating in this country, the American carrier sends money to the foreign carriers who receive the call. This "settlement" system sent from America to other countries about $7 billion every year, because Americans made more international calls than they received.

The outbound payments exceeded the total of United States non-military foreign aid. Moreover, settlement charges raised international calling prices to an average of about a dollar a minute—ten times higher than domestic long distance. We proposed to block these payments unless the telephone companies lowered their settlement charges closer to the levels competition would set. That meant a cut of 70 percent, phased over a few years. This policy would cause international prices to drop quickly. Calling volume would surge with lower prices, and communications would wrap the world in a "nerve of intelligence," as Al Gore had finely quoted Nathaniel Hawthorne in the 1994 Buenos Aires speech. As a result of the settlement rate decision and the WTO deal, more than a trillion dollars will be added to the world economy within 10 years. The Vice President had fulfilled his international vision for the communications industry. And that was the story we won from the *New York Times*.

In early January 1997, I sat with my team in one of our early morning conferences and read out loud an article reporting that I was a "spineless weasel" because of my refusal to block the giveaway of digital television spectrum to the broadcasters.

Blair responded, "No one thinks 'spineless' is fair."

Although I would have dearly loved to auction the digital television spectrum, the broadcast lobby enjoyed a congressional mandate in the telecommunications law that the FCC should give every existing analog television station spectrum for a new digital television channel. At the same time, the broadcasters did not want the Commission to impose new public interest duties such as kidvid or free time for political debate. Their reason was that the new spectrum licenses were probably money-losing propositions.

Blair and I wanted to use the giveaway as the basis for getting something back. Specifically, we wanted the broadcasters to grant free time for political debate. A billion dollars of air time would be small recompense for tens of billions of dollars in free licenses. Moreover, our public debate on the giveaway had increased the willingness of the broadcasters to make some gesture toward serving the public interest. It was a unique opportunity for John McCain again to be a hero.

I believed McCain would seize the moment to demand that the FCC pass a rule requiring free time for political debate. If he did so, I could get Commissioner Chong's vote, because she would hope that McCain would support her for reappointment. If I appeared to be able to pass a free-time rule, broadcasters would beg Congress to block me. The strategy was unstoppable. To repeal or bar my free-time rule, Congress would have to pass the McCain-Feingold campaign finance reform bill. Even if the legislation did not provide for free time by FCC rule, at least it would limit soft money contributions and other excesses of today's corrupted system.

To my dismay, McCain disavowed his earlier support for my rulemaking. Without McCain, Rupert Murdoch was unwilling to stay with me. Bill Bradley was nowhere in sight. Our coalition dissolved.

As an apparent quid pro quo for protecting the broadcasters from free time, Majority Leader Lott promised to allow McCain and Feingold time to debate their bill on the Senate floor. The deal proved worthless, as the Republican Senate leadership killed the campaign finance reform bill even after brave Chris Shays, Republican from Connecticut, pushed it through the House over Newt Gingrich's opposition.

With Dole gone, and McCain reversing himself, we lacked any congressional support for withholding the giveaway or extracting specific public interest commitments, like free time. Some congressional support was always necessary for me to take a strong stand on any issue. Otherwise, Congress would amend a bill that was destined to pass, such as an appropriations bill, to add explicit instructions to the FCC. These dictates might be phrased in a manner unintelligible to a layperson; they rarely would be debated by more than one or two Senators. Yet the instructions would strip us of authority at the FCC to interpret existing law as we thought best. But even one Senator could usually block such assaults on our authority.

The solution crafted by Blair and Julius Genachowski, after the loss of McCain's support, was that the broadcasters would agree to the principle of concrete public interest obligations, the Vice President would create a commission to define more specifically the public interest obligations owed by the broadcasters in return for the new licenses, and the Commission would vote clearly that the public interest had to be served.

The broadcasters' argument was part of the historic tradition of the FCC: namely, that government should make sure all communications companies were profitable. Our new approach was to use the authority of the telecommunications law to rescind the compact between government and the status quo in the information sector. In the benign but dramatic communications revolution, companies might fail, service might be interrupted, choice could confuse consumers. But we would unleash the power of change.

To this purpose, we interpreted the Telecommunications Act to form a deregulatory wall around the Net. For instance, we received a petition to restrict the sale of Internet phones—devices that would let you make a voice telephone call not on the traditional circuit-switched telephone technology, but on the new packet-switched Internet. My staff persuaded the Commission to reject this attempt to impose old regulations on new technology. With the support of the Administration, I vowed not to "pour new wine into old bottles." As a result, the United States has the cheapest Internet access in the world.

Our pro-data, pro-Internet policies also led us to exclude Internet traffic from charges normally imposed on long distance voice communications. A prominent Republican Senator, who had provided helpful advice on many occasions, called me to his private office high in the Capitol, where the view down the Mall was a look across the history of the country.

"Look at this," he demanded.

I turned to the window.

"I mean the computer," he said. He was one of the first Senators to use a PC. He jabbed at the screen. I saw an e-mail message.

"From my daughter. She's a schoolteacher."

I began to smile, assuming that he had summoned me in order to thank me for my efforts in connecting all classrooms to the Internet.

"This is an outrage," he continued. "She's bypassed the access charge system. If everyone sends e-mail instead of calling, the telephone companies will be severely hurt. They won't be able to collect fair access charges from the long distance companies. They will have to raise local rates. Then look what you will have done: hurt every consumer in the country!"

"But everyone can send e-mail for free."

"Fiddlesticks," he said. "If you don't let the telephone companies charge for the Internet, you'll destroy the phone system."

I returned to the office and related this conversation to my team. We calculated that letting telephone companies impose a charge for Internet access equal to the charge they put on long distance voice calls would amount to about five cents a minute, or $150 a month, for the average Internet user. Such access charges would stifle the Internet boom.

The biggest business victim would be Steve Case, the co-founder of America Online. Blair and I met with Case to explain that the Senator apparently intended to lead a Bell charge against the Commission's exemption of Net communication from the access-charge system. Did Case have any reaction?

Case shook his long hair away from his face. He had been in tougher spots than this. He said he "got it."

In the few weeks that followed the meeting, more than 400,000 e-mails rained across the Net down to the PCs of Senators, Congressmen, and FCC commissioners. Case had orchestrated the first Internet lobbying campaign in history. The e-mails urged that the Congress support the FCC's decision not to regulate the Internet. That was the way AOL spun the access-charge issue. Never had so many said the same thing to so few.

The Bells still complained, and the Senator joined them. But their campaign against our pro-data, pro-Internet exemption from access charges sputtered out. The free-market conservatives of Congress were particularly reluctant to alienate the new wealthy of the Internet economy.

Karen Kornbluh said later, as we sat over late morning coffee, "You realize Case saved the Snowe-Rockefeller provision?"

"How do you figure?" I asked.

"If you let the telephone companies raise access charges to the long distance companies for Internet communications, then the long distance companies would be unwilling to fund the Snowe-Rockefeller provision in addition. From their perspective, they pay either to connect classrooms or for new access charges. They don't like doing either, but they'd strongly oppose doing both. They'd fight us on the classrooms initiative."

"And if a big company goes against the teachers, the teachers might lose."

"That's the way it could have worked here," she explained.

"Now tell me how to get Chong and Quello to vote for the Snowe-Rockefeller rule."

On a day in March 1997, bandy-legged Commissioner Jim Quello walked into my office. He rolled from side to side like the old salt on the ship.

"You're always welcome, Jim. Make yourself at home," I said.

I shook his hand firmly, in imitation of some of the best shakers I had met on the Hill. (In public office you need a gradation of welcomes, from the nod toward an empty chair to the chest-to-chest embrace for same-sex friends, known as the "full clutch.") Jim had a strong grip. He was wiry and athletic, an avid tennis player.

"Sit down, Commissioner," I said.

Jim gingerly sat in one of my chairs, reluctant to make himself at home. He said, "I can't agree with you on this. [When he visited, he never agreed with me.] I've been talking with some folks. This time we will just agree to disagree. [Only Commissioner Ness devoted serious efforts to discussing rulings with my staff and me.] You're just so headstrong. It's impossible to talk to you about some things. You just don't appreciate broadcasters. Broadcasters do a great deal for the community."

He was referring to my insistence on creating free time for political discussion by candidates in connection with the digital television giveaway. After his visit, Jim announced that I had gone "way too far with these expansive ideas." He would fight this last broadcast battle with vigor.

I had learned much from Jim Quello, but our public disagreements over free time and children's television and many other matters had made it possible to prevent his reappointment by President Clinton. In 1997, Jim's Democratic seat, for the first time in 20 years, would go to a true Democrat, effectively picked by the Vice President.

Commissioner Chong also would be leaving the Commission. She had wanted a President Dole to make her the chairwoman as I left in bitter defeat following the November repudiation of Bill Clinton. After the election, her next choice was to seek Republican lobbyists' support for reappointment. But Commerce Committee Chairman Larry Pressler had been defeated for re-election in the Senate.

John McCain was the new Republican chairman of the Senate Commerce Committee. He wanted Colin Powell's son, Michael, to be on the FCC. Tom Bliley, chairman of the House Commerce Committee, wanted one of his aides to represent him on the Commission. The Republican Congress thus divided its two seats. No one on the Hill wanted Commissioner Chong back at the Commission.

If she had been loyal to the Democrats from her Republican seat, I would have fought hard for her reappointment. Instead she had made her pact with the other side of the aisle. Yet because she was a Clinton appointee, the Republicans had never really accepted her. Deserters are never accepted.

My particular problem was how to get departing Commissioners Quello and Chong to vote to connect all classrooms to the Internet. In leaving, why should they give me what I had most wanted for four years? From their perspective, they owed me nothing but a hard time.

Unbeknownst to the Gang of Two, they were not the only departing commissioners. As soon as the election was over, Judy Harris, now thriving in private law practice, had come to see me.

"Have you got it figured out?" she asked.

"Probably not," I responded. People were always asking me that question.

"It's time to go," she said. "You're finished. You have done what you wanted. You are exhausted. Your family doesn't know you. You're probably broke. There's a time for everything, and it's time to go."

"But I've got to pick a successor, get the classroom connections vote, find a way out that doesn't lead to the collapse of what we've done," I said.

"Everyone thinks they are irreplaceable," she replied. "You're not."

In December and January, I thought at great length about Judy's comments and talked with my wife about the stress of the chairmanship on me and on my family. By February I had concluded that Judy was right. I had indeed begun to think that perhaps the country needed me as chairman. Nothing could be less true. The job was an opportunity and a privilege. It should go to someone with the energy to think anew. I was deeply tired; my whole team was worn out. It was time to make way for someone else.

Blair and I would go out together, as we had come in together, but we needed an exit strategy. Sitting in my car outside his rented house late at night, for several weeks' worth of nights, we worked out our plans, listening to Blair's ever growing dog barking at my ever deteriorating 1987 Century. Blair thought two essential duties remained. We had to pass a rule that followed the congressional edict to give away the digital television spectrum, but it had to maximize the possibility that the spectrum would be used, required the broadcasters to build the digital television transmission towers, returned as much spectrum to the public as quickly as possible, and addressed the broadcasters' commitment to serve the public interest. He and Julius Genachowski would manage that. The other uncompleted job was to pass the rule that connected the classrooms. That would be part of the May "universal service" ruling on how to guarantee affordable local telephone service to all Americans.

"What if we could get a real Democrat in Jim's seat?" I asked. "Then we could reform the campaign finance laws, too."

"This Congress will never give you the third vote," said Blair. We would do the two rulemakings, and then exit the stage.

In March, congressional leaders wrote to demand that the FCC expedite the gift of digital television licenses to broadcasters. We had persuaded the editorial pages of most large newspapers in the country to opine in favor of auctioning the licenses. But editorial page consensus against the giveaway had not altered congressional ardor for it. Bob Dole and Barney Frank had been almost our only vocal congressional supporters. The former was now a Washington lawyer and the latter could not protect us from the entire Congress.

We wanted to eliminate the Commission's commitment to ordering high-definition television. We believed that the best use in the marketplace for this spectrum was not, in any event, video broadcast. Instead, it was for high-speed access to the Internet, also more generally called wireless data. This particular swatch of spectrum (frequencies of radio waves) was ideal for penetrating buildings. (That is why you can watch television indoors!) Consequently it would be desirable to use this spectrum for wireless connections.

The solution was to eliminate the FCC's requirement that the digital licenses be used only for video. The Gang of Two accepted this point as well, in order to overcome my now notorious intransigence. Two years later, as we predicted, broadcasters began to discuss publicly the possibility of using the new licenses for data transmission. If we had auctioned the licenses in the first place, as we wanted, the auction winners would almost certainly have been firms that had wireless data business plans.

Our last point was to demand that the broadcasters use the spectrum. As we approached the moment of actual giveaway by rulemaking, the NAB explained that it was unwilling to promise that any station would construct digital broadcast facilities in the near future. We took to the press the story that broadcasters wanted gifts but then would not unwrap them. The other commissioners took the NAB's side, but we bluffed Commissioners Quello and Chong into thinking that we would postpone the spectrum giveaway until after the April NAB convention. That distressed them. They wanted to be thanked at their last NAB. They voted for our compromise package.

We also insisted on getting back from broadcasters twice the amount of unused spectrum the previous Commission had sought, speeding up the build-out, and in all other respects eliminating the government-mandated planning for what broadcasters would do with the licenses. Although we had not been able to prevent the entire giveaway of spectrum to the broadcasters, we had achieved most of our objectives. On the eve of the NAB convention, the FCC issued the digital television rulemaking and finally gave the licenses, free, to the broadcasters. The broadcasters are now on their own in the marketplace, wondering how to use the spectrum instead of depending on the government and the NAB to tell them what to do.

When the National Association of Broadcasters gathered in Las Vegas in April 1997, I took the occasion to attend a performance of George Carlin's stand-up comedy act. Carlin had been the subject of the most famous lawsuit involving the FCC, a 1978 case called *FCC v. Pacifica*. The Pacifica lawsuit arose from the broadcast on the radio of Carlin's disquisition on seven dirty words. The FCC received a complaint from a listener that Carlin had polluted the public airwaves. The Commission fined the station. The case went to the Supreme Court. The Court ruled in favor of the Commission. The airwaves belonged to the people, and the FCC was the representative of the people. As such it could set standards of decency and otherwise issue rules that preserved the public interest.

Thirty years later, FM radio had killed AM almost dead, CDs had overwhelmed records, digital had conquered analog, and Carlin's dirty words had snuck on television via cable. But we still had the duty of enforcing the public interest standard.

There were two options for interpretation: prohibition or promotion. We could continue to monitor the airwaves for language inappropriate for children. That, broadcasters would support. Or we could make broadcasters deliver some television that served public purposes. That, broadcasters considered an assault on the First Amendment. The economic difference between the two approaches was that "prohibition" did not reduce broadcasters' revenues, because mainstream advertisers did not want to buy time on raunchy shows. By contrast, "promotion" cut revenues, because public interest shows were not attractive for advertisers. Our team favored promoting public interest programming, for kids and democracy.

In my lightly attended NAB speech, I predicted that fundraising in future elections would be in the billions. The search for money was limiting who could run for office and what they could do in office. Most of the money was spent to buy access for public debate on the public's air-waves. In pre-television America, Lincoln and Douglas could debate for free in the town squares of Illinois. In our modern age, why didn't we give the debaters free access to the air? The broadcasters knew that with the licenses given away, I no longer had any power to extract concessions from them. Their applause at the end of the speech arose from relief that the hectoring was over.

Before I went to Vegas, I had decided it would be my last NAB. The broadcasters had been a necessary opponent, and in truth I had enjoyed the intellectual and political dimensions of the battles. But even if they had known this was my last speech to their industry convention, I do not think they would have spent any sentiment on memories of their debates with the departing chairman.

Twelve Exit and Outcomes

May 1997–November 1997

One's grand flights, one's Sunday baths,

One's tootings at the weddings of the soul

Occur as they occur.

Wallace Stevens, "The Sense of the Sleight-of-Hand Man"

As we approached the vote on the FCC rule to connect millions of children to the Internet, I feared that if news leaked that I intended to leave the Commission, I might be unable to muster a majority. I imagined that the Gang of Two might seek delay, hoping that we would leave the decision to our replacements. Although no one except Blair and Betsy knew my intentions, I was already frequently denying the imminence of my departure. Yet I needed to explain my real plans to one person in the White House—the Vice President. I could not let him be surprised by my decision, which I wanted to announce after the vote.

By coincidence, Al Gore and I were both going to Seattle in May 1997 for a "summit" of business and government leaders called by Bill Gates. My staff negotiated for me to meet with Al during the trip. Al gave a speech about the power of education to fuel the information economy. Afterward, the hoi polloi (celebrated business executives) filed into buses for transportation to the boat that would take us to Gates's never-before-visited dwelling. Al would go by motorcade to the lake, so that he could march last on board the boat, waving to the watching crowd on the shore. Timing is the secret of life, and politics. Besides, public figures cannot stand on line; they disturb the queue.

A benefit of the plan was that Al had to wait in a holding room for a few private minutes. When the Secret Service let me in the room, Al's eldest daughter, Karenna, was offering him a critique of his presentation. He looked at her with wordless admiration as she dissected his presentation. Daughters often leave fathers speechless. After Karenna finished, I claimed his attention. She stepped away, out of politeness.

"There's something I have to tell you," I said.

Al looked distracted by Karenna's trenchant remarks.

"Your speech was great," I said, "but I need to talk to you about me."

He frowned, guessing what was to follow. Politics had made him highly intuitive about people. He had foretold, for instance, that John McCain would let me down on the free-time issue.

"It's time for me to go," I said.

"I was hoping to reappoint you." He was distressed.

"I haven't been fully part of my family for four years. I spend time with them but I can't pay the right level of attention. The job consumes me."

"Is it as bad as that?" Al asked softly.

"Yes, it is," I said. "Of all the things I admire about you, the most is the way you just keep at it. Year after year. You don't quit."

"I put up limits," he said, blushing. "I block off time." I knew he was referring to the fact that he scarcely ever missed watching his big son play football or one daughter play all-star soccer or the other daughter lead her field hockey team.

"I don't know how to do that," I said. "It's seven days a week for me. I just have to bring it to an end."

"Will you stay until I can confirm a replacement?" Al asked.

"Of course I will," I said. I owed him that.

Then we went out to the motorcade.

On May 20, 1997, the FCC commissioners were scheduled to vote on whether to accept the joint board's recommendation to pass a rule paying for the Internet in every classroom. The issue was part of a complicated proposal. For consumers, we would order lower long distance prices for low-volume users. For Internet users, we would make access cheap by prohibiting local phone companies from charging extra tolls for Internet communication across state lines in the way they did for long distance voice traffic—just as Steve Case's e-mails had urged. We proposed to order all communications companies to contribute about one percent of revenues every year to the fund for connecting classrooms. However, we would let local telephone companies reimburse themselves by charging long distance companies higher access charges in an amount equal to the contribution. At the same time, we ordered a reduction in those charges on the grounds that technology made telephone networks cheaper to operate.

So we raised access charges by including in them the payments to the classroom funds, and we lowered them by ordering the local telephone companies to reflect their productivity gains. The net result was a slight lowering. That in turn led to the possibility of lower long distance prices.

We insisted that AT&T translate this reduction specifically to a one penny drop in long distance rates for low-volume users—typically senior citizens. In this way we effected an immediate consumer benefit from the law's changes. It was fair and right, and it rebutted the criticism of the classroom connections on the grounds that it raised prices to consumers. We also postponed for a year the decision on how to subsidize rural consumers. We had no intention of driving rural users off the telephone networks, but we sought to separate this controversial constituency's lobbying from the other issues.

Under Senator Rockefeller's aegis, Bell Atlantic, Nynex, AT&T, and the education groups had worked out this complicated compromise on the Snowe-Rockefeller rule. By muting industry opposition—at least at this stage—the Senator had won us the breathing space necessary to present to Commissioners Quello and Chong the appearance of lack of opposition to the proposed rule.

In the days before the May 20 vote, the Vice President and Secretary of Education Dick Riley wrote to all the commissioners. Riley walked the eighth floor to make his points. George Lucas encouraged the commissioners to vote for the rule: the power of the Force was with us. An army of lobbyists from education groups swarmed over the Commission. Senators Snowe and Rockefeller called and visited with the commissioners. Jim Quello was easily converted by the industry compromises and the lobbying. But Chong vacillated. No one could understand why she would not go along. (Senator Snowe was particularly surprised.)

In public office, you inevitably define yourself in the eyes of others, and their view can become the truth for you. Indifference to the views of others is the thick skin recommended to me by John Dingell. The problem, I think, for Commissioner Chong was that the May 20 vote made her worry about her reputation. As she saw the matter, she could leave office perceived as an enemy of education or as a supporter of Gore's biggest technology and education initiative. She did not care for either version of herself. The night before the vote, my senior adviser Jackie Chorney persuaded Chong that she would be less damaged by a vote for Gore's dream than by a vote against children. In that light, and in the dawn's early hours, at 5:00 A.M. on May 20, the commissioner gave us her vote. We had unanimity. Ira Fishman's strategy of quiet persuasion had been vindicated. He shrugged off my praise, but said it had been a year well spent. Then he resigned just as he had said he would and devoted the next six months to reacquainting himself with his family.

In a ceremonial press conference, the Vice President announced the victory. Senators Rockefeller and Snowe, to whom we owed the success, spoke warmly of the Commission's accomplishment. Commissioners Quello and Chong refused to attend the ceremony. They had given us their votes, but they took no pleasure from the fact that Al Gore's dream had become reality. Their disgruntlement foreshadowed the future congressional hostility to the Commission's rule.

A financial analyst praised our staff's complicated funding technique. Our decision was "remarkably even-handed," the analyst wrote. "It is difficult for us to find areas that the [local telephone companies] could complain about." Bell stocks rose. Nevertheless, the chief telephone company lobbyist, Roy Neel, who had helped me become the chairman, complained to Congress that our decision "will jeopardize universal telephone service." You can please some of the people none of the time. A few days later, I wrote to the President, asking him to begin the process of selecting my successor.

In the previous four years my staff and I had managed 1,500 votes at the Commission. Although we never had a reliable majority of allies, by innumerable stratagems, stubbornness, and a proclivity for public debate, we had obtained unanimous votes on 99 percent of the items. In a memorable day for everyone in my office, the *New York Times* ran an editorial praising our "legacy of a focused agenda and energetic leadership."

Blair, true to his California roots, was more delighted by the *San Jose Mercury News* story:

"On the intellectual playing fields of Silicon Valley, one of the highest compliments is to be considered someone who instinctively 'gets it.' And to the area's storm-the-world digital evangelists, Reed Hundt, who

Tuesday announced he's resigning as chairman of the Federal Communications Commission, clearly 'got it.'"

Even Senator John McCain, who remained a friend notwithstanding our disagreements, said much of the criticism directed at me was "very badly misplaced." He went on: "It was Congress's fault for writing a law that handed him so much power, like letting him define what was in the public interest." But, of course, what Senator McCain disparaged is exactly what my team considered to be our luck—to have the legal authority to do what we thought was the right thing. As Al Gore had said to me four years earlier, public service had been a "privilege."

Injected with anti-allergens to guard against the pollen of a Washington spring, feet on the desk, feeling great about my press for a change, and waiting on the White House nomination process to select my general counsel as my successor, I opened the paper on a day in late May 1997 to read that the giant long distance company AT&T was holding merger talks with its arch rival, the huge local telephone company Southwestern Bell.

"Blair, this isn't what we wanted," I said.

"We're not going to make more trouble, are we?" he asked.

"AT&T is supposed to compete in the local phone business. It's the premier national communications company selling to every residential consumer. It has to take on the Bells, not merge with them. That was the deal of the telecommunications law."

"So what are we going to do about it?" he asked.

He referred to the fact that when a merger announcement is made, it is customary for public officials in reviewing agencies to say they will have no opinion until the matter is presented for review. In this case I would have departed long before the proposed AT&T-SBC merger hit the Commission. According to tradition, I was supposed to zipper my lips.

However, the Telecommunications Act had been passed on the assumption that AT&T would compete against the Bells. If AT&T needed facilities giving them access to customers, then they would have to use wireless or cable, rather than buy the telephone companies who already served the customers. Moreover, the FCC's competition policies might not survive if AT&T's lobbying forces joined the side of the Bells and opposed pro-competitive rules in the local market. An SBC-AT&T merger could undo all the benefits of our competition policy.

I asked Craig McCaw, Andy Grove, and other business leaders if the merger was a good idea. Grove's blunt assessment—"It would hurt the country"—was convincing.

I asked Senator Bob Kerrey, Democrat of Nebraska, if he agreed with my view about the proposed merger. He had fought to assure that the law gave the Commission the authority to open the local markets. He had spent political capital in reliance on AT&T's promise to compete in the local telephone market.

"If you try to stop the merger I will support you," he said.

My staff visited the antitrust subcommittee of the Senate Judiciary Committee, led by Republican Mike DeWine and Democrat Herb Kohl. They shared Kerrey's opinion. They agreed to write a joint letter supporting any criticism of the merger that I would make.

Blair called AT&T and urged them not to pursue the deal, explaining that "the purpose of the new law was to allow AT&T to bet the ranch, but not sell it." He suggested that the FCC would not have a problem with the acquisition of GTE, because its scattered properties would provide a geographical base for attacking Bell monopolies in some part of about two dozen states. But the AT&T representative said the company did not want GTE—its properties were too rural and costly to maintain. My staff called the Department of Justice, but Justice insisted on following the normal procedure of waiting for the deal to close and then reviewing it. Justice would not join us in a preemptive statement.

Without Justice's support, I was concerned that if I spoke out against an unannounced merger, I would be perceived as intemperate. I could undo the reputation we had spent years constructing from the broken shards of cable rate regulation. Furthermore, as a lame duck, I probably would not be in office when the proposed merger came to the FCC for approval or rejection.

Then I caught a break. Bob Allen, the CEO of AT&T, said in a speech that AT&T merging with a Bell was "not unthinkable." Executives of companies in merger discussions are never supposed to speak about a deal in advance. Apparently Blair's warnings had caused AT&T to make an exception to this rule.

"Now if you speak out, we won't be initiating anything," said Blair. "We will be responding."

"They broke the first rule of information age politics. Don't go first," I said.

"The front page of the business section above the fold might be interested in your reaction to Allen," Blair mused.

Blair negotiated with the Brookings Institution to obtain a venue for the speech I would give on the merger. We met with economists and lawyers inside the Commission and wrote a draft articulating our merger policy. He cut a deal with the *New York Times* to trade good coverage of my speech for an exclusive leak. As the *Times* predicted in a banner headline on page one of the business section the day of my speech, I said the proposed merger would be "unthinkable." Based on the antitrust theory for the information sector set forth in my speech, I concluded that the nation's biggest telephone company was supposed to compete against the Bells, not merge with one of them.

The AT&T-SBC merger discussions collapsed. For all we knew, the merger might not have occurred anyhow, but from most observers in Congress, the media, and business, the FCC got the credit for stopping it. Predictably, the *Wall Street Journal* ran a piece blasting me for interfering with business. They called me Al Gore's "stunt double." When it was published, I was in Japan to explain certain details of the World Trade Organization deal. A phone call from the Vice President awakened me at midnight my time, noon his time.

"Hello, Stuntman," he said. "I just read in the *Wall Street Journal* that you rejected that merger on my behalf."

I mumbled an acknowledgment.

He continued, "I wanted you to know you can do this sort of trick for me anytime. I'm proud of you."

Within a few months, Bob Allen and his designated successor, John Walter, were gone. As I left the government, Mike Armstrong roared onto the scene at AT&T and bought TCI, the country's biggest cable company, from John Malone. Armstrong was determined to make cable an alternative to the telephone line as a communications pipe for America's homes. AT&T's purchase of cable took everyone by surprise after its century of copper network building, but this new strategy was exactly the kind of bold, pro-competitive decision we had hoped to force when we opposed the Southwestern Bell merger. Armstrong promised to make our competition policy real, guaranteeing every American a choice in local phone service. (And he more than doubled AT&T's stock price in a year.)

"Sorry. I blew it," said Blair on a day in June, entering the light, clean, air-conditioned chairman's office.

"What now?" I said, wondering why we were not past the era of crises.

Blair frowned, "You know how I keep getting calls about how you are trying to become secretary of commerce?"

I nodded. Initially anxious that Al Gore would think I was promoting myself, I had become resigned to the fact that in Washington such rumors are the political equivalent of a good report card in high school.

Blair said, "I got so bored denying it, I said, 'Well, that's not true but you ought to follow that rumor about commissioner of baseball.'"

"There's no truth to that at all," I said. "Is there?"

"None whatsoever. Bud Selig is going to keep the job. And more power to him. Still, why should George Mitchell get all the fun of being mentioned for baseball commissioner? Here's my pitch: 'A commissioner for Commissioner.'"

I suppose Blair should not have done it. The *Post, Business Week,* and the AP all reported that I was being considered for the job of commissioner of baseball. Reading the accounts, I almost thought I might get the job. In Washington, after you have announced your departure, day by day your agency, your lobbyists, your congressional friends, and adversaries gradually ignore you more and more—unless they believe you are going on to something even more important, like baseball commissioner.

Blair talked with a Congressman who, before he read the baseball story, had routinely attacked me. He sheepishly asked Blair if the rumor about my future were true.

"In Washington and Hollywood all rumors are true," Blair responded.

The Congressman said he hoped he could go to a game with me sometime.

"Congressman," said Blair, "let me assure you that we always remember our friends."

Blair was smiling a synthesis of his two smiles when he told me this story.

If Calvin Coolidge was right that the business of America is business, then it is also true that the leaders of America are its business leaders. They are polymaths, heroes, creative geniuses, gurus, visionaries, and decathlon champions—when they succeed. They are narrow-gauged, myopic short-termers—when they do not make money for their companies. But when they are in power, their thoughts and actions matter a great deal to our economy and our society. I went to the Allen and Company conference

in Sun Valley, Idaho—called each year by the New York financier Herb
Allen—to enjoy a last chance to deliver my message. Barry Diller and Andy
Grove had arranged for my participation on a panel that ran stage left
to right: Rupert Murdoch, David Geffen, me, Grove, Edgar Bronfman,
Diller, and Jerry Levin. After four years on stage as chairman, I was beyond
pinching myself.

Backstage at the UCLA conference in 1994, Barry Diller had asked
for two pipes to the consumer to give him a choice in providers of carriage
for his content. In fact, by 1997, wireless, satellite, cable, and telephone
companies were each competing to build high-speed, big-bandwidth
pipes. The vision of a monopoly conduit—the idea behind Ray Smith's
failed TCI–Bell Atlantic merger in 1994—was now defunct. In Sun Valley, I told the audience that, as a result of competition in communications,
bandwidth, like pizza, will be delivered hot to your door, small, medium,
or large. You could get anything you want on it: voice, video, or data. And
there would be many bandwidth sellers—wireless, satellite, cable, and telephone. None would be a monopoly provider regulated by a Federal Pizza
and Bandwidth Commission.

I said that instead of buying albums or CDs, folks would download
music from the Net—and also movies, and application software. The Net
would take audiences from broadcast television, but if broadcasters started
buying sports franchises they would still have uniquely valuable content.

On the Internet, a little interactivity goes a long way. If the consumer
had only a smidgen of capability to choose on the Net, I said, that would
change every industry. By the time of the Allen conference, I and many others were convinced that the Internet's power to change business and society was unstoppable, as long as the United States maintained its pro-competition policies. The Net would spark creativity in every CEO of every
company in America, and the world. The changes of the telecommunications reform law had not caused the Internet to be invented—indeed there
was no single invention—but they had made America the hotbed of entrepreneurial change. As long as our government's policies did not take a
turn back to the preservation of the status quo and the discouragement of
initiative, the long boom had many years left to roll.

In October 1997, my successor, the former general counsel of the
FCC, William Kennard, walked the Hill to hear the demands of Senators
who had barred the vote on his nomination in order to negotiate with him.

The Republican Senate leadership had negotiated with the White House the simultaneous replacement of Quello, Chong, and me, but individual Senators demanded specific Commission actions from Kennard before they would release their hold on voting for him. He was obliged to negotiate with a half dozen Republican Senators. While he suffered this education in Republican realpolitik, I packed my papers.

Finally the Senators agreed to vote my friend into office as the new chairman. I was very proud to swear him in. It is a rare treat in public office to have a colleague take your place. As planned, three new commissioners were sworn in simultaneously; Commissioners Quello, Chong, and I went out together on November 11, 1997.

After four years of amazing intensity, I was suddenly no longer Mr. Chairman. When I was young, my mother was in the habit of saying to me, "Remember who you are." I misunderstood her. I thought that I had a consciousness inside that was separate from the outer self engaged in the world of action and expression. I believed that my mother meant that I should conduct myself in accordance with the wishes of that inner person. Only in my time in public office did I understand that I had her teaching exactly wrong. She was trying to explain not that an individual can separate the self from the outer world's rewards and punishments, but that you are the choices you make in the world.

My father had a complementary, although darker, view. He believed that a person's life was a generally desperate battle against impersonal, authoritarian forces. But in public service I came to believe that my father's pessimism was only his style of confronting the world. In truth, his life taught the same lesson that my mother wished to impart: remember that you have an inalienable right to choose your ideas. They will give you power. You have an inviolable right to select your battles. They give your life its meaning. Remember, you may select your side, your team, your leaders, your companions of the heart. In our American experiment with freedom and democracy, wise and fortunate choices will give victory to you, and the country.

A week later Blair had his official going-away party at the Comedy Club. Center stage, doing stand-up seemed an appropriate ending, he said. Someone in the crowd called out that he hadn't been that funny for the previous four years. Rueful laughter. The gaggle of lobbyists expressed respect; they acknowledged that he had mastered their trade and often bested them.

A few days afterward was my own fine good-bye party at the National

Press Club, where I had given my critique of the broad[c]
1995. Al Gore, Bill Kennard, Peggy Charren, Ed M[?]
of teachers' groups, minority groups, and women's g[ ]
sons from my own team at the FCC had come to praise o[ ]
ments.

Before the speeches, my family and I met backstage with the Vice
President. Al explained to my daughter Sara what to do. She should wait
with him behind the curtain until he was introduced, and then they would
walk on stage together. I and the rest of my family would follow.

"Stagecraft," he said to her. She looked up at him with a studious gaze.
Like any child, she was always learning in a new way.

"Okay," she said. He took her hand and led her out to the applaud-
ing crowd.

In January 1999, more than two and a half years after we had written the interconnection rules to open the local phone markets to competition—and after the Eighth Circuit Court of Appeals in Kansas City had
declared that the states and not the federal government had this power—
the United States Supreme Court overturned the Eighth Circuit decision
that had invalidated our August 1996 rules. One of the most conservative
of the Supreme Court justices, Antonin Scalia, wrote the opinion that in
short order dispensed with the Eighth Circuit's rejection of my view that
the Congress had given the FCC the authority to write national rules ordering competition everywhere. The FCC was again the rightful authority
on competition in communications.

By 1999, more than $30 billion had been invested in new companies
competing in the local telephone market against the incumbent Bells and
GTE. Virtually none of the capital would have been committed without
the Telecommunications Act and the Commission's regulations. Meanwhile, the new and incumbent local telephone companies were adding new
lines—especially for connecting to the Internet—faster than ever before.

Wireless competition that began as a result of our airwave auctions
and our flexible policies of spectrum use had dropped cellular phone prices
by 75 percent, and they were still falling. The country was on a path toward having on average one or more mobile phone devices per person.

The World Trade Organization agreement had opened almost all the
world's communications markets to competition and investment. Glob-
ally, the information sector was growing at a record 8 percent a year.

The communications revolution energized the entire American economy. It led to increases in spans of control, the elimination of layers of organization, and faster, more efficient, and more consensual decision making. Meanwhile, because of widespread entrepreneurship and competition, two-thirds of all new jobs since Bill Clinton's first inauguration were in the information economy. Our policies had served Main Street and Wall Street.

The miracle of low inflation, high growth, and continued consumer confidence in the face of foreign crises was attributable in significant part to the communications revolution. In July 1997, Alan Greenspan had said that "an expected result of the widespread and effective application of information and other technologies would be a significant increase in productivity and reduction in business cost." He told Congress in January 1999 that the economy was enjoying "higher, technology-driven productivity growth." And in May 1999, Greenspan said that economic expansion had continued without a corresponding rise in inflation as a result of the burst in productivity that came from heavy investment by businesses in computers and other high-tech devices of the information age. He also noted in May that over the preceding 12 months, productivity (a measure of output per hour of work) had been rising at nearly a three percent annual rate, three times the one percent rate of the early 1990s. Higher output from the same number of workers allows businesses to pay those workers more and enjoy higher profits without raising the price of goods and causing a concomitant rise in inflation.

As of 1999, 42 percent of American adults are regular Net users. Every month, some 65 million adults go on-line. There were 26,000 Web sites in use in 1993. By 1999, there were 5 million.

In 1995, when Andy Grove was readying the packet-switched battalions for war against the circuit-switched networks—the Internet versus the telephone system—revenue generated by the Internet totaled $5 billion. Three years later, in 1998, the Internet generated $301 billion. The telecommunications industry captured $270 billion in revenue in 1998. By comparison, the energy and auto industries were measured at $223 billion and $350 billion, respectively.

The data explosion was of particularly unforeseen dimension. In 1999 data traffic was doubling every 90 days, as connected personal computers spread across the globe. The Web invited the creation of innumerable sites, and most of them were in the United States. As a result, Internet traffic into the United States from abroad began to balance the historic pattern of telephone callers normally calling out from this country on voice circuits. In time, the settlement rate fees charged to Americans by other countries for international phone calls would be cut back not only by the FCC's regulatory decisions to lower international phone prices, but also as a result of the Net drawing in bitstreams from all over the world.

We also could claim success in creating new public benefits from the information sector of the economy. New educational television programs appeared on every network. One television executive said, "As much as I find this difficult and imposing creatively, I welcome this over the 1980s, when every show was based on a toy. That was the nadir in creativity. This is a much better direction to be going." Indeed, in spring 1999, the only audience increase for ABC was in the children's television segment. And in the highest form of flattery known to television, I was lampooned in an episode of the cartoon show *Animaniacs* as a regulator named "Reef Blunt," who forced kids to watch shows they did not like.

No fight in politics ends. It evolves. As I left, the Republican Congress attacked our classroom connection program, otherwise known as the "e-rate" program. They claimed that the funds were poorly administered, although they made this assertion before monies were distributed. They argued that the program was a tax, and they encouraged the telephone companies, led by the Bells, to challenge it in court.

John McCain led the congressional effort to attack the program. In the heart of much of modern conservatism is a dark judgment that inequality of opportunity is a part of fate that government should leave unaddressed. But my successor used his majority to fend off the Republican attacks in 1999, winning by a 3–2 vote renewed and full funding of the classroom program. In August, the FCC also defeated the legal appeals against the classroom program filed by GTE. By 2001, virtually all classrooms can be connected and a revolution in education will follow. Now, Senate Commerce Committee Chairman John McCain supports the e-rate. In announcing his presidential candidacy, he said, "I have fought to make sure that every American child has access to the technological wonders that are remaking our world. Some day very soon every school in America will be wired to the Internet. Children on the Navajo reservation in Northern Arizona and children from the wealthiest neighborhoods will have access to the same information."

Bill Gates had declined to promote our classroom connection program. But in 1997 he called me to say that he would install computers and software in every library in the country. In 1999 he created what will be the largest charity in history.

Technology shapes possibility in the long run, but politics determines results in the short run. The Commission's policies were aimed at letting entrepreneurs exploit the potential of technology. By choosing a policy that favored competition, we promoted packet-switched technology. Because of the Internet, this policy then stimulated the growth of the data-driven economy. What followed was all this: sales of computers overtaking those of phones and televisions, growth stocks soaring, venture capitalists creating prodigious wealth, youth triumphing over age, the West rising, bandwidth spreading, entrepreneurs growing rich, the power of ideas exceeding the power of the status quo. Some of these results we consciously sought; others were happy accidents. Taking all these results into account, we could reasonably say that opportunity had become more equitable and broadly distributed in America, in part because of our decisions.

As businesses, libraries, classrooms, and homes came on the Net, we believed that democracy would be strengthened. Always government would have the challenge of writing laws and regulations that open monopoly businesses to new entrants and new innovation. Again and again, government would need to renew the community of America by creating and sharing equitably new public goods born from the confluence of technology and economics. Over and over individuals would gain the privilege of public office, by a combination of chance and will. And in their time, each would have rare opportunities to find themselves by sharing in the renewal of the American Dream for another generation.

ABC (American Broadcasting Company), 75, 225
Adams, Gerry, 116–17
AirTouch, bidding in spectrum auctions, 96
Allard, Nick, 22
Allen, Bob, 95, 133, 152–53, 218–19
Allen, Herb, 221
Allen, Paul, 102
American Psychological Association, 121
America Online, 207, 214
Ameritech, 17, 155, 197
Andreesen, Marc, 10, 105, 133
Animaniacs, 225
Anstrom, Decker, 52
Armstrong, Mike, 96, 219
Arrow, Kenneth, 25
Arthur, Brian, 25
Atlas, Larry, 182
AT&T: breakup of, 7, 92, 107, 178; competition under new rules, 152–53, 155, 178, 214–15; and local phone market, 108, 217; and low-volume users, 214–15; McCaw Cellular Communications acquisition, 95; and mobile phones, 92; regulation and monopoly, 38–39; Southwestern Bell merger talks, 217–19; as spectrum bidder, 95–96; TCI acquisition, 219; and telecommunications reform bill, 107, 133, 138, 143–44
AT&T–SBC merger, 217–19

Bak, Per, 25
Barrett, Andrew (Andy), 12, 31, 75–76, 114, 123, 158–59

Barshefsky, Charlene, 202–3
Bell Atlantic, 22, 26–27, 33, 43, 54–55, 66, 153, 221. *See also* Bell companies
Bell Atlantic–TCI merger, 22–24, 26–27, 33–34, 45, 54–55, 134, 170
Bell companies: and classroom Internet connections, opposition, 184, 195; competition under new rules, 155; FCC attacks, 180; interconnection charges, 57, 92, 157, 178–79, 193, 195; Internet use, free ride, 134–36, 206–7; long distance market entry, 66, 107, 153, 178, 197; Snowe-Rockefeller rule compromise, 215; stock prices, 179, 216; telecommunications reform bill and, 66, 85, 107–9, 125–26, 133, 143–44, 152–53, 180
Bennett, William J., 119
Berners-Lee, Tim, 41
Bingamann, Anne, 8
Bischoff, Carol Ann, 111–12
Bisson, Peter, 184
Blackstone Group lunch, 54–56
Bliley, Thomas J., 151, 165, 208
Boasberg, Tom, 183
Bomb threats against FCC, 115–16
Bradley, Bill, 174, 205
Broadcasters' association. *See* National Association of Broadcasters
Broadcasting & Cable, 8, 50, 75, 127
Bronfman, Edgar, 221
Brown, Ronald H., Jr., 8, 166
Browner, Carol M., 4
Bryant, Anne, 185

Budget cutting, 128–29
Buffett, Warren, 141, 187, 188–89
Bush, George, ix, 20, 36
Business Week, 52, 220

Cable Act (1984), 31
Cable Act (1992), 20–21, 31, 49–52
Cable rate regulation, 20–24, 30–
  34, 45, 49–50, 56, 59, 86, 131,
  170
Cable shopping channels, 51–52
Cable television, 9, 14, 51, 64, 76,
  125, 170, 219
Campaign finance, 82–83, 107, 132,
  172–74, 205
Campbell, Tom, 191
Candidates, free TV air time, 171–
  75, 181, 208, 211–12
Carlin, George, 211
Carter, Jimmy, 35
Case, Stephen M., 207, 214
CBS (Columbia Broadcasting Com-
  pany), 73, 146–47
Cellular telephones, 14–15, 23, 64,
  92–93, 223; spectrum auction,
  91–97
Charren, Peggy, 35–37, 72, 75, 128,
  132, 190, 223
Children's Defense Fund, 122
Children's television, 36, 121–22,
  124–25, 132, 171, 181, 190–91,
  225. *See also* Educational television
Children's Television Act (1990), 36,
  125
China, 198–99
Chong, Rachelle: and candidates' air
  time, 205; and children's television, 37, 75, 114, 125, 181, 190;
  departure from FCC, 208; Dole
  loyalty, 16, 37, 86; and telecommunications rules, 158–59, 182,

215–16; and universal service rule,
  157
Chorney, Jackie, 183, 216
Classroom Internet access: Bell Atlantic–TCI merger to offer, 26–
  27; Bell company opposition, 184;
  Bliley opposition, 165; Democratic House telecommunications
  bill provision, 58; e-rate tax argument, 225; EdLink and, 185; FCC
  vote on, 214–16; funding for,
  167, 184, 201, 215, 225; Gang of
  Two and, 209; Gates-Hundt meeting, 105–6; Gore communications agenda, 9–11, 165–67, 194;
  GTE challenge, 225; Hundt's
  FCC agenda, 98; lobbying for
  FCC position, 184–85, 187–89,
  191–92, 201; Net Day (1996),
  166–67, 192; reforming education, 183; schoolgirl in Carthage as
  Gore's example of, 9, 11, 94, 151,
  165, 216; spectrum auction funding, 94; telecommunications bill
  provision, 109–12, 119, 125–26,
  137–38, 143; universal service
  and, 107, 109, 167, 209
CLECs (competitive local exchange
  carriers), 156–57, 157, 179, 194
Clinton, Bill, ix; candidates' free air
  time for, 174–75; children's television commitment, 123; classroom
  Internet connections advocated by,
  151, 184, 201–2; Democratic National Convention (1992), 4; Gingrich Congress and, 97, 145–46;
  Lewinsky affair, 131; and Net Day
  (1996), 166–67; re-election of,
  201–2; Renaissance Weekend
  (1992), 6; signing of telecommunications bill, 151–52; television-

newspaper mergers opposed by, 147

Clinton, Hillary Rodham, 4

Coase, Ronald, 126

Comcast Cable, 52, 54, 55, 76, 95

Communications Act (1934), 11, 13–14, 35–37, 48, 73, 127–28

Communications technology: advances bridge industries' legal divisions, 14; analog versus digital data, 57, 106; circuit-switched, 39–40; developing countries, 42; digital television, 63–64; educational opportunity and, 10–11, 120; expansion goal, 7; FCC policy, 226; high-definition TV, 63; lines or pipes, physical connections, 11, 26, 134, 221; packet-switched systems, 39–41, 134–36, 226; political campaigns and, 171–75; Public Switched Telephone Network, 38–39, 57; rich and poor, bridging gap between, 42

Competition: cellular phone companies, 14, 93–94, 223; computer and telephone companies, 57; deregulation of telecommunications, effect, 15; digital television and cable, 64; FCC goal, 98, 177, 221; FCC rulemaking authority, 11, 58; FCC rules and monopolies, 14; Gingrich view on, 89, 117–18; Hollywood studios and networks, 75; interconnection order, 193–97, 223; Internet and, 206–7, 221; level playing field and FCC mission, 136; local and cellular phone service, 92; local telephone service, 66, 107–8, 152–55, 178–79, 193; long distance

telephone service, 107, 217–19; Markey's support of, 181; Republican deregulation, 85; telecommunications reform bill, 107–8, 144, 152–55, 214–15; telephone and cable companies, 9; telephone and Internet technology, 136, 206; television-newspaper mergers, 147; television syndication rights, 74–75; two-pipe systems, 26, 134, 221

Congress: ambiguous laws, regulations for, 52, 68, 177, 217; Commerce Committees, 72, 84, 93, 110–11, 180; constituent complaints, 72; digital television licenses, 210; FCC regulations and, 19–21, 169, 205; government shutdown of 1995, 142–43, 146; Hundt confirmation, 8; Kennard confirmation, 221–22; Republican control of, 81, 84, 98–99, 125, 142–46, 183

"Contract with America," 81

Coolidge, Calvin, 220

Cosby, Bill, 191

Cowhey, Peter, 203

Cox Communications, 47, 95

Cullen, Jim, 22

D'Amato, Alfonse M., 169

Dancey, Ruth, 18–19, 116

Democratic National Convention (1992), 3–4

Democratic National Convention (1996), 194

Deregulation, 15; cable industry, 125; cellular phones, 98; Gilder advocates, 23–24; Gingrich plan, 82, 89, 118; House telecommunications bill, 125–26; Hundt's

Deregulation (*continued*)
"New Paradigm," 112, 124, 126, 177, 179–80; Republican plans, 82, 85, 180; television, 112–13
DeWine, Mike, 218
Digital television: analog versus, 106; build-out time, 211; cable competition, 64; candidates' free air time, 175, 208; congressional pressure on, 210; Disney sought as ally, 199; FCC rulemaking, 209–11; Gates sought as ally, 105–6, 159–60; license delay, Dole letter, 147–48, 160; Microsoft and transmission standard, 160, 202; public interest obligation, 170; spectrum auction proposals, 99–100, 105–6, 126–27, 181, 204, 210; spectrum giveaway, 64–65, 100–101, 106, 126–27, 142, 147–48, 160, 170, 204–5, 209–11; transmission specifications, 175; value to computer industry, 105; wireless data transmission, 210
Diller, Barry, 25–26, 50–52, 54–55, 127–28, 146, 174, 191, 221
Dingell, John D., 28–29, 30, 100, 182, 215
"Dirty words," 169, 211
Disney Company, 24, 75, 197–200
Distance learning, 6, 26, 109–10. *See also* Classroom Internet access
Dole, Bob: broadcast industry attacks, 127, 147; and digital broadcast licenses, 147–48, 160; elections, and FCC inaction, 77; FCC concessions, 11–12, 16; Hundt criticism, 47; as presidential candidate, 165, 173, 197; and spectrum auctions, 126–27, 147–48, 210; and telecommunications reform, 66–67, 107, 144, 153; television ads by, 173
Downey, Thomas J., 28
Dreyfuss, Richard, 199
Duggan, Ervin, 12, 19, 132
Dukakis, Michael S., 3

Eastwood, Clint, 185
Earth in the Balance (Gore), 25
Ebbers, Bernie, 108, 178
E-commerce, 180
Economic growth: communications revolution and, ix–x, 9, 42–43, 118, 156, 194, 224; education and, 185–86, 213; information sector, FCC regulation, 13; Internet economy, 133, 136, 224; telecommunications rules and, 156, 179, 206–7
Edelman, Marian Wright, 122–23
EdLink, 185
Educational television: advocating kidvid rule, 35–37, 72–75, 112, 125–28, 131, 171, 176, 181; CBS, Westinghouse acquisition, 146–47; Clinton and Gore support, 123, 194; constitutional arguments, 127–28; FCC goal, 98, 181; Fields's criticism of FCC, 85; Gang of Three on, 114, 123, 128; party politics of, 131–32, 189–90; public opinion campaign, 181, 189–90; supported by Ann Landers, 132–33; White House summit, 190–91
Eisner, Michael, 197
E-mail, 69–70, 206–7
Esrey, Bill, 95

Farquhar, Michelle, 182
Farrell, Joe, 182

FCC v. Pacifica (1978), 211

Federal Bureau of Investigation (FBI), 115–16

Federal Communications Commission (FCC): bomb threats, 115–16; budget cutting threat, 128–29; career staff briefings, 12–13; cellular telephone spectrum auction, 91–97; closing field offices, 129; and communications revolution, ix–x; e-mail and computer upgrade at, 69–70; Hammer Award, 96; Internet Web site, 183; radio car, 21–22; Republican plans for, 85–87, 126, 210; staff reorganizing, 69, 98, 178; threat of elimination, 82–83, 89, 120–21

—decision making at: "all who mattered," 132; ambiguous laws, regulations for, 52, 68, 177, 217; balance of power among industries, 14; committee style, 13; compromise, process of, 12–13, 67–68; congressional influence, 19–21, 210; court review, 68; Dole's commissioner, 11, 16; Gang of Three, 90, 114, 123, 128–29, 139–40, 146–47, 155, 157–59; Gang of Two, 159, 181–82, 188, 207, 210, 215, 222; industries seek regulatory advantage, 11; level playing field, 136–37; lobbying pressure, 20; online posting, 69; reforming process, 68, 181; regulatory imbalance, 13; unanimous votes, 157–59, 181, 216

Ferris, Charlie, 35

Fields, Jack, 31, 84–86, 87, 88, 117, 144, 175, 193

Film industry: Artists' Rights Dinner (1996), 160–64; and shape of television sets, 160–61, 199–200

Fishman, Ira, 184–85, 189, 192, 195–96, 201

Forbes, Malcolm S., Jr. (Steve), 173

Fortune, 38

Fowler, Mark, 29, 30, 35–36, 100, 124

Fox Television investigation, 73–74, 90–91

Frank, Barney, 99, 210

Free TV for Straight Talk, 174–75

Fritts, Eddie, 43, 46–48

Gabbard, Ralph, 190, 196

Gage, John, 166

Gang of Three, 90, 114, 123, 128–29, 139–40, 146–47, 155, 157–59

Gates, William H.: book signing party, 141–42; business beginning, 102; charitable commitments to education, 195, 225–26; and classroom technology, 185–87; Internet's effect on, 41, 141, 186; Paris communications conference, 37; PCs, vision described, 38; politics, studying, 105; spectrum auctions, support for, 159–60; summit of business and government leaders held by, 213; support desirable in spectrum giveaway, 103–6; wealth of, 186–87

Geffen, David, 51, 221

Genachowski, Julius, 72, 124, 127, 182, 190, 205

Gilder, George, 23–24, 55, 64, 82, 145

Gingrich, Newt: budget battle, 142–44; and campaign finance, 82, 205; classroom Internet connections opposed by, 125; FCC elimination advocated by, 82–83, 89,

Gingrich, Newt (*continued*)
120–21; information executives
meeting with, 83; philosophy of,
81–83, 88–89; and telecommunications reform bill, 117, 125,
151–52
Ginn, Sam, 96
Gips, Don, 91–92, 182
Global Crossing, 157
Gore, Al, ix; balanced budget vote,
15; Buenos Aires speech to ITU,
42–45, 204; cable industry
speech, 169–70; cable rates, views
on, 30, 34, 86; cellular phone pre-
dictions, 94; children's television
commitment, 123, 194; communications policy, 4, 7–9, 11, 25,
42, 87, 117–18, 164–65; economic policy, 6, 43, 118; education policy, 10–11; Gates's summit
attendee, 213; and Hundt departure, 213–14, 223; information
highway vision, x, 4–7; Internet
connections in classrooms advocated by, 106, 109, 138, 165–67,
184, 202, 215–16; leadership lesson of, 98; National Association of
Broadcasters speech, 169–70; and
Net Day (1996), 166–67; public
service role, 7; re-election of, 201–
2; schoolgirl in Carthage, Tenn.,
example, 9, 11, 151; and spectrum
auctions, 94–95; technology view
of, 131; telecommunications reform, signing ceremony, 151–52;
UCLA speech, 24–25
Gore, Karenna, 214
Government shutdown of 1995,
142–43, 146
Graham, Katharine, 49, 140–41
Greenspan, Alan, 224

Grove, Andrew S., 38, 57–58, 104;
circuit-packet switched network
war, 134–36, 224; FCC staff provided by, 69; financial forum
arranged by, 221; SBC–AT&T
merger views, 217–18
Gruley, Bryan, 160–64
GTE, 218, 225

Hammer Award, 96
Harriman, Pamela, 37
Harris, Judy, 28, 50, 66, 70, 72, 110,
121, 122, 209
Hawthorne, Nathaniel, 45, 168, 204
Hendrix, Jimi, 88, 183
Hennock, Frieda, 128
High-definition television (HDTV),
63, 65, 112, 210. *See also* Digital
television
Hollings, Ernest F. (Fritz), 11, 37, 67,
107–8, 110, 137, 181
Hollywood. *See* Film industry
Hostetter, Amos, 52
Hundt, Reed E.: baseball czar rumor,
219–20; broadcasting industry
and, 43–46, 112–14, 169, 211–
12; confirmation process and
swearing in, 8, 11–12, 16–17;
FCC agenda, 98, 131; Gore-
Clinton connections, 1–7; nomination, 5–7; personal objectives,
58, 61–62, 222; public school
teacher, 10, 116; "Reef Blunt,"
225; Republican revolution and,
97–99; resignation from FCC,
209, 213, 214, 222; "Shoot
Hundt," 53–56; Silicon Valley
and, 57–58, 216–17; summary of
successes, 225; telecommunications rules czar, 153–56, 164–65;
Woodstock experience, 88–89

Hunt, Jim, 155
Hypertext markup language (html), 10, 41

Information economy. *See* Economic growth
Information highway. *See* Internet
Intel, 38, 57, 135–36
Interconnection order, 157, 178–79, 193–97, 223
International telecommunications agreement, 45, 203–4, 223
International Telecommunications Union (ITU), 42, 43, 44–45
Internet, ix–x, 8, 10, 41, 221; browsing free, 133, 206–7; cable access, 170; cable rate decision impact, 31–34, 52, 54–55, 134; CLECs data networks, 157; consumer goods, 178; democracy and, 226; digital broadcast spectrum, 160, 210; e-mail lobbying, 207; education transformed by, 120; FCC decisions, 69; FCC role, 5, 41, 133, 206–7, 221; Gates's computer network vision, 38, 41; Gore's information highway vision, 4–7; growing use, 224; invention of World Wide Web, 10, 41; international calls to U.S., 225; library connections, 225–26; lines or pipes, physical connections, 11; multiple networks, multimedia, 134–35; Net Day (1996), 166, 192; packet-switched network, 39–41, 135–36, 226; pornography, 183; telephone access, 57, 134–36, 206–7, 214; "virtual" bandwidth, 38, 104; wireless access, 93, 210. *See also* Classroom Internet access

Internet service providers, 180
Internet telephony, 135, 206
Ireland, 116–17
Irving, Larry, 8

Jeffords, James M., 189
Jiang Zemin, 198
Johnson, Lyndon B., 99
Jones, Meredith, 182
Jordan, Michael, 146, 147

Kasich, John R., 100
Katz, Michael, 31
Katzen, Sally, 8
Katzenberg, Jeffrey, 51, 163, 197
Keeney, Gina, 69, 182
Kennard, William E., 69, 123, 124, 127, 155, 182, 221–23
Kennedy, John F., 112–13
Kerrey, Bob, 107, 111, 218
Kidvid rule. *See* Educational television
Knight, Peter, 25
Kohl, Herb, 218
Kornbluh, Karen, 106, 110–11, 122, 124, 125, 138, 167–69, 207

Landers, Ann, 132–33
Lawler, Greg, 35
Lawrence, Sharon, 163–64
Laybourne, Geraldine, 170
Level 3, 157, 197
Levin, Blair, 12, 60–62, 96–97, 155–57, 197–200, 204–5, 209, 217–20
Levin, Gerald M. (Jerry), 47, 83, 221
Lewinsky, Monica, 131
Lewis, Ann, 130–32, 136
License auctions. *See* Spectrum auctions
Lieberman, Joseph I., 183

Lincoln, Abraham, 89
Long distance communications: access charges, 134, 179, 196, 214–15; Ameritech, 197; Bell companies' as competitors in, 107–8, 152–53; international settlement system, 204, 225; low-volume users, 214–15; telecommunications reform bill, 107–8, 133, 152–54
Lott, Trent, 108, 205
Lucas, George, 76–77, 163, 215

McCain, John: and campaign finance reform, 173, 189, 205; and candidates' free air time, 174–75, 205, 214; e-rate tax argument, 225; and FCC nominee, 208; Hundt criticism, 66, 148, 217; school communications opposition, 111, 119; spectrum auction support, 99, 159
McCaw, Craig, 54, 95, 217
McCaw Cellular Communications, 95–96
McGinty, Katie, 4
McKinsey and Company, 27, 91, 184
McNealy, Scott, 191–92
McPherson, Harry, 83
Malone, John, 22, 26–27, 53–56, 219
Markey, Edward J., 28–30, 34, 94–95, 132, 181, 190, 223. See also Telecommunications Act (1996)
Maxwell, Elliot, 182
MCI, 108, 133, 138, 178
Metzger, Richard, 69, 182
Microsoft, 102–5, 141, 159–60, 185, 202. See also Gates, William H.
Milkman, Ruth, 182–83

Minow, Newton N., 112–13, 125, 126
Mitchell, George J., 220
Mobile phones. See Cellular telephones
Morris, Dick, 125
Motorola, 94
Murdoch, Rupert, 73–74, 90–91, 174, 205, 221
Murphy, Tom, 74
Myhrvold, Nathan, 104, 106

Nakahata, John, 183
National Association of Broadcasters (NAB): children's television position, 182, 190; convention, 43–47; digital transmission standard, 202; Dole attack, 127, 147; Gore speech, 169–70; Hundt speech, 112–14; public interest obligation, opposition, 181; and second broadcast channel, 64–65, 210; snubbing Hundt, 45–46, 112, 169
National Cable Television Association, 52–53
National Press Club, 124, 222–23
Neel, Roy, 5–6, 216
Negroponte, Nick, 23–24, 55, 64, 82
"Negroponte switch," 23, 55, 64
Ness, Susan, 37, 76, 157, 208
Net Day, 166–67, 192
Netscape, 104–5, 133, 134
Neukom, Bill, 104
"New Paradigm" of broadcast regulation, 112, 124, 126, 177, 179–80
News Corporation, 73
New York Times, 100, 127–28, 204, 216, 219
Nixon, Richard M., 141
Noam, Eli, 46

Oklahoma City bombing (1995), 115, 116
Omnibus Budget Reconciliation Act (1993), ix, 15, 91–93, 142–44
Ornstein, Norm, 28
Ovitz, Mike, 197–200

Pacifica, FCC v. (1978), 211
Pacific Bell, 96
Packet-switched networks, 39–41, 135–36, 226
Paramount, 25, 50, 54
Pepper, Bob, 182
Perot, H. Ross, ix
Perry, Wayne, 95–96
Personal communications services (PCS), 91–92. *See also* Cellular telephones
Pesci, Joe, 162
Pirate radio, 21
Platt, Lew, 191–92
Pressler, Larry, 84–85, 87, 88, 90, 95, 138, 208
Public Broadcasting System (PBS), 19, 82, 94–95, 125, 128, 132
Public interest obligation: broadcasters' agreement in principle, 205; Diller support of FCC, 127, 146; legal arguments, 72–73, 124–25, 127–28; NAB convention speeches, 112, 114, 169–70; promotion versus prohibition, 211; Quello's position, 48, 114, 208; Republican view, 85. *See also* Educational television
Public Switched Telephone Network (PSTN), 38–39, 57

Quayle, Dan, 123–24
Quello, James: cable rate decision, 31; children's television views, 37, 48, 76, 114, 132, 181, 189–90; classroom Internet access supported by, 215; FCC commissioner, 12–13, 139; FCC departure, 208; FCC swing vote, 18, 85; and Fox Television investigation, 90; mentoring new chairman, 15–17, 46–47; and public interest obligation, 114, 208; and spectrum auctions, 94; and telecommunications rules, 158–59, 182, 215
QVC Network, Inc., 25, 50, 51
Qwest, 157, 197

Reagan, Ronald, 29, 36, 70
Redstone, Sumner, 25, 54
Reich, Robert B., 4
"Reinventing government," 24, 94, 96
Renaissance Weekend, 6
Richards, Mary Beth, 183
Riley, Richard W., 166, 185, 195, 201, 215
Roberts, Brian, 52, 76, 94
Roberts, Oral, 185
Roberts, Ralph, 52, 54–55
Rockefeller, John D., 187
Rockefeller, John D., IV (Jay), 107, 109–11, 137–38, 169, 189, 194–95, 201, 215–16
Roosevelt, Franklin D., 97
Roots (Haley), 122
Rosston, Greg, 183

Safire, William, 100, 126–27
Sallett, Jonathan, 8, 10
San Jose Mercury News, 216–17
SBC. *See* Southwestern Bell
Scalia, Antonin, 154, 223
Schmidt, Eric, 166

Schulhof, Mickey, 69
Schwarzman, Steve, 54, 56
Scorsese, Martin, 162, 163
Selig, Bud, 220
Selleck, Tom, 160
Sesame Street, 181
Shays, Christopher, 205
Sheehan, Michael, 70–71
Simon, Greg, 8, 10, 151
Skrzycki, Cindy, 7–8
Smart Valley, Inc., 191–92
Smith, Jean Kennedy, 116
Smith, Ray, 22, 26–27, 33, 43, 54–55, 66, 153, 221
Snow, C. P., 41
Snowe, Olympia J., 110–11, 126, 137–38, 167–68, 189, 195, 201, 215–16
Southwestern Bell, 47, 155, 217–19
Spectrum auctions: broadcasters lobby against, 127; cellular telephone, 91–97; classroom wiring with funds from, 76, 94, 105, 137; computer industry help sought, 105–6; digital television, auction proposals, 99–100, 105–6, 126–27, 181, 204, 210; digital television, spectrum giveaway, 64–65, 100–101, 106, 126–27, 142, 147–48, 160, 170, 204–5, 209–11; Fowler proposal, 100; Frank support, 99; McCain support, 99, 159; minimum fair price, 95; OBRA authorization, 15, 91; television licenses, 99; *Wall Street Journal* supports, 179
Sperling, Gene, 8
Spielberg, Steven, 51, 163, 199
Sprint, bidding at spectrum auctions, 95
Stern, Howard, 169

Stiglitz, Joseph E., 8
Stone, Sharon, 162
Stringer, Howard, 73
Sun Microsystems, 40, 57, 166, 191–92
Sunstein, Cass R., 127
Supreme Court, decision on telecommunications rules, 154, 223

Tauzin, Billy, 193
Taylor, Paul, 174–75
Tedlow, Richard, 25, 69
Tele-Communications, Inc. (TCI), 95. *See also* Bell Atlantic–TCI merger; Malone, John
Telecommunications Act (1996), ix; AT&T position, 133, 143–44, 152; Bell companies and, 66, 107–8, 133, 137, 143–44; budget bill impact, 142–44; cable rate regulation repeal, 170; children's educational programming, 35–37, 72–75; classroom communications provision, 107–12, 125, 137–38, 143, 151; Clinton signs, 151–52; competition, FCC discretion, 58, 144, 177; computer industry interest, 57–58; conference committee, 126, 133, 137–38, 143; Dole's role, 66–67, 107, 144, 153; drafting details, 110; FCC goal, 98; FCC regulatory role, 101, 126, 142, 148, 155, 217–18, 223; Gore agenda, 87, 101; Hollings efforts, 107–8, 110, 137, 143; House Commerce Committee hearings, 180; House Republican bill, 117–18, 125–26; local phone service competition, 66, 107–8; long distance companies and, 133, 217; Markey's efforts, 107, 125, 137,

143; political contributions, 107; Republican post-election plans, 84–86; school telecommunications rates, 58; Snowe-Rockefeller provision, 110–11, 126, 137–38; universal service, 154; veto threat, 88, 108, 118, 123, 126, 138, 143–44

Telecommunications rules: access to local network, 156; AT&T concerns, 152; Bell companies and, 152–53, 156, 180, 193, 195–96; Bliley's warning, 165; classroom connections, funding, 169, 214–17; competition and, 177; core principles, FCC staff, 156; deadlines and FCC schedule, 157–58; digital television, 210–11; FCC staff work, 154–57, 177–79, 182–83; Gang of Three and, 157–58; Hundt's decisions, 153–54, 157; industry advisers and, 178; interconnection rules, 157, 178–79, 193–97, 223; Internet, access charge bar, 214; Internet service providers, 180; kidvid rule, 75–76; lobbyists and, 158; local phone service competition, 152–54, 156–57; long distance access charges, 214–15; national scope, 156; public benefits, 177; public support, pressure, 157–59, 182; rural telephone service, 215; Snowe-Rockefeller compromise, 215; state regulators, 156–57, 180, 193; stock prices, 179, 193; Supreme Court decision, 154, 223; unanimous FCC votes, 157–59; universal service, 157, 209

Telephone services: access charges, 134–36, 154, 179, 214–15; cable competition, 9; cellular phone competition, 93; circuit-switched, 39–40; competitive local exchange carriers (CLECs), 154–57; data transmission, growth, 57, 133–35; e-rate tax argument, 225; infrastructure, 39; Internet bypass, 135, 206–7; new market entrants, 154–55; rate hike, 173, 178; universal service, 154. *See also* Long distance communications

Television: advertising and children's programming, 35–36; candidates, free air time, 171–75, 181, 208, 211–12; CBS, Westinghouse acquisition, 146–47; children's educational programming, 35–37, 73–75, 112; children's viewing time, 121; Disney acquisition of ABC, 75; FCC review of *Washington Post* station, 140–41; foreign-ownership rule, 73–74, 90–91; high-definition, 63–65; Hundt's "New Paradigm" of regulation, 112; industry on-air lobbying, 127; Internet content transmission, 64; license auctions, 99; newspaper mergers, Clinton opposes, 147; politicians and, 171–75; prime-time access rule, 73, 112; Public Broadcasting System, elimination, 82; public service programming, 100–101; screen dimensions, 160–61, 200; syndication rights, 74–75; "vast wasteland," 113; V-chip, 123, 125, 128, 155, 183; violence and children, 121. *See also* Cable television; Digital television

Thoreau, Henry David, 168

Time, 83

Tisch, Larry, 73
Toon, Rhonda, 166–67
Turner, Ted, 58–59, 61, 86

UCLA conference, 24–27
Universal service, 107, 109, 154, 157, 167, 209
Unruh, Jesse, 172
U S West, 157

Vail, Theodore, 38
V-chip, 123, 125, 128, 155, 183

Wall Street Journal, 33, 74, 160, 164, 179–80, 219
Washington Post, 7, 33, 49–50, 52, 140–41, 173, 190, 220
Western Governors Association, 187–88

Westinghouse, 146–47
Wired, 53
Wireless communications. *See* Cellular telephones; Spectrum auctions
Wolfe, Tom, x–xi
Woods, James, 162, 163
Woodstock, 88–89
WorldCom, 95, 108, 178
World Trade Organization (WTO): telecommunications agreement, x, 203–4, 223
World Wide Web: invention of, 10, 41. *See also* Internet
Wright, Bob, 73–74
Wright, Chris, 124, 182

Yahoo! 192
Yang, Jerry, 191–92